解码常春藤招生

——美国本科文书成功申请解析

李 锦 [美]路易斯·胡适 王心艺 著

上海交通大学出版社
SHANGHAI JIAO TONG UNIVERSITY PRESS

内容提要

本书为“名校招生官告诉你系列”之一，由美国名校招生官和专业的美国升学指导顾问老师合著，本书围绕申请美国本科中的重要环节——文书展开分析，主要内容包括申请文书类型、作用、准备要点及其在美国大学申请中的重要性，并通过一系列获得美国顶级大学录取的中国学生的申请文书使读者体会什么是好的文书。本书适用于计划申请美国本科的中国学生及其家长阅读。

图书在版编目(CIP)数据

解码常春藤招生：美国本科文书成功申请解析／李锦，(美)路易斯·胡适，王心艺著．—上海：上海交通大学出版社，2022.1
(名校招生官告诉你系列)
ISBN 978-7-313-25736-9

Ⅰ．①解… Ⅱ．①李… ②路… ③王… Ⅲ．①高等学校—留学教育—介绍—美国 Ⅳ．①G649.712.8

中国版本图书馆 CIP 数据核字(2021)第 229820 号

解码常春藤招生
——美国本科文书成功申请解析
JIEMA CHANGCHUNTENG ZHAOSHENG
——MEIGUO BENKE WENSHU CHENGGONG SHENQING JIEXI

著　　者：李　锦　[美]路易斯·胡适　王心艺
出版发行：上海交通大学出版社　　地　　址：上海市番禺路 951 号
邮政编码：200030　　电　　话：021-64071208
印　　制：常熟市文化印刷有限公司　　经　　销：全国新华书店
开　　本：710 mm×1000 mm　1/16　　印　　张：16.75
字　　数：260 千字
版　　次：2022 年 1 月第 1 版　　印　　次：2022 年 1 月第 1 次印刷
书　　号：ISBN 978-7-313-25736-9
定　　价：58.00 元

序言 1

我和作者李锦的认识，源自我任职上海市民办平和双语学校校长时，她当时是我们学校学生的家长。

记得那一年夏天，李锦领着儿子来到我们学校招生办，为刚从英国回来上小学的儿子咨询转学事宜。时间飞逝，她的儿子如今已经从美国的大学毕业，学业有成，进入新的事业。

2013 年的一天，李锦联系我，告诉我她写了一本《我是孩子的品牌总监》。我很惊讶她会写这样内容的书籍。她当时捧着新书对我说："我在帮助陪伴儿子申请美国大学的经历中，就像陪伴儿子重新成长了一番。"因为在准备大学申请过程中，除了鼓励儿子要在学习上努力取得好成绩，还需要准备一份申请文书。在准备文书的日子里，她和儿子一起回顾总结了一回人生。

在帮助儿子成功申请上美国的大学后，李锦就在思考，如今还有很多希望去美国留学的学生和他们的家长，会经历一番与自己一样的历程。这其中是跨文化的迷茫，是信息差的弯路，是试图表达自我时的困顿，是父母与子女之间不可避免的不理解、难沟通。她想把自己的体验和收获带给更多的学生和家长，以专业的方式给他们提供更为清晰的指引。于是她辞去美国华特迪士尼公司大中华区市场执行总监的职位，创办了峰越教育，专注于升学指导服务。听完她的想法，作为管理学校国际课程的校长，我给李锦的忠告就是要做就要做有质量的升学指导工作，因为这项事业是帮助更多的学生实现进入优秀大学深造学习的造福之事。

八年了，如今李锦创办的峰越教育不仅帮助很多学生圆了美国大学梦，更引导这些学生在申请美国大学过程中，实现了反思生活经历、感悟成长快乐、思考人生价值、确立学术追求的境界提升，让这些学子们带着理想的翅膀，畅游在世界知名学府。这些都是作为一位教育者，而非经营者，对年轻求学者的美好期冀。

随着高中国际课程的开展，我们对国内的“考”大学和国外的“申请”大学之间的差别不断加深了解。国外申请大学除了需要具备相应的学业成绩(GPA)、标化考试成绩要求以外，还需要提供个人学习收获、成长感悟、对未来研学的专业追求的书面陈述，这对我们国内学生和家长习惯了“考”大学的思维模式是一种挑战。本书通过分析多个实践经验和成功案例，总结归纳出如何让申请大学的个人文书以更真切、生动、精彩的形式呈现在招生官面前，使申请学生成为令大学招生官们欣赏并期待的申请人。

本书从分析美国大学的升学情况到发展趋势，从申请规划流程到递交申请书的时间节点，从入读国际课程的三年时间规划到完成文书的关键环节，都做了非常专业而详细的介绍，不失为一本实用、严谨且专业的升学指导书。本书不仅可以为国际课程学校的招生专业老师所使用，更是正在学习国际课程，准备去美国优秀大学深造的学生和家长们的必备书籍。

希望峰越教育能够在引领国际课程学生走向世界名校之路上，贡献更多的成功案例，成就更多学生实现大学深造和学业发展的梦想，为培养更多高水平、专业化的国际化人才做出贡献。

任国芳

上海浦东新区民办宏文学校总校长，上海市民办平和双语学校前校长

序言 2

李锦一直说她的工作是个圆梦人的角色。我知道她把很多孩子送到了他们梦想中的高校。这次她又推出新作,请我写序。

作为一个留学生的父亲,我曾经说起,将来哪天小女若能考进罗素集团成员大学,我就心满意足了。于是立刻被李锦老师批评,她告诉我经她们团队之手无数 CASE 中,她的 KPI 考核,进"哈耶普斯麻"属于第一梯队,进牛津、剑桥属于第二梯队。这次她出版新书,是对各位学生和家长有益的事。

我把书稿从头到尾看了,作为一个读书人、爱书人,做了 30 年新闻工作后现在转行做卖书人的我,觉得本书还真值得一看。此书是成功申请世界顶级名校的典型文书撰写过程及修改思路的集成,书中展现了一个个向世界讲好中国学生故事的教案。我一直觉得即使用双方母语沟通也未必顺畅,更何况是试图用外语表达自己。本书不仅解决了如何让国外招生官了解中国申请者这一难题,更提供了让他们认可、欣赏当代中国学生的办法。

本书是一册升学秘籍,将复杂的申请过程拆解成各个清晰的部分,以直接明了的方式呈现给学生、家长、行业从业者。即便像我一样并不太了解留学申请的读者,读完此书,我也在短时间有了明显的知识提升。此外,对于在跨国公司上班的年轻人,本书也值得深读。

钮也仿

上海新华传媒连锁有限公司执行董事

上海财经大学兼职教授

序言3

说起美国的高校，就不得不提到美国常春藤联盟八大名校（以下简称“藤校”）。“藤校”对于每一位想要去留学美国的申请者来说都是梦寐以求的归属。作为美国的顶尖高校，每年都有大批学生将“藤校”作为自己申请的最高目标，都争相申请希望得到它们的offer。

一、“藤校”的魅力

历史悠久、治学严谨、学术水平高是“藤校”的标签，从“藤校”走出了众多杰出科学家、政商各界的重要人物。在“藤校”你不仅能跟着杰出人物学习最新、最前沿的知识，你所拥有的校友资源也是其他学校难以相比的。

学生的成就越好，学校荣誉越高。

学校荣誉越高，来这里读书的好学生也就越多。

好学生越多，未来取得的成就也会越高。

二、“爬藤”的技巧

知彼——了解你申请的学校。你得先了解这所大学的招生情况究竟是怎样的？它录取学生的标准是什么？这些信息在各大院校的官网里面基本都会有。

知己——了解自己当前学术能力水平及方向。通过自我评估和专业导师对自己的评价，找出自己的发光点，清楚自己的优势和劣势，这很关键。

匹配申请——根据自身情况选择合适的学校，同时根据目标高校标准努力提升自己的硬实力。大家在选择学校及专业的时候，一定要结合自身的能力和实际条件筛选出适合自己的，一定要明确自己的喜好，清楚自己未来想做什么。

三、文书的“魔力”

美国大学生招生咨询委员会（NACAC）报告显示：“申请文书”和“强烈兴趣”将成为最重要的软性因素。在现在这个时代，对于中国学生们来说，标化考试拿到高分不是最难的，最难的是在后面的考核中脱颖而出。在具有同等竞争力的学生中，如果文书出众，那么被录取的概率将会大大提升。而对于标化考试略有不足的学生，一篇强有力的文书可以帮学生在申请时实现翻盘。这就是为什么越来越多的美国大学在网申中设置“为何选择本校”一类的命题。因为这些题目可以让招生官更好地了解学生是如何认识学校的，学生又是否花了相当长的时间来确定这所大学与自己的匹配度等。

文书是申请材料的灵魂所在。申请文书，可以帮助招生官了解申请人的个性特征，判断其是否适合这个专业。大家都知道文书对于申请名校的重要性，也知道名校的文书都不好写，往往都有很个性化的要求，而名校正是希望通过文书这几乎唯一的途径去了解学生的内在特点，所以我们必须认真对待，尽力做到最好。本书旨在破解中国学生申请“藤校”文书写作之谜，为广大读者解码文书的写作步骤，剖析写作思路，分享写作技巧，期待用文书的“魔力”，点亮留学生的未来。

“藤校”是多少莘莘学子的梦想，“藤校”的光环加持，对以后人生的发展也大有裨益。“藤校”的价值还体现在人文精神上，在“藤校”你会有机会与杰出教授们一起攻克科研难题，探索未知领域，这种精神上的快乐和成长更让人愉悦。

最后想说的是，在留学申请这件事情上，一定要做到从自我出发、从实际出发。这是你自己的人生，要跟着自己的心走，才能过上想要的生活，并不是大学排名靠前的就是最好的。适合你的，你喜欢的，才是最好的。希望大家在追梦的路上都能一路顺风，希望能有更多的学子获取梦想美国名牌大学的 offer，有一个美好的未来。

徐　俭
上海世外教育集团总裁

序言 4

七月流火，八月未央。暑假中的一天，李锦老师找到我，非常诚恳地邀请我为她的新书《解码常春藤招生——美国本科文书成功申请解析》写序，并将该书的初稿寄给了我。我和李锦老师在五年前的一次活动中相识，由于我俩同在从事与国际教育相关的工作，因此有了很多共同语言，也成了朋友。所以，为李老师新书写序的事情，我欣然应允。

当我翻开书稿，一章章细细品读下去——从"解码美国常春藤大学""解码常春藤申请文书"，读到"好的文书到底怎样写"，再到"获得美国顶尖大学录取的'牛娃'的文书赏析"，以及大量真实的数据和典型的成功案例，心中不禁惊喜连连。书中宝贵的资料和建议不正是我们这些申请美国名校的家长和学生一直想要的"升学秘诀"吗？

众所周知，美国高校的招生制度和中国高校的招生制度大相径庭。中国高校的招生制度长期以来偏重学生的分数，学生分数达到了录取分数线就可以拿到录取通知书，所以相对简单、客观，学生也没有太大的选校烦恼。而美国大学招生实行申请制，学生能否进入心仪的学校，成绩不是被大学录取的最关键因素，招生官才是决定申请是否成功的最关键人物。而招生官是非常注重全面、综合地评价申请学生的，所以需要学生提交很多信息和资料。有些申请美国高校的硬性标准，对于学生来说只要照实罗列即可，如学校的 GPA、年级排名、标化考试成绩、教师的推荐信、课程的挑战性、课外活动等。唯独特殊的是申请文书这一项，它没有统一的评价标准，也不能量化，用一个词来形容就是——主观。对于申请学生而言，它是自己主观的作品，反映自己的个性、观点和思想；对于招生官来说，阅读申请文书，喜欢或不喜欢，欣赏或不欣赏，往往也是非常主观的判断，自己在脑中生出文书作者的画像。鉴于这一点，文书的撰写就非常讲究和关键了。正如李锦老师在书中写道:“文书就像是一个最为宽大的舞台,能够让申请者在其中以自己独特的方式完美呈现‘个人品牌’,而坐在台下的招生官从中可以看到的是申请者与众不同的闪光点。”我们也常说,“好看的皮囊千篇一律,有趣的灵魂万里挑一。”当硬性条件千篇一律的情况下,如何让你的申请文书展示你“有趣的灵魂”? 李锦老师的这本书给出了最好的解答,它不仅告诉了你,让申请文书引人入胜的“五步法”、独立升学顾问是助你挖掘自身个性的强大的“背后力量”,它还列举了各个美国顶尖名校的文书题目和分析,以及展现了真实的文书修改案例。我相信本书对于希望本科阶段去美国留学的学生将是一场及时雨,尤其是在国际形势日益严峻、申请竞争愈发激烈的当下,它能给广大申请美国本科的学子和家长提供专业的指导和帮助,使我们获益匪浅。

我经常感慨,我们中国的孩子选择了国际教育和出国留学之路,就好比美国诗人罗伯特·弗罗斯特的诗歌《未选择的路》中描述的情形一样,就是选择了“the road less travelled by”——一条少有人走的路,一条人迹罕至、布满荆棘的道路。然而,当我品读完此书,慢慢合上的时候,我由衷地感到,国际教育和出国留学之路其实并不人迹罕至,并不布满荆棘。因为,这里有一大批老师和专家同走在这条路上,不断给我们的孩子专业的指导、人生的规划甚至还有心灵的启迪和陪伴。所以,我们的孩子并不孤独,当初在勇气和冒险精神驱动下做出的决定很值得。同时,我也坚信,哪怕眼前充满未知的挑战,他们在这条路上也一定能走得踏实而成功,将来定有足够的力量去承载和完成家长的期待和时代的使命,去实现自己人生的追求和价值。

姚瑞丹
上海交大附中 IB 课程中心校长
2021 年 8 月 14 日于上海

大咖说

本书专业系统地介绍了海外大学招生办在招收中国学生时的侧重点和选择标准，针对目前主流的申请系统（如美国大学通用申请系统、英国大学和学院招生服务中心 UCAS、美国 UC 申请系统）对申请者的主文书和辅文书构思给出了切实、有效的建议和说明。本书将给申请中的学生提供有益的专业帮助！

唐盛昌
上海市首届教育功臣，上海中学原校长

文书，是美国本科申请的要义之一。如何理解自己，讲好自己的故事，让大学招生官从纸面上还原鲜活的申请人样貌，是中国留学生的一大申请难点。本书包括申请文书类型、准备要点和各类文书范本，是一本系统、细致的文书指导手册。

贾博
WLSA 上海（复旦）学校校长
世界名中学联盟执行理事兼秘书长

从 0 到 1 全面解剖申请美国大学中举足轻重的文书写作——你将会看到实例文书从初稿到终稿的演变过程，以及招生官顾问精确的修改意见和点评。

赵立楠
美国斯坦福大学 2020 级本科生

本文书写作秘籍简直比中国学生自身还要更了解中国学生！要是我能在申

请季读到它就好了！

姚诗怡

美国纽约大学 2020 级本科生

这是一本实战指南。本书从招生官的角度揭示了美国大学是如何通过文书来快速了解和评价一个学生。据此再提出一系列有针对性的方案，帮助中国学生应对挑战、脱颖而出。实用和可操作性是本书的特点。

李晨玉

美国克莱蒙特·麦肯纳学院 2016 级本科生

这本书涵盖了美国本科申请的所有方面，内容翔实且可靠。对于国内申请者常见的盲区和误解，本书能很好地为大家答疑解难，来避免犯一些错误，最大程度上展现自己的优势。对于缺乏各路大学信息、英语写作训练的本土学生来说，参考本书内容可以有效提升我们与招生官之间的信息传达的质量和效率，以获得最佳的申请结果。

朱一杰

美国康奈尔大学 2017 级本科生

本书值得仔细阅读，通过鲜活的文书案例分析，结合自身经历，能得到很好的启发，助力名校申请！

徐亦如

美国范德堡大学 2018 级本科生

大家都说美国大学的申请文书很重要，但本书具体谈到了这些文书为什么重要（why it is important）以及在申请审阅过程中的具体意义（how it is important）。带着这些背景知识和书中提到的写作技巧，相信大家都能写好申请文书，讲好属于自己的故事。

张奇正
美国芝加哥大学2018级本科生

本书逻辑性很强，不只是在说文书，把申请的每一步都解释得很清楚，而且解释的方式不只是一行行的专业术语，还用了很多例子。对申请一点都不了解的同学也可以看懂，本科申请招生官看重哪些，为什么看重这些，怎么在这些方面脱颖而出。文书写作是本书的侧重点，我觉得同学们看过之后得到的帮助甚至可能比学校指导老师给到的帮助更大，因为同学们可以对照着书里给出的步骤自己一步一步来策划自己的文书内容，题材是非常重要的。书里涵盖了绝大多数常见的文书题材和热门大学的文书例子，最棒的一点是有一篇作文从初稿到终稿的记录以及老师的点评和修改，非常详细，这是其他关于申请文书书籍里比较少见的。尽管文字、结构等方面还是建议留给老师修改，但有了这本书做参考，学生就会准备得更充分，文书就比别的同学需要修改的次数少，多下来的时间可以在别的方面做准备。

邵文奕
美国埃默里大学2019级本科生

当我看到本书的时候，申请大学时写文书的情景再一次浮现在脑海。回忆过去17年并不算长的经历，什么事对我来说最深刻而有意义的呢？在我看来，都太过平凡；但是，当顾问和我把这些平凡的日常一点点聚集起来，从不同的角度去看它，仿佛就赋予了不同的内涵，这些灵感，对我来说必须立刻抓住。文书的打磨工作相当艰巨，但我知道这是通往成功之路，众所周知，文书在申请中占有非常重要的地位，它能够展示一个真实、生动的自己；而最后，你的形象一定会跃然于纸上。感谢本书能够让我重温文书写作过程，回顾那段时光，一切都是值得的。最后给即将申请的同学们一个小小的建议，在申请前请一定提高自己的写作能力。

林若贤
美国康奈尔大学2020级本科生

前言 1

美国的大学招生官通常会告诉你，你高中的课程强度以及你的课业成绩是决定录取结果的最关键因素。即使一篇大学申请文书再优秀，也不能拯救一张不合格的成绩单。那么，优秀的申请文书可以有什么样的作用呢？你可以把它理解为一场“决胜局”，它是帮助招生委员会从一众拥有相似学术能力的申请者中筛选更适合候选人的关键因素。顶尖美国大学的申请者，大多都在高难度的高中课程体系中拥有优异的学校课业成绩和标化考试成绩，这使得大学招生官很难单单凭借学术表现就在他们之中做出选择。这也就是申请文书存在的重要原因。不过，文书只是区分高水平学生的三大方式之一(另外两个是课外活动、特殊才能、奖项等学生的课外成就和推荐信)。

本书能帮助你学会从招生委员会的角度来看待大学申请文书。我甚至会带你经历一遍招生委员会讨论、评判文书的过程，以便你了解这其中的步骤和评价要素。你会发现，招生官们也是和我们一样的人。就同你一样，他们也会在阅读时，被某些东西惊喜到，也会对某些东西感到无聊。他们有时也不得不顶着工作压力读完那些不感兴趣的材料。他们的“阅读季”(在申请提交和学校最终放榜之间的数周)里，充斥着令人疲倦的、不曾停歇的材料阅读，委员会会议和一个接着一个紧凑的截止日期。因此，本书既提到了什么样的文书开头会抓住招生官的眼球，又告诉你如何将你的人生经历变成有趣的叙事。你所陈述的这个“故事”并不一定是重大的事件，但它们是能够向招生官展示你是什么样的人，是帮助招生官明白他们的校园将会如何因你而精彩的人生故事。

我在美国大学招生领域已有超过 35 年的工作经历，其间我担任过招生办主任，领导过美国大学招生咨询协会(NACAC)和波托马克大学招生咨询协会(PCACAC)中的招生规范委员会。

Louis L Hirsch

2021 年 10 月 18 日于美国特拉华

前言 2

自 2013 年创立以来，峰越教育已不知不觉经历了 8 个申请季，正迎来第 9 个申请季。在过去的 8 年里，家长们经常会问我，"美国大学的申请文书到底重要吗?""写文书有模板吗?""到底什么样的文书才是有成效的?""怎样的文书才会让'藤校'的招生官喜欢?"……确实，相比学校 GPA、标化考试成绩、课外活动、推荐信这些有着相对具体标准的申请材料而言，文书的好坏听上去有些虚无缥缈，很容易让人摸不着头脑。文书中应该写什么和不应该写什么，对于很多准备申请的中国家庭，尤其是学生本人来说是一个不小的难题。

既然文书没有确切的标准，难以捉摸，那我们为什么要呈现这样一本专注于文书写作的书籍呢？这是因为文书在整个申请中扮演着非常重要的角色，在一众申请材料中，文书就像是一个最为宽大的舞台，能够让申请者在其中以自己独特的方式完美呈现"个人品牌"，而坐在台下的招生官从中可以看到的是申请者与众不同的闪光点。在我与曾在美国做过几十年招生官的外籍老师们交流的时候，他们经常会说："文书是申请中的灵魂，我们会从文书中去判断一个学生的个性和发展潜力，看是不是我们学校所需要的学生。"总而言之，文书是申请过程中最不容易被完成的部分之一，它没有标准、没有套路，却偏偏又是招生官们最为关注的部分之一，它是整个申请过程中最能展现学生特质的部分。

不过，即便文书有如此的重要性，家长们仍然需要注意，文书在留学申请中并不具有"起死回生"的功效。在一份申请材料中，招生官最先看到的还是成绩单。成绩是影响录取最重要的因素之一，这是国内外通用的真理。在申请者的成绩达到一定标准之后，招生官会开始综合评估申请人的影响力和贡献，参考学生的活动、推荐信及文书。一篇好的申请文书，不仅让招生官想录取这个学生，还会让他想在这位学生入学后与他一起聊聊。外籍老师曾这么开玩笑地说："它

(文书)可以治疗病人,但无法让死人起死回生。”所以说,在一份申请跨过了成绩、学校排名等初步的门槛,具备了一定质量的课内外活动、推荐信等方面后,好的文书或许可以改变最终的录取结果。

因为我们深知文书在美国大学这样注重全面、综合性评估的招生流程中的重要性,在过去的8个申请季中,峰越教育的每一位升学顾问老师都会指导学生花费大量的时间来一轮一轮打磨文书。即便是很优秀的学生,在写作文书时,我们也会指导学生反复审视、思考、修改手中的文字。我们通过一次次的头脑风暴去助力学生努力挖掘自己的个性,并且指导学生精雕细琢每一篇文书。8年间,这样的坚持也让我们收获了优异的成绩,我们有许多学员欣喜地拿到了常春藤名校以及其他美国顶尖大学的录取通知书,得以继续自己学术、思想或是职业上的追求。

正是在对文书无数次重复修改的过程中,我们找到了一些写作规律。本书浓缩了8年的文书指导经验,外籍老师们指导文书的方式方法,以及一篇篇过往优秀学生的真实文书分享。我希望通过这样理论加案例的全方面展示,能够帮助中国家长们更好地理解文书为什么如此重要,文书到底应该是什么样子的,又该如何品鉴文书的好与不好。我们也希望帮到更多想要留学的学生找到文书写作的技巧,在努力备考、参加活动之余,创作出真正属于自己的,并且能够完美呈现自己“闪光点”的文书,让自己踏入世界顶尖学府的大门!

2021年9月28日于上海

鸣　谢

本书从构思设计到策划成稿，历经多个申请季，其间获得了诸多国际教育专家、国际学校资深从业者和亲历美国留学申请过程的优秀学生的支持，他们阅读了本书并给予了中肯的评价。

峰越教育全体辛苦耕耘的同事和始终无条件默默支持我的家人们，在此，对他们的信任，鼓励和付出表示衷心感谢！同时，也要向将自己的美国大学申请文书在本书刊出的几位同学致以诚挚的谢意，他们是(这里用学生的笔名，排名不分先后)：

斯坦福大学 Frank 同学

纽约大学 M 同学

克莱蒙特・麦肯纳学院小李同学

康奈尔大学 Jerry 同学

范德堡大学 Louisa 同学

宾夕法尼亚大学 LXJ 同学

埃默里大学邵文奕同学

康奈尔大学奥特曼同学

斯坦福大学 Bambi 同学

乔治城大学 Nijedan 同学

芝加哥大学 Emma 同学

在此，对他们开诚布公地分享和大力支持表示衷心感谢！

李峰

2021 年 9 月 18 日

目 录

第一章 解码美国常春藤大学

第一节

为什么选择美国大学

随着中国家庭经济条件、文化和教育水平的逐年提升，越来越多的人有能力、有意识将子女送至海外接受高等教育。每每提及海外升学的"择校问题"，中国家庭普遍热衷于将目光紧紧锁定世界上排名最前的、最顶尖的院校。但是到底哪些学校算是"最好"的大学呢？

《美国新闻与世界报道》(*U.S. News*)根据全球研究声誉、地区性研究声誉、发表论文、出版书籍、学术会议、标准化引用影响、被引用次数、国际合作、高频被引文献数量(在引用最多文献的前 10%)、高频被引文献百分比(在引用最多文献的前 10%)、高频被引文献数量(在各自领域被引次数最多的前 1%)、高频被引文献百分比(在各自领域被引次数最多的前 1%)等数据，在 2021 年调查了全球上千所大学并进行了排名。其中我们发现，在排名前 50 的大学中，美国大学占据了 24 个席位，占整个榜单的近一半。英国则仅有 6 所大学进入榜单前 50。如表 1.1 所示。

表 1.1　2022 *U.S. News* 世界大学排名

排名	学 校 名 称	中 文 名 称	所属国家和地区
1	Harvard University	哈佛大学	美国
2	Massachusetts Institute of Technology	麻省理工学院	美国
3	Stanford University	斯坦福大学	美国

续 表

排名	学 校 名 称	中 文 名 称	所属国家和地区
4	University of California-Berkeley	加州大学伯克利分校	美国
5	University of Oxford	牛津大学	英国
6	Columbia University	哥伦比亚大学	美国
7	University of Washington	华盛顿大学	美国
8	University of Cambridge	剑桥大学	英国
9	California Institute of Technology	加州理工学院	美国
9	Johns Hopkins University	约翰霍普金斯大学	美国
11	University of California-San Francisco	加州大学旧金山分校	美国
12	Yale University	耶鲁大学	美国
13	University of Pennsylvania	宾夕法尼亚大学	美国
14	University of California-Los Angeles	加州大学洛杉矶分校	美国
15	University of Chicago	芝加哥大学	美国
16	Princeton University	普林斯顿大学	美国
16	University College London	伦敦大学学院	英国
16	University of Toronto	多伦多大学	加拿大
19	University of Michigan-Ann Arbor	密歇根大学安娜堡分校	美国
20	Imperial College London	伦敦帝国理工学院	英国
21	University of California-San Diego	加州大学圣迭戈分校	美国
22	Cornell University	康奈尔大学	美国
23	Duke University	杜克大学	美国
24	Northwestern University	西北大学	美国
25	University of Melbourne	墨尔本大学	澳大利亚
26	Swiss Federal Institute of Technology Zurich	苏黎世联邦理工学院	瑞士
26	Tsinghua University	清华大学	中国
28	University of Sydney	悉尼大学	澳大利亚
29	National University of Singapore	新加坡国立大学	新加坡

续　表

排名	学 校 名 称	中 文 名 称	所属国家和地区
30	New York University	纽约大学	美国
31	Washington University in St. Louis	圣路易斯华盛顿大学	美国
32	University of Edinburgh	爱丁堡大学	英国
33	King's College London	伦敦国王学院	英国
33	Nanyang Technological University	南洋理工大学	新加坡
35	University of British Columbia	不列颠哥伦比亚大学	加拿大
36	University of Queensland Australia	澳大利亚昆士兰大学	澳大利亚
37	University of Copenhagen	哥本哈根大学	丹麦
38	University of Amsterdam	阿姆斯特丹大学	荷兰
39	University of North Carolina-Chapel Hill	北卡罗来纳大学教堂山分校	美国
40	Monash University	莫纳什大学	澳大利亚
41	University of New South Wales	新南威尔士大学	澳大利亚
42	University of Pittsburgh	匹兹堡大学	美国
43	University of Texas-Austin	得克萨斯大学奥斯汀分校	美国
44	King Abdulaziz University	阿卜杜勒阿齐兹国王大学	沙特阿拉伯
45	Peking University	北京大学	中国
46	Sorbonne Universite	索邦大学	法国
46	University of Munich	慕尼黑大学	德国
48	Catholic University of Leuven	鲁汶天主教大学	比利时
48	Karolinska Institute	卡罗林斯卡学院	瑞典
48	Utrecht University	乌得勒支大学	荷兰

（资料来源：*U.S. News* 官网 https://www.usnews.com/education/best-global-universities/rankings?int=top_nav_Global_Universities）

除了 *U.S. News* 排名外，2021 年，英国泰晤士高等教育根据教学（学习环境）、研究（规模、收入和声誉）、引文（研究影响力）、国际展望（员工、学生、研究）、行业收入（知识转移）这 5 个维度对全球 99 个不同的国家和地区的 1 662 所大学进行排名(见表 1.2)。在全球 TOP100 大学的排名中,美国上榜高校最多,一共有 38 所,其次是英国和德国,分别是 11 所和 7 所。中国内地进入前 100 的院校一共有 6 所。

表 1.2　泰晤士高等教育 2022 年全球 TOP100 大学

排名	学 校 名 称	所在国家/地区
1	牛津大学	英国
2	加州理工学院	美国
2	哈佛大学	美国
4	斯坦福大学	美国
5	剑桥大学	英国
5	麻省理工学院	美国
7	普林斯顿大学	美国
8	加州大学伯克利分校	美国
9	耶鲁大学	美国
10	芝加哥大学	美国
11	哥伦比亚大学	美国
12	帝国理工学院	英国
13	约翰霍普金斯大学	美国
13	宾夕法尼亚大学	美国
15	苏黎世联邦理工学院	瑞士
16	北京大学	中国
16	清华大学	中国
18	多伦多大学	加拿大
18	伦敦大学学院	英国
20	加州大学洛杉矶分校	美国
21	新加坡国立大学	新加坡
22	康奈尔大学	美国
23	杜克大学	美国

续　表

排名	学 校 名 称	所在国家/地区
24	密西根大学安娜堡分校	美国
24	西北大学	美国
26	纽约大学	美国
27	伦敦政治经济学院	英国
28	卡耐基梅隆大学	美国
29	华盛顿大学	美国
30	爱丁堡大学	英国
30	香港大学	中国香港地区
32	慕尼黑大学	德国
33	墨尔本大学	澳大利亚
34	加州大学圣迭戈分校	美国
35	伦敦国王学院	英国
35	东京大学	日本
37	不列颠哥伦比亚大学	加拿大
38	慕尼黑工业大学	德国
39	卡罗林斯卡学院	瑞典
40	洛桑联邦理工学院	瑞士
40	巴黎文理研究大学	法国
42	海德堡大学	德国
42	鲁汶大学	比利时
44	麦吉尔大学	加拿大
45	佐治亚理工学院	美国
46	新加坡南洋理工大学	新加坡
47	得克萨斯大学奥斯汀分校	美国
48	伊利诺伊大学香槟分校	美国
49	香港中文大学	中国香港地区

续 表

排名	学 校 名 称	所在国家/地区
50	曼彻斯特大学	英国
51	圣路易斯华盛顿大学	美国
52	北卡罗来纳大学教堂山分校	美国
53	瓦赫宁根大学与研究	荷兰
54	澳大利亚国立大学	澳大利亚
54	昆士兰大学	澳大利亚
54	首尔国立大学	韩国
57	莫纳什大学	澳大利亚
58	悉尼大学	澳大利亚
58	威斯康星大学麦迪逊分校	美国
60	复旦大学	中国
61	京都大学	日本
62	波士顿大学	美国
63	南加州大学	美国
64	布朗大学	美国
65	阿姆斯特丹大学	荷兰
66	香港科技大学	中国香港地区
67	加州大学戴维斯分校	美国
68	加州大学圣塔芭芭拉分校	美国
69	乌得勒支大学	荷兰
70	细腻新南威尔士大学	澳大利亚
71	莱顿大学	荷兰
72	鹿特丹伊拉斯姆斯大学	荷兰
73	柏林大学医学院	德国
74	柏林洪堡大学	德国
75	代尔夫特工业大学	荷兰

续　表

排名	学 校 名 称	所在国家/地区
75	浙江大学	中国
75	苏黎世大学	瑞士
78	图宾根大学	德国
78	华威大学	英国
80	格罗宁根大学	荷兰
80	麦克马斯特大学	加拿大
82	埃默里大学	美国
83	柏林自由大学	德国
84	上海交通大学	中国
85	俄亥俄州立大学	美国
86	格拉斯哥大学	英国
86	明尼苏达大学	美国
88	蒙特利尔大学	加拿大
88	中国科学技术大学	中国
88	索邦大学	法国
91	香港理工大学	中国香港地区
92	布里斯托大学	英国
93	马里兰大学帕克分校	美国
93	密西根州立大学	美国
95	巴黎理工学院	法国
96	哥本哈根大学	丹麦
96	根特大学	比利时
98	加州大学欧文分校	美国
99	达特茅斯学院	美国
99	韩国科学技术院	韩国

（资料来源：THE World University Ranking 官网 https://www.timeshighereducation.com/world-university-rankings/2022/world-ranking）

通过这两个排名我们不难看出，美国大学的优势位于世界大学的最前列。学校能拥有如此高的地位和排名与美国整体的教育理念息息相关。

1. 美国的大学更愿意“招贤纳士”

较之只看重高考分数的有些亚洲国家，美国大学对于学生的考核更为全面，美国学校更关注每一位学生的个性和潜力，愿意给那些英文成绩不佳但在某一领域表现突出或有才能的学生有进入大学或就读名校的机会。

2. 美国的教育是阶梯持续性的

从教育机制上来看，美国的教育不是一次性的而是阶梯持续性的。也就是说美国持续不断地将教育给那些曾经想放弃受教育的人。所以美国学生在选择大学的时候，往往是自主选择的，而不像大多数中国学生那么被动，只能确定自己不想做什么，而不知道自己究竟想做什么。

3. 美国大学拥有丰富的教育资源

美国是世界上教育质量最高的国家之一，拥有的教育资源也位列世界前茅。很多美国大学拥有最前沿的实验室、国外学术交换项目、实习项目以及强大的师资力量，这些都能让学生在各个领域学习到顶尖的知识。同时，美国大学在知识传授方式上也是多种多样的，学校中有些课程是单向的知识讲授，学生可以安静地听课和记笔记，而有些课程则是以讨论的形式展开，学生在其中可以选择适合自己的学习方式。

在美国，无论公立还是私立大学，其目标都是尽可能地减少课堂人数，通过小班化、个性化的教学让学生更全面深刻地理解知识，通过这样的方式可以激发学生新的想法和新的思路。所以美国大学课堂更注重“授之以渔”，多维度的教授方法来真正培养学生的学习能力、研究能力、创新能力、实践能力。

4. 美国大学的多样性不可忽视

美国校园更具有多样性。如果你的同学来自其他国家，且与你有着不同的社会经济背景，拥有不同的兴趣又或者信仰不同的宗教，那么你通过他们会见识到许多新事物。当你听到不同观点时，就会迫使你重新审视自己的观点。这种多样性有助于形成你的批判性思维。因此大学更希望招收已经接触过多个学科领域并拥有多种思维方式的学生，这就是所谓的多样化。

当然美国大学优势并不仅仅只是以上几个方面，还包括了学校的学术贡献、科研水平以及科技创新能力。尤其是中国家长们口中经常提到的像普林斯顿大学、哈佛大学、耶鲁大学、斯坦福大学、麻省理工学院等更是受到世界范围内教育专家们的认可。此外，美国大学所提倡的通识教育以及自身的包容性、多元化和丰富的教育资源确实令很多学生和家长向往。

第二节 美国大学招生官让学校“与众不同”

美国的大学之所以能与众不同、多姿多彩，这与学校自身的风格和招收的学生息息相关。例如纽约大学，地处纽约市的中心地带，邻近华尔街，而且时代广场、第五大道商业区、洛克菲勒中心、百老汇剧院区、唐人街等也都在这里。学校周边多元化的环境，也使得很多追求时尚、思想活跃、多元化的学生希望就读于此，而整个纽约大学的风格也就自然而然地时尚、活泼了起来。这也是为什么我们常说美国大学都有自己的风格。

而帮助学校守护“校风”的便是招生官，他们会根据学校自身的情况去审核每一位申请者。不同学校的招生官们在招生时所考虑的范围也大有不同。

接下来我们将把大学分为“极度挑剔”“非常挑剔”“较挑剔”和“不太挑剔”①这四类。那么招生官是如何给美国大学进行归类的呢？

1. “较挑剔”和“不太挑剔”的大学

如果大学对学生的筛选“较挑剔”（招生录取率为 50%～75%）或“不太挑剔”（招生录取率为 76%～90%），那么其主要关注点是该学生是否为取得学业成功做好了准备。招生官将重点关注：

（1）在 9 年级至 12 年级期间，学生修了多少门学术课程？

（2）这些课程是否满足该大学对每学期英语、数学、实验科学、社会科学和

① “极度挑剔”“非常挑剔”“较挑剔”和“不太挑剔”的定义引用自美国大学委员会网站（https://bigfourture.collegeboard.org/college-search）。

外语课程的最基本要求？

(3) 学生是否达到大学的最低数学水平？

(4) 学生是否符合大学的最低平均成绩要求？

(5) 如果需要考试，学生是否达到该大学最低考试分数线？

(6) 如果学生的母语不是英语，那么学生是否达到该大学在英语能力测试方面的最低分数要求？

总结：对于这些大学，审查申请主要是看学生是否满足该大学在课程、成绩和考试分数上的最低要求。除了下面列出的例外情况，如果学生没有达到要求，学校将不考虑活动、奖项和荣誉、申请文书或老师和独立升学顾问的推荐信等其他的申请材料。

例外情况：

(1) 该学府荣誉学院的申请人。

许多高等学府都设有一个小型的荣誉学院或荣誉课程，这类课程具有更高的录取标准，其为最有才华的学生提供更具挑战性的课程工作并开设小规模研讨类课程。有些课程极具有声望，录取苛刻。在这种情况下，可能会要求提交申请文书以及老师的推荐信。

(2) 某些竞争激烈专业的申请人。

即使某大学在入学方面的竞争总体来说不是特别激烈，它提供的某些专业可能仍会极具竞争性(一般是工程、计算机科学或护理学专业)。申请这一类专业时可能需要申请文书。

(3) 学术奖学金，特别是全额奖学金的申请人。

即使一所大学在常规申请中不将文书列为必需项，它仍可能要求申请奖学金的学生递交申请文书。有些申请人可能会被学校要求进行一对一面试。

(4) 特殊情况。

想要在高中毕业之前考上大学的学生，或者高中成绩受到不可控因素(例如严重的疾病或家人死亡)影响的学生。

2. “非常挑剔”和“极度挑剔”的大学

“非常挑剔”的大学录取率为 25%～49%，而“极度挑剔”的大学录取率低于25%。由于申请这些大学的绝大多数学生都有很突出的学业成绩和丰富的学术知识储备，并且由于大多数人具有相似的高分成绩，仅凭他们的分数等级和考试成绩招生官很难抉择是否录取申请人。招生官也表示，有些天赋和才能是无法通过平均学分绩点（以下简称GPA）或考试成绩来评估的。

这就是为什么你会听到这些大学讨论如何“综合评估申请人”的原因。这意味着他们除了查看学生成绩外，还考虑申请文书、推荐信以及课外成就的广度和深度。当综合考虑所有这些因素时，他们的关注点是哪些候选人能为大学做出最多的贡献。

但是，当我们说“做出最多贡献”时，是什么意思呢？以下是招生部长及其招生委员会必须考虑的事项：

1）学校的学费收入目标

美国大学即使拥有巨额捐赠，但本身仍然需要依赖学费来支付一部分运营费用。如果学生需要有经济资助才能入学，这将减少大学从录取这名学生中获得的收入。

美国只有一小部分大学是既对“需求盲目（need-blind）”（即他们录取学生时不考虑学生是否有经济需要），又可以满足所有入学学生的经济资助需求。

有些大学会充分满足被录取学生的资金需求，但它们在做出录取决定时会有“需求意识（need-aware）”。这意味着它们会限制对有经济需求的学生的招生数量。所以对于那些需要经济援助入学的学生，升学申请的竞争压力会更大。当然有一些大学会对美国当地申请人提供充分经济援助，但却不能满足非美国籍申请人的全部经济援助。

2）各专业的招生目标

美国大学在招收学生时，必须要招收足够的学生，以填补每个专业的招生名额。当然学校也必须保证每个专业不会因超额招生而导致超负荷。

因此美国大学各专业经常会出现一种情况，假如某一学年，申请生物学专业的学生过多，而申请物理专业的学生远远不足，那么这一年计划申请物理专业的学生将具有绝对的申请优势。

3）特殊专业内部的招生目标

在美国音乐和视觉艺术等专业尤其复杂，音乐专业需要会演奏特定乐器的学生。视觉艺术则需要特定的熟悉2D、3D和数码技术的学生。假如在某一年，申请小提琴专业的学生过多而申请大提琴专业的学生不足，那么申请大提琴专业的学生会占有优势。

4）各种大学运动队和其他学生活动的招生目标

众所周知，体育在美国非常重视，因此大学的体育教练为了招收到有潜力的运动员，许多大学会提供体育奖学金给有潜力的优秀运动员。在录取学生之前，招生办公室必须评估被招募的运动员是否具备在大学取得成功的学术潜力。大学也可能需要完成其他学生活动的招生目标。例如，如果一所大学拥有出色的辩论队，它则可能正在寻找优秀的高中辩论者。

5）增加学生群体多元化的目标

许多美国大学认为，保证每届学生的多元化能促进不同背景、文化和生活经历的学生们之间的交流学习，这有利于帮助大学提供优质的教育。

学生的多元化体现在每个专业所录取的学生群体在种族、地理位置、性别和社会经济水平等多方面的差异。例如，就性别差异而言，招生官会留意某些以往对于某一性别代表性不足的专业，这意味着申请工程专业的女同学或申请护理专业的男同学可能在录取方面占据优势。

6）公立大学会为本州的学生预留入学名额

例如，北卡罗来纳州法律规定北卡罗来纳大学教堂山分校的州外一年级本科生入学率不得超过18%。这就导致北卡罗来纳大学教堂山分校的州内学生录取率为40%，而州外学生的录取率仅为11%（国际学生被视为“州外学生”）。

7）申请人高中课程的难度

申请人在高中阶段学习了几门美国大学预修课程（以下简称AP）或国际预科证书课程（以下简称IB）？其AP或IB考试成绩又如何？大多数招生官明白学生的平均成绩有可能被夸大，因为有些学生的GPA会因为课程相对简单容易获得高分。

有些高中提供的高级课程较少。招生官在评估学生的过程中会尝试了解学生在多大程度上充分利用了所在学校提供的有挑战性的学习机会。

8）应届新生的整体学术概况

大学网站和大学指南，如*U.S. News*和美国Niche大学排名等，提供了每届大学新生的学术数据，其中包括标化考试成绩和高中平均成绩的范围。

一所大学的学术概况通常被认为是该大学声望的衡量标准，也是影响其排名的一个因素。如果学生的学术成绩远远低于这些平均水平或范围，那么即使有出色的申请文书或出色的课外活动成就也无法保证学生会被录取。

9）申请人的才能及生活经历能为校园带来的贡献

这包括获得国家级、省部级或国际奖项的学生，也包括能使其他学生受益的具有宝贵生活经验和观点的学生。

10）非英语母语学生的英语语言水平

有些大学在校园内设有英语语言学院（ELI）。如果学生在除英语水平以外的其他所有方面都非常优秀，学校会考虑为学生提供有条件录取。学生需参加语言学院且当英语语言水平得到充分提高后才被允许入学。

11）“全才”的学生，也可能是整体普通但在某一学科或课外活动领域尤为突出的学生

尽管大学希望招收到一届“全面发展”的学生，但这并不意味着每个学生都必须做到全面发展。在理想情况下，大学希望同时招到这两类学生：真正全面发展的学生和仅在一两个领域表现卓越的学生。

想象一下在一个宿舍楼里，其中一些学生各个方面都非常优秀，而其余有的学生在化学工程专业表现出色，有的已经出版过小说，有的是已赴多国演出的舞者，有的达到奥运会水准的滑雪运动员，还有数学天才和正在为国际职业生涯做准备的钢琴家，等等。总的来说，这栋宿舍楼的学生“多才多艺”，尽管其中的学生并不都是十项全能。

12）履行学校的社会责任

在美国，为来自低收入家庭的学生提供高等教育是帮助提升他们未来经济发展的传统手段。所有公立学校和许多私立学校都将促进这一社会进步作为其使命的一部分，并会在预算允许的范围内提供经济援助，帮助低收入的申请人减轻大学开销。

学校也将公平视为一种社会责任。在选择应届新生时，他们会考虑到学生遇到的困难，例如申请人就读于一所课外活动非常有限的高中。许多美国大学也承受着降低美国高考（以下简称 SAT）或美国大学入学考试（以下简称 ACT）等标化考试要求的压力，因为有数据表明，这些考试偏袒生在富裕家庭，能享受

专业辅导和暑期课程的孩子。

而针对在大学毕业后可能对社会做出积极贡献的学生，许多学校也认为他们有义务向这类学生伸出援手。结合招生官们的考虑范围，也就不难看出为什么美国大学的录取“扑朔迷离”，其主要的原因就是它受到了很多方面的影响，并不是由一个成绩做决定。因此才会让各位学生和家长焦虑，捉摸不透。

第三节

近年来美国大学录取数据与趋势解读

前文提到，美国大学招生官在录取学生时会综合各个方面来考虑。这种情况下，美国大学每年都会录取多少人呢？通过历年统计数据，我们能看出怎样的录取趋势呢？中国学生近几年的录取情况又是如何呢？

美国部分大学 2015～2021 年的申请人数及录取数据如表 1.3 所示。

表 1.3　美国部分大学 2015～2021 年的申请及录取数据　　（单位：人）

学校名称	录取情况	年份						
		2015	2016	2017	2018	2019	2020	2021
哈佛大学	申请人数	34 919	37 307	39 041	39 605	42 749	40 246	57 435
	录取人数	1 944	2 080	2 110	2 037	2 024	1 980	1 968
	录取率	5.57%	5.58%	5.40%	5.14%	4.3%	4.92%	3.43%
哥伦比亚大学	申请人数	36 250	36 292	37 389	40 203	42 569	40 084	60 551
	录取人数	2 222	2 279	2 263	2 260	2 245	2 465	2 218
	录取率	6.13%	6.28%	6.05%	5.62%	5.27%	6.15%	3.66%
宾夕法尼亚大学	申请人数	35 866	37 268	38 918	40 413	44 491	44 961	56 333
	录取人数	3 718	3 787	3 674	3 757	3 110	3 246	3 202
	录取率	10.37%	10.16%	9.44%	9.30%	6.99%	7.22%	5.68%
布朗大学	申请人数	30 431	30 396	32 390	32 723	35 437	38 674	46 568
	录取人数	2 661	2 875	3 014	2 799	2 718	2 733	2 537
	录取率	8.74%	9.46%	9.31%	8.55%	7.67%	7.07%	5.45%

续　表

学校名称	录取情况	年　份						
		2015	2016	2017	2018	2019	2020	2021
康奈尔大学	申请人数	43 037	41 900	44 965	47 039	51 324	49 114	67 000
	录取人数	6 105	6 315	6 337	5 962	5 448	5 330	5 836
	录取率	14.19%	15.07%	14.09%	12.67%	10.61%	10.85%	8.71%
塔夫茨大学	申请人数	19 059	19 063	20 223	21 101	21 501	22 766	31 000
	录取人数	3 287	3 069	2 889	3 127	3 143	3 404	3 469
	录取率	17.25%	16.10%	14.29%	14.82%	14.62%	14.95%	11.19%
波士顿大学	申请人数	54 190	54 781	57 441	60 825	64 481	62 224	75 733
	录取人数	18 701	17 871	16 907	15 273	14 247	11 786	13 884
	录取率	34.51%	32.62%	29.43%	25.11%	22.09%	18.94%	18.33%

（资料来源：根据各高校 2015～2021 年通用数据报告(CDS)整理）

我们从表 1.3 可以发现，美国大学录取的人数越来越少，如哈佛大学 2017～2019 年的录取人数虽然都在 2 000 人以上，但也是逐年递减。而在 2020 年，哈佛大学的录取人数直接跌至 1 980 人，2021 年则在这个基础上又减少了 12 人的录取。

哈佛大学官网就曾经发布新闻称，2021 年收到的申请比去年增加了约 42%，2020 年有 40 246 名学生申请了 2024 届的入学。2025 届的申请人数创下新高，而两年前的 2023 届申请人数曾创下 42 749 人的纪录。

2021 年秋季的申请季，哈佛大学应该是申请人数增长幅度较为明显的学校之一。据了解，哈佛大学在早申请阶段增长了 57%，加上常规阶段的学生，总申请人数达到 57 435 人，而总录取率也跌至 3.43%。要知道，哈佛大学去年的总录取率为 4.92%，录取人数为 1 980 人，而今年总录取人数为 1 968 人，申请人数的继续上涨和录取人数的持续下降使得哈佛大学的录取率创了新低。

而这种录取率大幅度下降的学校也不仅仅是哈佛大学，表 1.3 中哥伦比亚大学、宾夕法尼亚大学、布朗大学、康奈尔大学近 7 年的录取率都有不同程度的下降。尤其在 2021 年的申请季，录取人数和录取率都发生了很大的改变。

那么在这种情况下中国学生被美国大学录取的情况究竟如何呢?

全球范围内对美国教育资源的争抢如此激烈,中国更是如此。根据 2020 年美国门户开放报告数据(见表 1.4)显示,中国仍然是美国最大的生源国。而且每年还呈递增趋势。

表 1.4 2020 年美国门户开放报告 (单位:人)

国家和地区	2018~2019 年人数	2019~2020 年人数
中　国	369 548	373 532
印　度	202 014	193 124
韩　国	52 250	29 809
阿拉伯	37 080	30 957
加拿大	26 122	25 992
越　南	24 392	23 777
中国台湾地区	243 369	23 724
日　本	18 105	17 554
巴　西	16 059	16 671
墨西哥	15 229	14 348

(资料来源:2020 美国门户开放报告 https://www.iie.org/en/Research-and-Insights/Open-Doors)

从表 1.4 中我们不难看出,在 2019~2020 年美国高校国际学生人数整体略有降幅的情况下,中国学生依然相比 2018~2019 年增长了 1.8%,留学美国高校总人数为 373 532 人,占国际学生总数的 34.6%,再次位居第一,连续 11 年成为最大国际生源国。其次是印度,留美学生人数占国际学生总数的 18.0%。中国和印度的留美国际学生占据了全美国际学生半数以上。

美国部分 TOP20 大学 2020 年申请季和 2021 年申请季两年录取中国学生的数据如表 1.5 所示。

表 1.5 美国部分 TOP20 大学 2020 年及 2021 年中国学生录取人数 (单位:人)

学 校 名 称	2020 总人数	2021 总人数
普林斯顿大学	24	22
哈佛大学	13	19

续　表

学 校 名 称	2020 总人数	2021 总人数
哥伦比亚大学	43	44
麻省理工学院	23	24
耶鲁大学	31	25
斯坦福大学	35	48
芝加哥大学	91	124
宾夕法尼亚大学	80	63
西北大学	64	54
约翰霍普金斯大学	82	99
加州理工学院	11	7
杜克大学	65	54
达特茅斯学院	26	30
布朗大学	43	52
范德堡大学	92	100
莱斯大学	75	83
圣路易斯华盛顿大学	82	78
康奈尔大学	144	159
圣母大学	34	34

（资料来源：我样（WOWYOUNG）平台统计数据汇总整理 https://mp.weixin.qq.com/mp/homepage?__biz=MzU2MTU1NjI3NQ==&hid=4&sn=e0e23ee6ac00d8a9c0e58c09920469b4&scene=18&uin=&key=&devicetype=Windows+10+x64&version=63030532&lang=zh_CN&ascene=7&fontgear=2）①

通过表1.5的数据我们发现，2020年申请季中国学生进入美国TOP20大学的人数仅有1 058人，但进入美国大学的中国学生总人数高达373 532人，进入美国TOP20大学的中国学生，仅占美国大学中国学生总人数的0.28%。

而2021年，美国TOP20大学录取人数虽然相较于2020年的录取人数有所增加，但变化幅度也并不大，仅有1 119人进入美国TOP20大学，比去年仅仅多了61人，这种人数的变化，相较于每年进入美国学习的近40万的中国学生总数

---

① 数据为人工统计，2020年数据在5月统计完成，其中包含了候补名单（waitlist）转正数据，2021年数据在4月统计完成，以上数据仅供大家参考。

来说，基本可以忽略不计。

因此我们可以得出，虽然每年有许多进入美国大学的中国学生，但是能够进入美国 TOP20 名校的学生还是少之又少的，想要踏进美国顶尖大学的校门，并不是一件简单的事情。

第二章 解码常春藤申请文书

第一节

为什么申请美国顶尖大学时的文书很重要

美国大学理事会的“Big Future”网站曾经要求上千所美国大学参与评估“课程、校内成绩、标化考试成绩、活动、申请文书和推荐信”对申请者的重要性，并将这些因素列为“非常重要”“重要”和“会考虑”。

这次评估中我们发现常春藤院校的反馈非常相似，但还是有一些有趣的区别。我们列举了几所具有代表性的美国大学，如表 2.1 所示。

表 2.1 美国大学申请因素

重要程度	学校名称		
	耶鲁大学	康奈尔大学	宾夕法尼亚大学
非常重要	GPA 申请文书 个性/个人特质 年级排名 课外活动* 推荐信 中学课程的挑战性 标化考试成绩 才能/能力	GPA 申请文书 个性/个人特质 年级排名 课外活动 推荐信 中学课程的挑战性 标化考试成绩 才能/能力	GPA 申请文书 个性/个人特质 推荐信 中学课程的挑战性 标化考试成绩
重要		班级排名	年级排名 课外活动 面试 才能/能力

续 表

重要程度	学校名称		
	耶鲁大学	康奈尔大学	宾夕法尼亚大学
会考虑	校友关系 是否是家中第一代大学生 居住地地理位置 面试 种族 本州居民/公民身份 志愿者经验 工作经验	校友关系 是否是家中第一代大学生 居住地地理位置 面试 种族 本州居民/公民身份 志愿者经验 工作经验	校友关系 是否是家中第一代大学生 居住地地理位置 面试 种族 本州居民/公民身份 志愿者经验 工作经验

重要程度	学校名称		
	维克森林大学	密歇根大学	加州大学伯克利分校
非常重要	GPA 申请文书 个性/个人特质 年级排名 中学课程的挑战性	GPA 中学课程的挑战性	GPA 申请文书 中学课程的挑战性 标化考试成绩
重要	课外活动 面试 推荐信 才能/能力	申请文书 个性/个人特质 是否是家中第一代大学生 推荐信 标化考试成绩	个性/个人特质 课外活动 志愿者经验 工作经验
会考虑	校友关系 是否是家中第一代大学生 居住地地理位置 申请人就读该校的意愿 种族 宗教隶属关系或联盟 标化考试成绩 本州居民/公民身份	校友关系 课外活动 居住地地理位置 申请人就读该校的意愿 本州居民/公民身份 才能/能力 志愿者经验 工作经验	是否是家中第一代大学生 推荐信 本州居民/公民身份

* 重点阐述的申请环节做了底色标注

通过表 2.1 我们发现"**非常挑剔**"(参见第一章中对大学的分类)的大学会对学生进行全方位的审核,如表 2.2 所示。

表 2.2　“非常挑剔”大学因素评估

	“非常挑剔”大学
非常重要	GPA 申请文书 个性/个人特质 班级排名 课外活动 推荐信 中学课程的挑战性 标化考试成绩

而我们深知中国学生想要申请像耶鲁大学、宾夕法尼亚大学、康奈尔大学这些录取率不超过 25%的学校，学生自身能力都很强，尤其是高中成绩、标化考试成绩以及学校课程难度方面，大家这方面的能力不相上下。筛除那些在绝大多数申请人中差异不大的因素后，剩下的因素如表 2.3 所示。

表 2.3　“非常挑剔”大学重要因素

	“非常挑剔”大学
非常重要	~~GPA~~ 申请文书 个性/个人特质 ~~班级排名~~ 课外活动 推荐信 ~~中学课程的挑战性~~ ~~标化考试成绩~~

在申请文书、个性/个人特质、课外活动、推荐信这几项中，申请文书以及老师和辅导员的推荐信最能体现学生的“个性和个人品质”，但我们知道老师和辅导员的推荐信内容并不受学生控制，所以学生们真正可以自我控制的因素只剩下两项，如表 2.4 所示。

表 2.4　“非常挑剔”大学生控制因素

	“非常挑剔”大学
非常重要（足以区分申请人）	申请文书 课外活动

现在你能理解了吗？为什么独立升学顾问会花费大量时间给你提供有关大学申请文书的建议并规划你的课外活动履历？因为这两项内容是学生可控的，同时这两项也是最能展现学生自身与众不同的特质，并能帮助申请者，在标化考试成绩、GPA、班级排名大家基本相似的情况下脱颖而出最有效的方法。

但我们也发现了一个有趣的现象，耶鲁大学和康奈尔大学将“课外活动”列为“非常重要”，而宾夕法尼亚大学则将其列为“重要”，可见不同大学对学生的要求各有不同，而文书的作用也不言而喻。

因此，我们得出结论，这些学生应该对申请文书十分关注：

(1) 所有申请“极度挑剔”大学的人——尤其是排名前50的大学!

(2) 也包括每个申请“非常挑剔”大学的人，特别是如果他们的考试成绩排在该大学入学新生成绩的前25%之后。

(3) 还有申请“较为挑剔”的大学的学生，如果其学习成绩参差不齐或考试成绩低于该大学的中位数，或有特殊情况影响其成绩(如疾病、家庭成员死亡、学校变更等)。

因此，这些美国顶尖大学的招生官会非常关注每位申请者的文书，他们通过美国大学通用申请系统中的主文书了解一个学生的个人品质、知识技能、择校动机、你将如何从你感兴趣的研究项目中获益以及你与其他申请者的区别。

通过各个学校的辅文书，他们可以了解该学生身上是否有学校所需的特质，是否对学校真的了解，学生是否真的想进入该大学学习以及学生是否能让学校和社区变得更好。因此我们常说文书就是你最佳的“传声筒”。

第二节

要写好文书，先了解你的读者——揭秘美国大学招生委员会工作流程

撰写有效的大学申请文书，从了解你的读者开始。你申请的每所大学的大学招生委员会都是你的读者。因此，让我们先了解这些人是谁，以及他们会如何阅读你的入学申请材料。

1. 大学招生委员会都有哪些成员？

(1) 大学招生委员会的成员包括70岁以上的退休人员、22岁的大学毕业生等。他们受雇专职审核大学申请材料，每年会收到的成千上万份申请。

(2) 这些成员多数来自不同的民族，有着不同的学术背景。

(3) 如果该大学招收了大量的国际学生，那么招生委员会的一名或多名成员可能会专门审阅国际学生的申请。他们了解各类国际教学体制的评分系统，了解哪些海外高中因学术严谨而享有盛誉。他们大多数去过很多国家(尤其是中国)，访问过当地高中，并参加过海外主要城市的大学博览会。

2. 有多少人会阅读申请材料呢？他们如何决定哪些招生委员会成员来阅读我的申请材料？

(1) "较挑剔"的大学，可能只会有一个人来审核你的申请。只有当你的GPA和标化考试成绩高于最低分数门槛时，你的材料才有可能被其他人看到。

(2) "非常挑剔"和"极度挑剔"的大学可能会有"第一"审阅人和"第二"审阅人来对申请材料进行批注，之后才将材料送达正式委员会。或者只有当两个审

阅人意见不一的情况下，文书才会交由正式委员会决定。一些大学（如宾夕法尼亚大学）由一个审阅人来审核学术情况，另一个审阅人来审核申请的“主观部分”，如申请文书、推荐信和课外成就。

(3) 小规模的且“非常挑剔”和“极度挑剔”的文理学院极有可能由全体委员会来审核申请。

(4) 一些大学可能会指派某个招生官审核特定专业的申请（例如，某个招生官可能只审核工程专业的申请或商学专业的申请）。

(5) 有些大学更为常见的情况是招生委员会成员可能会根据申请人的高中来将申请分类审核。

3. 在大学招生委员会工作是什么体验？

实际上，这是份充满挑战且烦琐的工作。在申请审核季（每年秋季末至春季），招生人员几乎每天都会阅读文件到晚上。许多大学设置了每日审核预期指标。对于招生人员来说，保持阅读进度的压力很大。这里需提醒一下，每所大学收到的是成千上万份申请材料，并且学校有严格的“早申请”和“常规申请”期限，以通知学生申请结果。

招生人员没有很多时间细读每一份申请，他们通常在 5～10 分钟内读完一份申请，其中包括审核成绩单、活动列表、推荐信，当然，还有充满闪光点的申请文书。这就是为什么申请文书必须要有能吸引招生官的开篇的原因。因为你要在相当短的时间内给招生官留下一个良好的印象。

竞争越激烈的大学，筛选申请人的难度越大。顶尖大学可能出现 10 个或更多的申请人竞争 1 个录取名额，并且其中的大多数申请者都已具备极其优秀且难分上下的学术成绩和考试成绩。

即使大学在综合地审核申请，筛选学生仍然很难。例如，在一位获得过两次国际法医学金牌冠军的学生与另一位撰写出你迄今读过的最感人的申请文书之一的学生之间，你会如何选择？这些决定通常是非常主观的。

正是由于许多决定都是主观的，招生委员会成员之间往往会产生意见分歧。

许多大学招生委员会被要求优先考虑对本校表现出“明显兴趣”的申请者，如查看学生是否参观过校园，有无浏览学校网站上的各个页面，回应学院的面试请求，参与在线聊天等表现。

从大学的统计上看，对一所学校表现出“明显兴趣”的学生更有可能收到该校的录取通知书。在所有收到录取的学生中，接受录取的学生所占的百分比称为录取接受率。高的接受率被视为衡量大学“声望”的标准，并可能影响大学排名。

招生委员会权衡的因素可能是申请人不可控的，因此可能你提交了很出色的申请资料，却仍然被拒绝录取或列入候补名单。例如，在审查每份申请时，委员会成员可能会问自己以下问题：

我们很喜欢这个孩子的文书和活动，但是她的 GPA 和 SAT 会降低我们入学新生的学术成绩统计结果，这可能会降低 *U.S. News* 的排名，我们要冒这个风险吗？

我们很喜欢这个孩子的文书和活动，但是他申请的专业有超额录取的风险。我们还能再招其他学生吗？（如果超额录取，那个专业的部门领导们也会不高兴）

如果我们录取这名学生，我们的教授们会满意吗？许多教授都是更看重成绩，并不十分注重学生的综合条件。

我们打造的是真正多元化的一届学生吗？还是只是一次又一次地接纳同一类的学生？

我们是否招收了太多来自同一地区或高中的学生？是否做到了地理位置多元化？

在男女失衡的专业中，有兼顾到性别多样性吗？

我们的财政援助预算会超支吗？这个孩子需要大额经济援助吗？

4. 招生官是如何“在内部”开会讨论一份申请的？

招生委员会由多人组成。就像其他人一样，他们有时也会感到疲倦或劳累过度，也可能会错过申请中的重要内容并由此产生误解。他们也带有偏见，包括一些他们自己都还未察觉的偏见。

让我们来听听一个大学招生委员会是如何深入讨论一位中国申请人的。该委员会包括了主要负责审核国际学生申请的招生官 Kate。第二审阅人为 Bob。Kate 和 Bob 都已读过申请文件，委员会还包括另外三名招生官员。首先，Kate 向委员会介绍了申请人的情况如表 2.5 所示。

表 2.5 招生委员会对一名中国申请人的讨论

招生官 Kate	Wei 来自中国一所很好的高中,并且已经开始上国际课程,包括数门 AP 课程。她的 AP 宏观、微观经济都是 5 分(满分),现在正在读微积分和高等数学。 她的 GPA 在 4 分制里是 4.3 分(已经考虑各科目成绩的比重)*。从材料中也可以看到她的 TOEFL 和 SAT 成绩都很不错。 她计划主修数学,也许会修数学和计算机双专业。
招生官 A	我们学校对 Wei 所在高中历年来的申请人感觉如何?
Kate	今年这所高中有 15 名学生申请我们大学,Wei 的 GPA 在他们之中排名第五。 去年我们收到 12 份来自这所高中的申请。我们录取了其中 3 个学生,选了 3 个学生加入候补列表,然后拒绝了其余的申请人。被录取的 3 人中 2 位学生接受了我们的 offer。Wei 的一篇文书中提到她认识这两位学生其中的一位,并且是因为与他的交谈而申报了我们学校。
招生官 A	有意思。我能理解为从 Wei 的高中来的学生一般在我们大学的表现都很出色吗?
Kate	是的。Wei 的总体学术背景(选课难度、GPA、标化考试成绩)在我们国际申请人中排前 10%。我们一般会在和 Wei 学术背景相似的申请人中录取一半人数。
招生官 A	你喜欢她哪些方面?
Kate	在她的活动列表上你们可以看到她参加过一些高端的比赛。最值得一提的是她的队伍在国际奥数竞赛中的优秀表现。 不过我最喜欢的是她在"你最骄傲的是什么"这篇文书中的回答。她强调了团队合作以及鼓励他人。我承认我们的第二审阅人并不和我一样热衷于录取她。对吧,Bob?
第二审阅人 Bob	没错,Kate。我也觉得这篇文书不错,但我并不觉得它特别独特或者出挑。不过我们两个都很喜欢她通用申请里的主文书。
Kate	对!她围绕她对几何分形的兴趣写了一篇很好的文书。她多年前在一本旧杂志里读到一位数学家阐述如何用几何分形来描绘海岸线的形状以及测量过程中遇到的挑战,因而产生了极大的兴趣。我是英语专业毕业的,所以我也不能装作完全读懂了她的文书,但是我能理解的部分看上去都非常有趣!
Bob	我也不是数学家,但我也被她那篇文书吸引了,尤其是她描述如何自学高等数学知识和电脑编程来更好地理解几何分形的部分。我们的教授会很喜爱她——她有很强烈的求知欲,这是肯定的。 我觉得她的第三方机构面试也很好。她的英语口语很好,而且她强调了她对于学习新东西的热情。
招生官 B	她的缺点是什么?

续　表

Kate	是一个在国际申请人中比较常见的缺点。她的老师们写的推荐信并不是很有帮助。老师们当然都夸了她,但是他们没有提供能展示这名学生在班级里或在他们教授的优秀学生中与众不同的具体细节。
Bob	还有一个顾虑,就是虽然她的成就让人印象深刻,但我不敢肯定她这些成就在我们考虑的其他申请人中会更胜一筹。
招生官 A	和她同一高中的其他申请人表现如何?你们刚提到她的 GPA 在同高中申请人中排第五?
Kate	嗯,她和同高中其他申请人在 GPA 上差异其实很小。从她的第三方机构面试和文书上来看,我觉得她比其他申请人有着更“有趣”的思想。她虽然没有最高的标化考试成绩,但是她的成绩仍是非常好的。求知欲和创新的想象力看来是这个学生的优势。像她这样的案例,我们很难判断该把 SAT 和 GPA 看得多重。
招生官 A	说的一点都没错。
招生委员会主任	好吧。我们来投票吧。我们该暂时把她列为录取、候补、还是回拒?请大家举手表决。

* 表示 GPA 最终得分超过了满分,所修科目已经超过了高中阶段的学科难度要求

从整个招生委员会的讨论中,我们可以发现招生委员会对 Wei 同学作了全方位的评判,包括 Wei 同学所在高中的学长、学姐进入该大学后的情况以及 Wei 同学自身在学校的排名和个人经历,可见招生官们在招收一位学生时,审核的方面非常全面。

但在这个对话中,我们也能发现,招生官们对学生的主文书都予以高度评价,尽管她和同高中的其他申请人在 GPA 上差异其实很小,但招生官们从她的文书中,看到了她比其他申请人有着更“有趣”的思想,以至于招生官们将差异很小的 GPA 成绩和 SAT 成绩忽略不计,单独从 Wei 同学的文书中去决定是否录取。通过这里我们也能看出一篇好的文书真的会改变一个学生申请的命运。

第三节

强大的“后背力量”助你挖掘自身个性

牛顿有句名言:“如果说我比别人看得更远些,那是因为我站在了巨人的肩上。”的确,站在巨人的肩上能让我们看到遥远处最美丽的风景,也能使我们更靠近成功。如果把美国大学申请比作远处的风景,那么,寻求升学顾问/指导机构的帮助就好比站在巨人的肩膀上一样,这能使申请者不断提升自身水平来获得名校的认可。

很多家长认为,美国人都是让孩子自由发展,但实际并非如此。不少获得成功的美国年轻人,他们的成功有很大一部分都是其父母和升学顾问精心策划的结果。而独立升学顾问在美国的大量存在并形成一个行业,也说明了人生设计和职业规划的必要性。不过,很多中国家长对独立升学顾问这个概念还不是很理解。在美国,升学顾问是一个专门为学生和家长提供升学咨询服务的角色。他们的服务对象主要是生长在美国的本土学生。

或许你会说美国高中不都是配有校内学生顾问,为本校学生免费提供选课指导、心理辅导、大学申请等项目的咨询服务吗?可惜的是,不管是私立还是公立高中,相对大量的申请人来说升学顾问总是太少。美国公立高中的每个升学顾问平均要负责指导上百名学生!而校内升学顾问对学生的个性化申请指导几乎为零,充其量也就是尽到他们的义务。也正因此,“独立升学顾问”也越来越被家长们认可,因此在美国也有三分之一的学生通过“独立升学顾问”来助力自己申请美国大学。

而独立升学顾问并不是每个人都可以胜任的,美国专业的升学顾问每年要花大量时间研究搜集美国大学的情况，走访大学，参加全国和地区专业性会议，了解大学入学的最新动向及变化，有专门而丰富的专业信息渠道。他们常年与大学招生人员保持联系并经常与其他升学顾问互动，交换信息。好的独立升学顾问能帮助学生扩大视野，发掘潜能，整体规划高中生涯，正确评估学生的各项升学指标，并引导学生选择最适合自己的大学。除此之外，独立升学顾问还会指导学生进入大学后的转学、奖学金申请、实习、研究等，并能超前的对学生大学毕业以后的升学、就业、发展进行规划和指导。这个职业需要有一定的专业资历。因此，有着美国大学招生办任职经历的独立升学顾问，将会对学生的帮助非常大。

一位在美国大学招生办工作过的独立升学顾问，会非常了解美国大学的招生流程，首先，他们熟悉美国各个大学的情况，知道学校录取学生时会考虑哪些方面，了解招生官审核学生的整个流程。其次，他们会从招生官的视角帮助学生，进行整体升学规划，无论是标化考试、课外活动，还是文书方面的建议。他们会帮助学生快速寻找出学生自身的闪光点，并根据学生的亮点迅速匹配适合学生的学校。

当然，有的中国家长会担心，虽然独立升学顾问对美国大学很了解，但他们能融入中国的教育文化当中吗？这种情况下，中外双顾问的模式，将会弥补双方的不足，让学生申请美国大学事半功倍。

第三章 好的文书到底怎样写

第一节 五步让文书“引人入胜”

前几章我们了解了招生官的审核流程以及文书的重要性，那么到底如何写出一篇“引人入胜”的文书呢？我们常说，如果申请文书很优秀，那一定是因为用特有的方式讲述了一个有趣的故事。既然同学们的目标是让自己从成千上万的申请人中脱颖而出，那么最理想的情况是，你打造出一篇具有自身特色的文书，因为文书的细节来源于你的生活经历，而每个人的生活都是独一无二的。

写出非凡的文书并不需要你做过多么非凡的事情，而是需要你对自己以往所做的事情进行深刻思考，并从中得出了令人赞赏的观点或结论。

你需要留意招生官的认知水平，用你的故事打动招生官。很多学生们在讲完故事后，会尽力地解释这个故事的含义，生怕招生官不够聪明，无法看清故事的重点(关于这一点，我们将在后续举例说明)。

还有些最不尽人意的文书则是学生用生僻的单词写成的，他们误以为这会给招生委员会留下深刻的印象，但其实并不会。

那么到底怎样的文书会打动招生官，如何找到吸引招生官眼球的故事呢？下面给大家介绍 5 个步骤，教你如何选择文书的主题：

第一步：对你的生活进行一次回顾。考虑自己以下这些问题并写下答案。

(1) 你对自己最引以为傲的是什么？描述你自己感觉良好的那些时刻。

(2) 你人生中的转折点是什么？

(3) 哪些事件发现塑造了你和你的价值观？

(4) 你一生中有哪些事件使你一想到就会笑?

(5) 你曾经为另一个人做过的最美好的事情是什么?

第二步:接下来进一步讨论。从你最早的记忆开始,思考自那时以来每年发生的最令人难忘的事情。

(1) 专注于特定事件:你所做的、见证的、阅读的或听说过的事情中对你影响深远的那些,将它们记录下来!

(2) 回想那些令人难忘的戏剧、视频、电影、电视节目、现场或录制的音乐表演、你观看的艺术品、体育赛事、阅读的书籍——对你有影响的任何事物。

(3) 你能想到的人生中的每一项成功,无论大小。你曾克服的困难也是一种"成功"。

(4) 你能想到的教会你道理并使你变得更坚强的失败经历。

(5) 你能想到的你一生中所帮助的人,然后描述你为他们做了什么。想想曾经帮助过你的人,然后描述他们为你做了什么。

(6) 其中一些可能不适合做文书或对写文书没有帮助。不用担心,只需专注地记录下来,你就可以了解你生活中最重要的事情。

表 3.1 是上述步骤可能会包含的一些例子。

表 3.1 生活记忆记录

5 岁

- 上幼儿园的第一天没有哭。为自己感到骄傲,因为几乎所有其他孩子都在哭。
- 和我父亲在我家附近的池塘钓鱼。他边走向池塘,边把我放到他肩膀上。我还记得年幼的我被他闪亮的黑发迷住。

7 岁

- 某天放学回家吃午饭,我为了走"捷径",走上一个结冰的池塘(我和父亲去钓鱼的那个池塘)。不幸的是,冰还不够厚,无法承受我的重量。我掉入冰冷的水中,水已漫过我的腰。我幸运地爬上岸,穿着湿漉漉的鞋子走回家。那天下午,令人难以置信的是,我最好的朋友在我跌倒的那个池塘里同一个地方也掉进了水里。
- 当化验结果证实我患有严重的肾脏疾病时,我的妈妈不得不直接带我去医院。在那里我待了两个星期,每 4 小时接受一次青霉素注射。之后,我在家里休养了一个多月。我仍然记得回到学校时我的二年级老师脸上的笑容。

13 岁

- 为了体验标准化测试的感觉,我与一群朋友一起去当地的私立学校参加奖学金考试。三天后,校长打电话告诉我的父母我获得了奖学金。

续 表

14 岁 ● 在我父亲的印刷厂里度过暑假。我学会设定印刷机的类型并给印刷机上油。父亲能从线性印刷机上拿下滚热的铅块的能力让我感到惊讶。我那时并不知道有一天所谓的"计算机"会淘汰线性印刷和凸版印刷。 **16 岁** ● 我自愿辅导四名在学业上落后的小学生，其中一个三年级的学生是个了不起的"艺术家"。作为感谢，他为我画了幅极其神似的笑脸肖像。我把照片框起来，打算带去大学。因为这幅画会时刻提醒我，人的生命里可以取得的成就。

第三步：开始写作。

(1) 从你刚写出的列表中，找出对你来说最重要的一两件事。

(2) 像讲故事一样描述你刚挑选出来的事件。

(3) 这点极其重要。先不必担心怎么得出结论，也不必担心你的招生官会有什么反应。你只要专注地叙述发生了什么。让招生官倾听你经历的、见证的或完成的，无论是悲伤还是喜悦的故事。不必想着润色，至少现在还不需要。只要你在纸上专心致志地描述你生命中的这一时刻，尽情去讲你的故事。

第四步：把你刚写的内容转化为大学申请文书草稿。

看着你刚刚写的"故事"，问自己以下问题：

(1) 我从中学到了什么？

(2) 这个故事让我看到我自己的哪一面？

(3) 我生活中的这个故事塑造我什么样的价值观或信念？

(4) 它如何成就了今天的我？

第五步：查看美国大学通用申请系统里的主文书题目（见表 3.2），问问自己，你的故事是否可以作为对其中一个或多个的回应？（答案通常是肯定的！）

表 3.2 2020～2021 年美国大学通用申请系统里的文书题目

第一题	有些学生的身份、背景、兴趣或才能很出色。他们认为如果申请系统里这些信息缺失，会非常遗憾。如果这是你的情况，请分享你的故事。

续 表

第二题	从困难中吸取的教训可能对我们以后的成功至关重要。重述你遇到的挑战、挫折或失败的事件。它对你有什么影响,你从经验中学到了什么?
第三题	回想一下你曾质疑或挑战某个信念或权威想法的时候,是什么促使你思考?结果怎么样?
第四题	描述你已解决的或你想解决的问题。这可能是一个才智上的挑战,一个研究课题,一个道德困境——任何对你个人重要的、可大可小的事情。说明这些事情对你的重要性以及你的解决方案或打算采取的步骤。
第五题	讨论一个激发你一段时期个人成长并赋予你对自己或他人新认知的成就、活动或领悟。
第六题	描述一个让你着迷到可以忘记时间的话题、想法或概念。解释你为什么会为之着迷?当你想学习更多相关信息时,你会怎么做或会向谁求助?
第七题	分享由你自定主题的一篇文书。可以是已经完稿的,也可以是你对不同问题的回答,也可以是你全新自创的文书。

当你写文书时,请记住这些:

(1) 最有效的文书通常聚焦在非常普通的青少年经历上:参加管弦乐队、其他乐队或文艺演出,参加体育比赛、志愿者活动,模拟联合国大会,参加科学和数学竞赛,辩论,课余工作经验,照顾孩子或年幼的亲戚等。

(2) 美国大学不会要求你做多么卓越的事情。毕竟,大多数申请人只有十七八岁。

(3) 他们不会要求你对世界上所有的问题都有答案,也不会要求你明白生命的意义。

(4) 但是他们确实希望你会思考自己的生活。你会玩乐器吗?参加体育运动、辩论、模拟联合国大会、剧院活动吗?竞选学生会吗?做志愿者工作吗?你是否克服了生活中的重大困难?你是创意作家吗?是的话就太棒了!现在,请告诉我们你为什么要做这些事情。它们对你意味着什么?你从中学到了什么?

撰写大学申请文书时应该问自己的问题:

(1) 当我回顾我的所有生活经历和成就时,哪些经历和成就对我成年的影响最大?

(2) 我的文书讲了一个故事吗?

(3) 我的故事是否从正确的地方开始叙述？我的开篇句子是否使招生官渴望继续阅读？

(4) 我的故事是否包含生动的细节和真实的事件？

(5) 我的句子怎么样？我是否可以通过包含以“since”“although”“because”“when”等词开头的句子来使它们更有效、更高级？

(6) 我可以利用“少即是多”的原则吗？是否有删除之后仍能读清内容的单词,短语或句子？(当我们使用尽可能少的单词时,我们的写作将变得更加强大)

(7) 文书题目询问我为什么要申请特定的大学或特定的专业,是在让我向招生委员会展示我对这个大学所做的研究。我的回答证明了这一点吗？

(8) 招生官会认为我是一个已经考虑过希望对世界产生影响,以及考虑过如何帮助他人的人吗？

(9) 招生委员会希望选出能通过相识而丰富彼此的学生,以及教授们会乐于教导的学生。通过阅读我的文书,人们会判断我是这样的学生吗？

通过这 5 个步骤来选择主题,同学们基本可以选定一些大方向,也的确可以写出一篇属于自己的文书,但这篇文书并不能直接递交申请,因为你无法确定你的选题角度在招生官眼中是不是真的新颖？你自身的特点是否全部展现,展现的方式是不是最恰当的？以及你的文书结构是否真的正确？

如果想要了解这三个方面,你需要一位有经验并且专业的老师来帮助你。

第二节

独立升学顾问如何帮你提升文书

前文说过独立升学顾问在整个申请过程以及文书写作中的重要性。那么我们通过下面的文书，看看学生的原始版本以及独立升学顾问的建议、评论和修改。然后我们再看看学生根据独立升学顾问的建议改写的文书。最后我们将两篇文书(见表 3.3 和表 3.4)对比，看看通过专业人士的指导，学生的文书会出现怎样的变化!

表 3.3　关于应对不良的溜溜球销售员的文书：版本 1

Common Application Personal Statement Response to #7："Share an essay on any topic of your choice. It can be one you've already written, one that responds to a different prompt, or one of your own design." (650 words) **通用申请系统主文书第七题的回复："分享你选择的任何主题的一篇文书。可以是你已经完稿的，也可以是你对不同问题的回答，也可以是你自己设计的主题。"(650 词)**	
学生的原始版本	**由独立升学顾问修改后**
I was pretty sure that I was in trouble now. Since morning, a large harassing phone calls and spam messages flooded in my cell phone. My parents asked me what happened through WeChat, because when they called me before, they found that the phone was always busy. "You must have been attacked by Call You to Death! You should carefully think about whom you have offended recently!" My classmates told me so, after I shared with	I was pretty sure that I was in trouble now. Since morning, large harassing phone calls and spam messages flooded in my cell phone. My parents asked me what happened through WeChat, because when they called me before, they found that the phone was always busy. "You must have been attacked by Call You to Death! You should carefully think about whom you have offended recently!" My classmates told me so, after I shared with

续　表

学生的原始版本	由独立升学顾问修改后
them what I met. Call You to Death is an online phone calling platform. After entering the target phone number, it will keep harassing the target number by calling and sending text messages. In China, this is illegal. However, I had to save my cell phone from the endless call-ins and messages at first. Finally, our class monitor, Tommy, suggested downloading a certain APP on my cell phone to intercept strange numbers and text messages, which was from his sister's experience. His sister had been attacked by "Call You to Death" because of bad reviews she left on Taobao. The APP was effective, the call-ins and text messages became much less.	them what I ~~met.~~ experienced. Call You to Death is an online phone calling platform. After entering the target phone number, it will keep harassing the target number by calling and sending text messages. In China, this is illegal. However, I first had to save my cell phone from the endless call-ins and messages ~~at first~~. Finally, our class monitor, Tommy, suggested downloading a certain APP on my cell phone to intercept strange numbers and text messages, which was from his sister's experience. His sister had been attacked by "Call You to Death" because of bad reviews she left on Taobao. The APP was effective; the call-ins and text messages became much less.
I had time to think about who made the attack. I was an ordinary student and had a good relationship with my classmates. Recalling Tommy's words, I suddenly realized that I had given a yoyo store a bad review on Taobao last week. The newly bought Yoyo was not good as its promotion, so when the seller asked me to write a product review, I gave my real feedback and then clicked "Bad Review".	I had time to think about who made the attack. I was an ordinary student and had a good relationship with my classmates. Recalling Tommy's words, I suddenly realized that I had given a yoyo store a bad review on Taobao last week. The newly bought yoyo was not as good as its promotion, so when the seller asked me to write a product review, I gave my real feedback and then clicked "Bad Review".
Thinking of this, I opened the conversation page with the seller. After I gave the bad review, the seller asked me to delete the bad review, and he even promised to offer me a big discount. But unfortunately, I missed all the messages. The most recent messages were sent out yesterday evening: "If you insist embarrassing us, I will teach you a lesson!" Now I was sure that all my suffering today was from the yoyo seller.	Thinking of this, I opened the conversation page with the seller. After I gave the bad review, the seller asked me to delete the bad review, and he even promised to offer me a big discount. But unfortunately, I missed all the messages. The most recent messages were sent out yesterday evening: "If you insist on embarrassing us, I will teach you a lesson!" Now I was sure that all my suffering today was from the yoyo seller.
My classmates started to criticize the seller, and some even suggested me to communicate with the seller and agreed to delete my review.[1]* I felt angry: I was the right side, but I had to compromise to the wrong side.	My classmates started to criticize the seller, ~~and~~ but some even suggested ~~me to~~ that I communicate with the seller and agreed to delete my review. I felt angry: I was the right side, but I had to compromise ~~to~~ with

续 表

学生的原始版本	由独立升学顾问修改后
Maybe compromising was the easiest solution, but I did not want to compromise this time. I sent messages to the seller and asked him to stop the illegal behavior, soon I received the reply: they denied the attack, and all my words were my imagination, since I did not have any evidence. I had to contact Taobao agent and received the same reply: no evidence to support my complaint, but they recommended an APP, which was what Tommy suggested. At last, I had to go to the police station near my school. After hearing all my suffering, the policeman got the seller's phone number and made a call, but after speaking few words, the seller hung up the phone. Few minutes later, shocking things happened: the phone of the police station was attacked by the "Call You to Death".[2] Then, the story went quite smoothly later. The police found the seller, and in addition to being held under administrative detention of 5 days, the seller was also asked to apologize to me. I will never forget this special experience, since it is my important attempt to insist my authentic ideas and not compromise with the wrong side. I know someone in my daily life often describe me as a stubborn and single-minded boy. I strictly follow rules: I never run the traffic lights, though there are no cars; I never have breakfast on the school bus, though almost all my classmates do it; and like this experience, I refuse to give fake reviews. Despite so, I think being stubborn and authentic are required qualities to do scientific research in the future.[3] (649 words)	the wrong side. Maybe compromising was the easiest solution, but I did not want to compromise this time. I sent messages to the seller and asked him to stop the illegal behavior. Soon I received the reply: they denied the attack and said all my words were in my imagination, since I did not have any evidence. I had to contact the Taobao agent and received the same reply: no evidence to support my complaint, but they recommended an APP, which was what Tommy suggested. At last, I had to go to the police station near my school. After hearing all my suffering, the policeman got the seller's phone number and made a call, but after speaking few words, the seller hung up the phone. A ~~F~~few minutes later, shocking things happened: the phone of the police station was attacked by ~~the~~ "Call You to Death". Then, the story went quite smoothly later. The police found the seller, and in addition to being held under administrative detention of 5 days, the seller was also asked to apologize to me. I will never forget this special experience, since it is my important attempt to insist on my authentic ideas and not compromise with the wrong side. I know someone in my daily life who often describes me as a stubborn and single-minded boy. I strictly follow rules: I never run the traffic lights, though there are no cars; I never have breakfast on the school bus, though almost all my classmates do it; and like this experience, I refuse to give fake reviews. ~~Despite so,~~ I think being stubborn and authentic are required qualities to do scientific research in the future.

续　表

<table>
<tr><td>Independent College Counselor's Notes to the Student
独立升学顾问的批注</td></tr>
<tr><td>1. "My classmates started to criticize the seller, and some even suggested me to communicate with the seller and agreed to delete my review"
我将"和"("and")更改为"但是"("but"),因为这样更通顺。你的意思是,即使你的同学认为卖家错了,他们还是认为删除负面评论比让他终止对你的网络攻击要容易得多。</td></tr>
<tr><td>2. "A few minutes later, shocking things happened: the phone of the police station was attacked by 'Call You to Death' ..."
虽然骚扰电话是一件很严重的事情,但我必须承认,溜溜球卖家向警察局发起了轰炸式骚扰电话的行为也太愚蠢了,当我读到这里时,我忍不住大笑。
与其说"几分钟后,发生了令人震惊的事情",不如说:"几分钟后,发生了令人震惊(和好笑)的事情"["A few minutes later, something shocking (and amusing) happened ..."]?如果认识到这个情况中的幽默点,我认为它可以完善你的故事。你怎么看?</td></tr>
<tr><td>3. "I think being stubborn and authentic are required qualities to do scientific research in the future"
你的文书结束语(固然)是成立的,但因为它似乎是"半路杀出",导致结尾很尴尬。在它之前需要一个过渡语句,例如:
固执和诚实也是我未来在职场中的价值观。我将自己视为科学研究者,这些价值观对于成功至关重要。例如,________________。
请参阅以下有关此问题的其他想法。</td></tr>
<tr><td>独立升学顾问的评论</td></tr>
<tr><td>你编写了一个引人入胜的故事,而且正如我在评论中提到的那样,它甚至还具有一些风趣的方面,读者会从中发现乐趣。
你的文书是对通用申请系统文书第七题的回应(选择你自己的主题)。你是否考虑过把它作为对第四题的回应呢?("描述你已解决的或你想解决的问题。这可能是一个才智上的挑战,一个研究课题,一个道德困境——任何对你个人都重要的,可大可小的事情。说明这些事情对你的重要性以及你的解决方案或打算采取的步骤。")
我问这个问题是因为你的文书既是关于解决一个实际的问题(如何阻止你手机上的网络攻击)又是解决一个道德问题(拒绝更改负面评论并拒绝被不道德的卖家欺负的问题)。作为对第四题的回应,这变成了一篇有关解决问题的文书,并且由于题目中包含"道德困境",因此我认为你所写的内容是适当的。
同理:尽管你的文书有很多值得称赞的地方,但我担心,招生官们会钦佩你的道德价值观,他们会感到对抗欺诈的溜溜球卖家仍然是一件小事。展示你的执着和诚实会对你的生活产生更大影响的方式,这样能优化你的文书。
你在结束语中暗示了对科研的兴趣,但为什么不通过举例说明你想探索的科学主题或问题呢?为什么不展示你的执着和坚持做正确的事情的特质在科学研究钻研答案的过程中的重要性呢?例如,当科学研究实验需要反复试验时,固执和持久就是美德。你可以引用</td></tr>
</table>

续 表

独立升学顾问的评论
自己在学校实验室工作中的经验，或者成功的发现或发明，因为很多研究人员会执着地自愿将大量时间投入到反复试验中。无论哪种方式，你都将向招生委员会展示你为从事科学研究事业做好的充分准备。 详细说明研究的这一点可能会让你的文书超过650个单词，不必担心。我可以帮助你找到减少文书的其他部分腾出字数来添加修订版的结尾。

＊表格中加深蓝背景色的字句，独立升学顾问会专门批注和评价

接下来，我们来看看学生在独立升学顾问的建议下怎么修改文书的结尾。正如独立升学顾问指出的，新的结尾要好得多。但有一个问题是：文书篇幅增加了，超出了650词的最大限制。为了解决这个问题，独立升学顾问为学生指出可以删除字数的内容(见表3.4)。

表 3.4 应对不良的溜溜球销售员的文书：版本 2

Common Application Personal Statement Response To ＃4:"Describe a problem you've solved or a problem you'd like to solve. It can be an intellectual challenge, a research query, an ethical dilemma — anything that is of personal importance, no matter the scale. Explain its significance to you and what steps you took or could be taken to identify a solution."(650 words) **通用申请系统主文书第四题的回复："描述你已解决的或你想解决的问题。这可能是一个才智上的挑战，一个研究课题，一个道德困境——任何对你个人都重要的，可大可小的事情。说明这些事情对你的重要性以及你的解决方案或打算采取的步骤。"**	
学生的原始版本	**独立升学顾问的编辑**
I was pretty sure that I was in trouble now. Since morning, large harassing phone calls and spam messages flooded my cell phone. My parents asked me what happened through WeChat, because when they called me before, they found that the phone was always busy.	I was ~~pretty sure that I was~~ in trouble now. Since morning, ~~large~~ harassing phone calls and spam messages flooded my cell phone. My parents asked me what happened through WeChat because ~~when they called me before, they found that the~~ my phone was always busy.
"You must have been attacked by Call You to Death! You should carefully think about whom you have offended recently!" My classmates told me so, after I shared with them what I experienced. Call You to Death is an online phone calling platform. After entering the target phone number, it will keep harassing the target number by calling and sending text messages. In China, this is	My classmates told me, "You must have been attacked by Call You to Death! You should carefully think about whom you have offended recently!" ~~My classmates told me so, after I shared with them what I experienced.~~ Call You to Death is an online phone calling platform. After entering the target phone number, it will keep harassing the ~~target~~ number by calling and ~~sending~~

续　表

学生的原始版本	独立升学顾问的编辑
illegal. However, I first had to save my cell phone from the endless call-ins and messages. Finally, our class monitor, Tommy, suggested downloading a certain APP on my cell phone to intercept strange numbers and text messages, which was from his sister's experience. His sister had been attacked by "Call You to Death" because of bad reviews she left on Taobao. The APP was effective; the call-ins and text messages became much less.	~~text messages~~ texting. In China, this is illegal. However, I first had to save my cell phone from the endless call-ins and messages. Finally, our class monitor, Tommy, suggested downloading an ~~certain~~ APP to ~~on~~ my cell phone to intercept strange numbers and text messages. ~~, which was from his sister's experience.~~ His sister had been attacked by "Call You to Death" because of bad reviews she left on Taobao. The APP was effective; the call-ins and text messages became much less.
I had time to think about who made the attack. I was an ordinary student, and had a good relationship with my classmates. Recalling Tommy's words, I suddenly realized that I had given a yoyo store a bad review on Taobao last week. The newly bought yoyo was not as good as its promotion, so when the seller asked me to write a product review, I gave my real feedback and then clicked "Bad Review".	I ~~had time to think~~ thought about who made the attack. I was an ordinary student ~~,~~ and had a good relationship with my classmates. ~~Recalling Tommy's words,~~ I suddenly realized that I had given a yoyo store a bad review on Taobao last week. The newly bought yoyo was not as good as its promotion, so when the seller asked me to write a product review, I gave my real feedback and ~~then~~ clicked "Bad Review".
Thinking of this, I opened the conversation page with the seller. After I gave the bad review, the seller asked me to delete the bad review, and he even promised to offer me a big discount. But unfortunately, I missed all the messages. The most recent messages were sent out yesterday evening: "If you insist on embarrassing us, I will teach you a lesson!" Now I was sure that all my suffering today was from the yoyo seller.	~~Thinking of this,~~ I opened the conversation page with the seller. After ~~I gave the~~ my bad review, the seller asked me to delete ~~the bad review~~ it and ~~he~~ even promised to offer me a big discount. But unfortunately, I missed ~~all~~ these messages. The most recent ~~messages~~ were sent out yesterday evening: "If you insist on embarrassing us, I will teach you a lesson!" Now I was sure that ~~all~~ my suffering ~~today~~ was from the yoyo seller.
My classmates started to criticize the seller, but some even suggested that I communicate with the seller and agree to delete my review. I felt angry: I was the right side, but I had to compromise with the wrong side. Maybe compromising was the easiest solution, but I did not want to compromise this time.	~~My classmates started to criticize the seller, but some~~ Some classmates ~~even~~ suggested that I ~~communicate with the seller and~~ agree to delete my review. I felt angry: I was the right side, but I had to compromise with the wrong side. Maybe compromising was the easiest solution, but I did not want to compromise ~~this time~~.

续 表

学生的原始版本	独立升学顾问的编辑
I sent messages to the seller and asked him to stop the illegal behavior. Soon I received the reply：they denied the attack and said all my words were in my imagination，since I did not have any evidence. I had to contact the Taobao agent and received the same reply：no evidence to support my complaint，but they recommended an APP，which was what Tommy suggested. At last，I had to go to the police station near my school. After hearing all my suffering，the policeman got the seller's phone number and made a call，but after speaking few words，the seller hung up the phone. A few minutes later，something amusing happened：the phone of the police station was attacked by "Call You to Death". Then，the story went quite smoothly later. The police found the seller，and in addition to being held under administrative detention of 5 days，the seller was also asked to apologize to me.	I ~~sent messages to the seller and~~ asked the seller ~~him~~ to stop the illegal behavior. ~~Soon I received the reply：they~~ He denied the attack and said ~~all~~ my words were in my imagination，since I did not have any evidence. I ~~had to~~ contacted the Taobao agent and received the same reply：no evidence to support my complaint，but they recommended the ~~an~~ APP ~~，which was what~~ that Tommy suggested. At last，I ~~had to go~~ went to the police station near my school. After hearing all my suffering，the policeman got the seller's phone number and made a call，but after ~~speaking~~ a few words，the seller hung up the phone. A few minutes later，something amusing happened：the ~~phone of the~~ police station's phone was attacked by "Call You to Death". ~~Then~~ Now，~~the story~~ things went ~~quite~~ smoothly：~~later. The~~ the police found the seller，and in addition to being held under administrative detention of 5 days，the seller ~~was also asked~~ had to apologize to me.
I will never forget this special experience，since it is my important attempt to insist on my authentic ideas and not compromise with the wrong side. I know someone in my daily life who often describes me as a stubborn and single-minded boy. I strictly follow rules：I never run the traffic lights，though there are no cars；I never have breakfast on the school bus，though almost all my classmates do it；and like this experience，I refuse to give fake reviews.	I will never forget ~~this special experience，since it is~~ my important attempt to insist on my authentic ideas and not compromise with the wrong side. ~~I know someone in my daily life who~~ Someone ~~often~~ describes me as a stubborn and single-minded boy. I strictly follow rules：I never run the traffic lights，though there are no cars；I never have breakfast on the school bus，though almost all my classmates do it；and，like this experience，I refuse to give fake reviews.
Stubbornness and persistence are also values that I will carry into my future career. I see myself as a scientific researcher，where these values are critical to success. Shuji Nakamura had been recognized as a crazy	Stubbornness and persistence are also values that I will carry into my future career. I see myself as a scientific researcher，where these values are critical to success. I want to be like Shuji Nakamura，who ~~had been~~

续　表

<table>
<tr><th>学生的原始版本</th><th>独立升学顾问的编辑</th></tr>
<tr><td>freak before he won 2014 Nobel Prize in Physics. Shuji Nakamura had been working in a small enterprise in Japan and dedicated to a hopeless research-making blue LED with gallium nitride, which was regarded to have obvious defects. However, others in the same industry were using promising zinc selenide. Regardless of cynicism and doubt from others, stubborn Shuji Nakamura insisted what he thought was right, and finally successfully invented high-efficiency blue light-emitting diode. Countless scientific achievements are from scientists' stubbornness and persistence. The path of scientist research maybe tough, but I'm confident and well prepared to pursue my dream with my stubbornness and persistence. (775 words)</td><td>~~recognized as~~ was considered a crazy freak before he won the 2014 Nobel Prize in Physics. ~~Shuji Nakamura~~ He had been working in a small enterprise in Japan ~~and dedicated to~~ on a "hopeless"[1] research project: making blue LED with gallium nitride, ~~which was regarded to have obvious defects. However,~~ while others in the ~~same~~ industry were using ~~promising~~ zinc selenide. ~~Regardless of cynicism and doubt from others~~[2] Nevertheless, stubborn Shuji Nakamura insisted on what he thought was right, and finally ~~successfully~~ invented a high-efficiency blue light-emitting diode. ~~Countless scientific achievements are from scientists' stubbornness and persistence.~~[3] The path of ~~scientist~~ scientific research may be tough, but I'm confident and well prepared to pursue my dream with my stubbornness and persistence.</td></tr>
<tr><th colspan="2">独立升学顾问给学生的建议</th></tr>
<tr><td colspan="2">1. "hopeless"
我在"无望"这个词上加上了引号，因为它们向读者表明，尽管其他人认为他的研究无望，但实际上并非如此。</td></tr>
<tr><td colspan="2">2. "Regardless of cynicism and doubt from others"
我相信我们可以删除这句话，因为当你说 Nakamura 被视为"疯狂的怪人"时，我认为你已经很清楚地表达了你的意思。</td></tr>
<tr><td colspan="2">3. "Countless scientific achievements are from scientists' stubbornness and persistence."
我删除了这句话，是因为你已经在写"我认为自己是科学研究员，因为这些价值观(执着和坚持)对成功至关重要"时已经指出了这一点。</td></tr>
<tr><th colspan="2">独立升学顾问的评论</th></tr>
<tr><td colspan="2">我喜欢你写的新结尾！这是一个很好的例子，可以极大地改进你的文书。如你所见，我建议你删除一些内容并重新编写一些内容，把字数控制在通用申请系统要求的 650 个词内。
我特别喜欢的是这个结尾展示了你的执着和不认输在你生活的各个不同方面发挥的作用。</td></tr>
</table>

现在我们来比较学生文书的原始版本与最终版本(见表 3.5),你会很好地理解独立升学顾问是怎么引导你调整大学申请文书的:

表 3.5 应对不良的溜溜球销售员的文书原始版本与最终版本的对比

原 始 版 本	最 终 版 本
I was pretty sure that I was in trouble now. Since morning, a large harassing phone calls and spam messages flooded in my cell phone. My parents asked me what happened through WeChat, because when they called me before, they found that the phone was always busy. "You must have been attacked by Call You to Death! You should carefully think about whom you have offended recently!" My classmates told me so, after I shared with them what I met. Call You to Death is an online phone calling platform. After entering the target phone number, it will keep harassing the target number by calling and sending text messages. In China, this is illegal. However, I had to save my cell phone from the endless call-ins and messages at first. Finally, our class monitor, Tommy, suggested downloading a certain APP on my cell phone to intercept strange numbers and text messages, which was from his sister's experience. His sister had been attacked by "Call You to Death" because of bad reviews she left on Taobao. The APP was effective, the call-ins and text messages became much less. I had time to think about who made the attack. I was an ordinary student, and had a good relationship with my classmates. Recalling Tommy's words, I suddenly realized that I had given a yoyo store a bad review on Taobao last week. The newly bought Yoyo was not good as its promotion, so when the seller asked me to write a product review, I gave my real feedback and then clicked "Bad Review".	I was in trouble now. Since morning, harassing phone calls and spam messages flooded my cell phone. My parents asked me what happened through WeChat because my phone was always busy. My classmates told me, "You must have been attacked by Call You to Death! You should carefully think about whom you have offended recently!" Call You to Death is an online phone calling platform. After entering the target phone number, it will keep harassing the number by calling and texting. In China, this is illegal. However, I first had to save my cell phone from the endless call-ins and messages. Finally, our class monitor, Tommy, suggested downloading an APP to my cell phone to intercept strange numbers and text messages. His sister had been attacked by "Call You to Death" because of bad reviews she left on Taobao. The APP was effective; the call-ins and text messages became much less. I thought about who made the attack. I was an ordinary student and had a good relationship with my classmates. I suddenly realized that I had given a yoyo store a bad review on Taobao last week. The newly bought yoyo was not as good as its promotion, so when the seller asked me to write a product review, I gave my real feedback and clicked "Bad Review". I opened the conversation page with the seller. After my bad review, the seller asked me to delete it and even promised to offer me a big discount. But unfortunately, I missed these messages. The most recent

续　表

原　始　版　本	最　终　版　本
Thinking of this, I opened the conversation page with the seller. After I gave the bad review, the seller asked me to delete the bad review, and he even promised to offer me a big discount. But unfortunately, I missed all the messages. The most recent messages were sent out yesterday evening: "If you insist embarrassing us, I will teach you a lesson!" Now I was sure that all my suffering today was from the yoyo seller. My classmates started to criticize the seller, and some even suggested me to communicate with the seller and agreed to delete my review. I felt angry: I was the right side, but I had to compromise to the wrong side. Maybe compromising was the easiest solution, but I did not want to compromise this time. I sent messages to the seller and asked him to stop the illegal behavior, soon I received the reply: they denied the attack, and all my words were my imagination, since I did not have any evidence. I had to contact Taobao agent and received the same reply: no evidence to support my complaint, but they recommended an APP, which was what Tommy suggested. At last, I had to go to the police station near my school. After hearing all my suffering, the policeman got the seller's phone number and made a call, but after speaking few words, the seller hung up the phone. Few minutes later, shocking things happened: the phone of the police station was attacked by the "Call You to Death". Then, the story went quite smoothly later. The police found the seller, and in addition to being held under administrative detention of 5 days, the seller was also asked to apologize to me.	were sent out yesterday evening: "If you insist on embarrassing us, I will teach you a lesson!" Now I was sure that my suffering was from the yoyo seller. Some classmates suggested that I agree to delete my review. I felt angry: I was the right side, but I had to compromise with the wrong side. Maybe compromising was the easiest solution, but I did not want to compromise. I asked the seller to stop the illegal behavior. He denied the attack and said my words were in my imagination, since I did not have any evidence. I contacted the Taobao agent and received the same reply: no evidence to support my complaint, but they recommended the APP that Tommy suggested. At last, I went to the police station near my school. After hearing all my suffering, the policeman got the seller's phone number and made a call, but after a few words, the seller hung up the phone. A few minutes later, something amusing happened: the police station's phone was attacked by "Call You to Death". Now, things went smoothly: the police found the seller, and in addition to being held under administrative detention of 5 days, the seller had to apologize to me. I will never forget my important attempt to insist on my authentic ideas and not compromise with the wrong side. Someone describes me as a stubborn and single-minded boy. I strictly follow rules: I never run the traffic lights, though there are no cars; I never have breakfast on the school bus, though almost all my classmates do it; and, like this experience, I refuse to give fake reviews.

续 表

原 始 版 本	最 终 版 本
I will never forget this special experience, since it is my important attempt to insist my authentic ideas and not compromise with the wrong side. I know someone in my daily life often describe me as a stubborn and single-minded boy. I strictly follow rules: I never run the traffic lights, though there are no cars; I never have breakfast on the school bus, though almost all my classmates do it; and like this experience, I refuse to give fake reviews. Despite so, I think being stubborn and authentic are required qualities to do scientific research in the future. (649 words)	Stubbornness and persistence are also values that I will carry into my future career. I see myself as a scientific researcher, where these values are critical to success. I want to be like Shuji Nakamura, who was considered a crazy freak before he won the 2014 Nobel Prize in Physics. He had been working in Japan on a "hopeless" research project: making blue LED with gallium nitride, while others in the industry were using zinc selenide. Nevertheless, stubborn Shuji Nakamura insisted on what he thought was right, and finally invented a high-efficiency blue light-emitting diode. The path of scientific research may be tough, but I'm confident and well prepared to pursue my dream with my stubbornness and persistence. (648 words)

第三节

关于写作风格

文书是让学生证明自己写作能力的途径之一。对于英语非母语、非美国本地长大的学生而言，有时可能会在写作上遇到困难。几年前，《大西洋月刊》曾刊登过一篇文书，阐述了文化差异是部分中国学生在撰写美国大学申请文书时的主要障碍：

> 中文写作讲究留白、委婉，经常会使用一些富有诗意的词和短语。鼓励使用四字短语，文书的最后通常是升华的段落，拔高整篇文书的立意。这些都是中文的魅力所在。但是在英文写作中，好的文书都是直截了当，使用清晰明了的单词，而鲜明的主旨往往都是通过个人的故事获得的。所以，中国学生在写文书的时候，需要跳出中文写作的思路，认真思考写作风格和内容。

1906 年，福勒兄弟编写了一本英语用法的经典著作《国王的英语》(*The King's English*)，书开头有一条建议对英语写作很有帮助：

想成为一个好的作者，他的文书首先要做到直截了当、简洁有力、清晰易懂，然后他才可以去尝试一些更华丽、炫技的写作风格。

这一原则可以被理解为关于词汇的实用规则：

(1) 使用常见词，而不是生僻词。

(2) 使用具体词，而不是抽象词。

(3) 使用单个词，而不是累赘词。

(4) 使用短词,而不是长词。

以下两个段落的对比可以帮助你理解为什么这些规则值得遵循:

段落一

My initial introduction to mathematical ratiocination was obtained from a reading material vouchsafed to me from my grandmother the losing of which would have been detrimental to my mathematical educational advancement and also from the instructional expertise of my teacher of mathematics.

段落二

I was first introduced to math when my grandmother gave me a math textbook. Without it, I would not have progressed so well in math. That and the skill of a math teacher taught me to reason mathematically.

请注意,第一个例句要比第二个难理解得多。冗长的单词、抽象的概念、令人费解的短语,就像在作者和读者之间设置了一层障碍,使阅读既令人不愉快,又使人困惑。

看完了独立升学顾问修改前后的文书以及独立升学顾问的建议,我们不难发现独立升学顾问更善于去发现学生本身的个性,并且会通过引导,让学生自身的能力和个性展现得"淋漓尽致",告诉学生美国大学的招生官最想在你的文书里看见哪些特点,并且还能给到学生充分的信心,就如同评论中写的那句话,"字数太多不要紧,我可以帮助你找到减少文书字数的方法,腾出空间来添加修订版的结尾。"而想要轻松打磨一篇文书,看透一位学生个性并给到同学们最有效的建议,这就需要这位独立升学顾问对美国大学招生体系有充分的了解和日积月累的经验。当然,如果独立升学顾问具有多年的美国大学的招生官经验,那么他更加会从招生官视角给到同学们更多的建议。这同样也是独立升学顾问的能力和作用所在。

第四节

如何撰写美国大学通用申请系统主文书

让我们再回到美国大学通用申请系统里的主文书题目(见表 3.6)。正如我们前面提到的,首先要回顾你的生活经历,并找到有关自己引人入胜的故事。找到"你的故事"后,思考它适用于哪些文书题目。

表 3.6　2020～2021 年美国大学通用申请系统里的文书题目

<table>
<tr><td>第一题</td><td>Some students have a background, identity, interest, or talent that is so meaningful they believe their application would be incomplete without it. If this sounds like you, then please share your story.
有些学生的身份、背景、兴趣或才能很出色。他们觉得如果这些信息缺失,他们的申请将不完整。如果这听起来像你的情况,请分享你的故事。</td><td rowspan="3">当你查看这些题目时,请记住以下几点:
1. 你的目标是写一篇能使你从诸多申请人中脱颖而出的文书。
2. 大多数文书题目都在引导你讲述自己的故事。实际上,第一题里的"故事"一词已经非常明显。
3. 没有一个学校会要求你在生活中有过多么惊天动地的经历,但他们确实要求你是一个愿意花时间审视自己生活的人。注意这些提示中的关键短语:"它对你有何影响?""你从这次经验中学到了什么?""是什么启发了你的思考""解释其重要性""讨论你的一个成就,活动或领悟""为什么吸引你?"</td></tr>
<tr><td>第二题</td><td>The lessons we take from obstacles we encounter can be fundamental to later success. Recount a time when you faced a challenge, setback, or failure. How did it affect you, and what did you learn from the experience?
从困难中吸取的教训对我们以后的成功至关重要。重述你遇到的挑战、挫折或失败的事件。它对你有什么影响,你从经验中学到了什么?</td></tr>
<tr><td>第三题</td><td>Reflect on a time when you questioned or challenged a belief or idea. What prompted your thinking? What was the outcome?
回想一下你曾质疑或挑战某个信念或权威想法的时候,是什么促使你思考?结果怎么样?</td></tr>
</table>

续 表

第四题	Describe a problem you've solved or a problem you'd like to solve. It can be an intellectual challenge, a research query, an ethical dilemma — anything that is of personal importance, no matter the scale. Explain its significance to you and what steps you took or could be taken to identify a solution. 描述你已解决的或你想解决的问题。这可能是一个才智上的挑战，一个研究课题，一个道德困境——任何对个人都重要的事情。说明这些事情对你的重要性以及你的解决方案或打算采取的办法步骤。	4. 即使你选择第七题开放式的题目，你选择的主题也最好能分享一些关于你自己的重要信息，作为美国大学通用申请系统里没覆盖的要点。 5. 招生人员只有几分钟的时间审核每份申请，因此你的文书应有一个吸引他们注意力并激发他们兴趣的开头。
第五题	Discuss an accomplishment, event, or realization that sparked a period of personal growth and a new understanding of yourself and others. 讨论激发你某段时期个人成长和赋予自己或他人新认知的成就或活动。	
第六题	Describe a topic, idea, or concept you find so engaging that it makes you lose all track of time. Why does it captivate you? What or who do you turn to when you want to learn more? 描述一个让你着迷到可以忘记时间的话题，想法或概念。解释你为什么会着迷？当你想学习更多相关信息时，你会怎么做或会向谁求助？	
第七题	Share an essay on any topic of your choice. It can be one you've already written, one that responds to a different prompt, or one of your own design. 分享你自定义主题的一篇文书。可以是你已经完稿的，也可以是你对不同问题的回答，也可以是你全新自创的文书。	

我们看看刚阅读的这篇“应对不良的溜溜球销售员”的文书都满足了哪些要点。它有一个有趣的开场白（“I was in trouble now”）。它讲述了一个有趣的故事。故事重点突出了招生委员会看中的学生素质：决心、毅力、自信和道德观。它回答了两个基本问题：我们的教授会喜欢教这个学生吗？其他学生会从结识的这个人中受益吗？

让我们看另一个例子(见表 3.7)。在阅读过程中,思考你对这个故事的看法。

表 3.7　有关中日文化的文书

通用申请系统的主文书	
学生原先的回答	由独立升学顾问修改后
“What is this kind of language, it is … Chinese, right?”	“What is this kind of language, it is … Chinese, right?”[1]
I can still remember once in my childhood I watched an animation on TV. The subtitle included some Chinese characters I knew well and some foreign letters I had not seen before. I asked my father what they were.	I can still remember once in my childhood I watched an animation on TV. The subtitle included some Chinese characters I knew well and some foreign letters I had not seen before. I asked my father what they were.
“Oh, they are Japanese characters named ‘kana’, In Japanese kana are used with Chinese characters. You may feel a sense of familiarity, but it is a totally different foreign language from Chinese.”	“Oh, they are Japanese characters named ‘kana’~~,~~. In Japanese kana are used with Chinese characters. You may feel a sense of familiarity, but it is a totally different foreign language from Chinese.”
Maybe that was my initial motivation to learn Japanese because it is amazing to find another language that shares Chinese characters but whose usage is different from Chinese, the original language. I wanted to figure out the role the Chinese letters play in Japanese.	Maybe that was my initial motivation to learn Japanese because it is amazing to find another language that shares Chinese characters but whose usage is different from Chinese, the original language. I wanted to figure out the role the Chinese letters play in Japanese.
In Japanese there exists a grammatical system including honorific and modest expression that is used when talking with someone whose status, whether in society, company or at home, are higher, which means one must use another way of expression differing from that used in daily conversation when facing his parents, teachers, bosses, etc., and of course it greatly increases the difficulty for people who are learning Japanese, like me. I doubt the necessity of learning honorific and modest expression, for without it we can still express respect to elders, and it doesn’t exist in English, nor in Chinese.	In Japanese there exists a grammatical system including honorific and ~~modest~~ humble expression[2] that is used when talking with someone whose status, whether in society, company or at home, ~~are~~ is higher, which means one must use another way of expression differing from that used in daily conversation when facing ~~his~~ one’s parents, teachers, bosses, etc., and of course it greatly increases the difficulty for people who are learning Japanese, like me. I doubt the necessity of learning honorific and ~~modest~~ humble expression, for without it we can still express respect to elders, and it doesn’t exist in English, nor in Chinese.

续 表

通用申请系统的主文书	
学生原先的回答	由独立升学顾问修改后
"Intriguing idea." My father said, "but remember, every language has its cultural background, since you are learning Japanese, why not learning something more about Japan the country?"	"Intriguing idea." My father said, "but remember, every language has its cultural background, since you are learning Japanese, why not learning something more about Japan the country?"
Actually, I was attracted by Japanese culture, both modern one and traditional one. I can still remember the time I sat in front of the television and filled in Japanese animation with joy and laughter, or played Japanese video games like Contra together with my brothers. In spring days I was charmed by the beauty of cherry blossoms, whose another name is sakura, national flower of Japan through which Japanese poets express their delightful or pensive emotions in ancient times. Every time I read these poems (of course the translated version), I could also catch poets' feelings that life comes and goes, like sakura being blown away by winds with a transient lifetime.	Actually, I was attracted by Japanese culture, both the modern one and the traditional one. I can still remember the time I sat in front of the television and filled in[3] Japanese animation with joy and laughter, or played Japanese video games like Contra together with my brothers. In spring days I was charmed by the beauty of cherry blossoms, whose ~~an~~ other name is sakura, the national flower of Japan through which Japanese poets expressed their delightful or pensive emotions in ancient times. Every time I read these poems (of course the translated version), I could also catch the poets' feelings that life comes and goes, like sakura being blown away by winds within a transient lifetime.
These poems reminded me of Chinese poems I learned before. It seems like a coincidence that both Chinese and Japanese poets love to leave their thoughts and feelings in natural objects like flowers, mountains, rivers, etc.	These poems reminded me of Chinese poems I learned before. It seems like a coincidence that both Chinese and Japanese poets love to ~~leave~~ express their thoughts and feelings in natural objects like flowers, mountains, rivers, etc.
As we know, kana derives from running style of Chinese calligraphy, and now Japan and China are only two countries that use Chinese letters around the world. When China was in a crisis of coronavirus at the beginning of this year, what made Chinese move was not only that Japanese people sent us many surgical mask, but also that they wrote an ancient Japanese verse on the package, 'Though we're oceans apart, a shared moon connects hearts'. The verse was once created by a Japanese prince in 7th	As we know, kana derives from the running style of Chinese calligraphy, and now Japan and China are the only two countries that use Chinese letters around the world. When China was in a ~~crisis of~~ coronavirus crisis at the beginning of this year, what ~~made~~ moved many Chinese people ~~move~~ was not only that Japanese people sent us many surgical masks, but also that they wrote an ancient Japanese verse on the package, "Though we're oceans apart a shared moon connects hearts".[4] The verse was once

续　表

<table>
<tr><th colspan="2">通用申请系统的主文书</th></tr>
<tr><th>学生原先的回答</th><th>由独立升学顾问修改后</th></tr>
<tr><td>century. Back to 1300 years ago, it was a period that China and Japan were in a good relationship and each was seeking for bilateral communications on politics, culture, religion, etc. Under this background, the Japanese prince sent thousands of cassocks to Chinese monks as a way to show his respect for the great Tang Dynasty and his will to study Buddhist dharma from Chinese scholars, with this verse in attached letter. A millennium or so later, though under different situation, but with the same verse, we can still show friendliness and care to each other with shared Chinese characters. That is why I am charmed by Japanese, for it is amazing to find a bridge between these two totally different languages through which we can share our emotions, from the ancient time to now.</td><td>created by a Japanese prince in the 7th century. ~~Back to~~ 1300 years ago ~~, it~~ was a period ~~that~~ when China and Japan were in a good relationship and each was seeking ~~for~~ bilateral communications on politics, culture, religion, etc. Under this background, the Japanese prince sent thousands of cassocks to Chinese monks as a way to show his respect for the great Tang Dynasty and his will to study Buddhist dharma from Chinese scholars, with this verse in an attached letter. A millennium or so later, though under a different situation, but with the same verse, we can still show friendliness and care to each other with shared Chinese characters. That is why I am charmed by Japanese, for it is amazing to find a bridge between these two totally different languages through which we can share our emotions, from the ancient time to now.</td></tr>
<tr><th colspan="2">独立升学顾问给学生的建议</th></tr>
<tr><td colspan="2">1. "What is this kind of language, it is … Chinese, right?"
这是好的开篇！激发了读者想要了解更多的好奇心，当然，这正是开篇句子应该做的。</td></tr>
<tr><td colspan="2">2. "honorific and modest expression"
以上的英语表达形式是"honorific and humble"。</td></tr>
<tr><td colspan="2">3. "filled in"
也许你想表达的是"回应"("responded to")日本动画。</td></tr>
<tr><td colspan="2">4. "Though we're oceans apart, a shared moon connects hearts"
这句诗相当唯美！我特别感动的是你将七世纪人们把这句诗写在长袍上与最近人们把它印在外科口罩上联系起来。</td></tr>
<tr><th colspan="2">独立升学顾问的评价</th></tr>
<tr><td colspan="2">这是一篇很好的文书，它揭示了你的一些特质：求知欲、对日语和日本文化的兴趣，对探索外国文化的渴望，分析和感知诗歌的能力，以及你的同情心。你的这些特质在美国大学招生官看来非常有吸引力。
你有没有想过这篇文书用来回答通用申请系统里的哪个文书题最有效？我认为第一题最有效。</td></tr>
</table>

续 表

独立升学顾问的评价
以下是我修改后的完整版： "What is this kind of language, it is ... Chinese, right?" I can still remember once in my childhood I watched an animation on TV. The subtitle included some Chinese characters I knew well and some foreign letters I had not seen before. I asked my father what they were. "Oh, they are Japanese characters named 'kana'. In Japanese kana are used with Chinese characters. You may feel a sense of familiarity, but it is a totally different foreign language from Chinese. " Maybe that was my initial motivation to learn Japanese because it is amazing to find another language that shares Chinese characters but whose usage is different from Chinese, the original language. I wanted to figure out the role the Chinese letters play in Japanese. In Japanese there exists a grammatical system including honorific and humble expression that is used when talking with someone whose status, whether in society, company or at home, is higher, which means one must use another way of expression differing from that used in daily conversation when facing one's parents, teachers, bosses, etc., and of course it greatly increases the difficulty for people who are learning Japanese, like me. I doubt the necessity of learning honorific and humble expression, for without it we can still express respect to elders, and it doesn't exist in English, nor in Chinese. "Intriguing idea." My father said, "but remember, every language has its cultural background, since you are learning Japanese, why not learn something more about Japan the country?" Actually, I was attracted by Japanese culture, both the modern one and the traditional one. I can still remember the time I sat in front of the television and responded to Japanese animation with joy and laughter, or played Japanese video games like Contra together with my brothers. In spring days I was charmed by the beauty of cherry blossoms, whose other name is Sakura, the national flower of Japan through which Japanese poets expressed their delightful or pensive emotions in ancient times. Every time I read these poems (of course the translated version), I could also catch the poets' feelings that life comes and goes, like Sakura being blown away by winds within a transient lifetime. These poems reminded me of Chinese poems I learned before. It seems like a coincidence that both Chinese and Japanese poets love to express their thoughts and feelings in natural objects like flowers, mountains, rivers, etc. As we know, kana derives from the running style of Chinese calligraphy, and now Japan and China are the only two countries that use Chinese letters around the world. When China was in a coronavirus crisis at the beginning of this year, what moved many Chinese people was not only that Japanese people sent us many surgical masks, but also that they wrote an ancient Japanese verse on the package, 'Though we're oceans apart, a shared moon

续 表

独立升学顾问的评价
connects hearts'. The verse was once created by a Japanese prince in the 7th century. 1300 years ago was a period when China and Japan were in a good relationship and each was seeking bilateral communications on politics, culture, religion, etc. Under this background, the Japanese prince sent thousands of cassocks to Chinese monks as a way to show his respect for the great Tang Dynasty and his will to study Buddhist dharma from Chinese scholars, with this verse in an attached letter. A millennium or so later, though under a different situation, but with the same verse, we can still show friendliness and care to each other with shared Chinese characters. That is why I am charmed by Japanese, for it is amazing to find a bridge between these two totally different languages through which we can share our emotions, from the ancient time to now.

我们再来看另一个例子如表 3.8 所示。

表 3.8 关于在数学和科学领域中的女性的文书

美国大学通用申请系统主文书第三题:"回想一下你曾质疑或挑战某个信念或权威想法的时候,是什么促使你思考? 结果怎么样?"(650 词)的回答。	
学生原先的文书	**由独立升学顾问修改后**
When I was a toddler, I always wanted to know how things worked. I attempted to take apart my father's DJI drone to get a feel why it flies. As got older, I was always wondering about the news about Elon Musk's SpaceX project and asking why this or that was a better way of implementing these or those ideas. Everyone around me was only concerned with things that were practical or had what I call "measurable value." However, this was never good enough for me. I challenge myself not knowing why things mattered, but why things were. I thought mathematics would be my answer to some extent.	When I was a toddler, I always wanted to know how things worked. I attempted to take apart my father's DJI drone to get a feel why it flies. As got older, I was always wondering about the news about Elon Musk's SpaceX project and asking why this or that was a better way of implementing these or those ideas. Everyone around me was only concerned with things that were practical or had what I call "measurable value." However, this was never good enough for me. I challenged myself to know not ~~knowing~~ why things mattered, but why things were. I thought mathematics would be an important part of the ~~my~~ answer. ~~to some extent.~~[1,2]
There is a common belief that "boys learn science and math easier than girls." Women remain vastly underrepresented in science fields. I believe that girls do not receive the same level of support and encouragement to do well in math and science as boys do.	There is a common belief that "boys learn science and math easier than girls." Women remain vastly underrepresented in science fields. I believe that girls do not receive the same level of support and encouragement to do well in math and science as boys do.

续 表

学生原先的文书	由独立升学顾问修改后
When I was in primary school, I was even the worst in the calculation test in grade two. After I practiced a lot and learned some mathematical methods beyond just calculations, I worked better on Math. Many mathematic skills can be practiced and memorized for improvement, no matter whether you are a girl or a boy. When I went to middle school, I continued to work better and better because I had more confidence in Math. However, when I entered high school, I again felt dejected by the fact that boys were getting full marks in Math and I was not. My Math teacher smiled and encouraged me instead of criticizing. With her encouragement, I retrieved my original status on the exams. I realized that by continuing to challenge myself I would succeed.	When I was in primary school, I was ~~even~~ the worst in the calculation test in grade two. After I practiced a lot and learned some mathematical methods beyond just calculations, I worked better on Math. Many mathematic skills can be practiced and memorized for improvement, no matter whether you are a girl or a boy. When I went to middle school, I continued to work better and better because I had more confidence in Math. However, when I entered high school, I again felt dejected by the fact that boys were getting full marks in Math and I was not. My Math teacher smiled and encouraged me instead of criticizing. With her encouragement, I ~~retrieved~~ regained my original status on the exams. I realized that by continuing to challenge myself I would succeed.
Since I regained my confidence, I wanted to empower other women too. I started a study group with several girls in my class who are poor at learning Math and even afraid of Math. Many of them want to give up and they have no confidence. I encourage them, tutor them, and share with them my experience. I believe that women can have more creative thoughts than men. I realize that I can provide some special solutions that other boys and even our teacher didn't think of. They can ask me some indeterminable questions or incomprehensive knowledge[2], and then I can explain these questions to them. I also recommend they watch the film "Hidden figures"[3] to know women can be mathematic geniuses and to break that old conception.	Since I regained my confidence, I wanted to empower other women too. I started a study group with several girls in my class who are poor at learning Math and even afraid of Math. Many of them want to give up and ~~they~~ have no confidence. I encourage them, tutor them, and share with them my experience. I believe that women can have more creative thoughts than men. I realize that I can provide some special solutions that ~~other~~ boys and even our teacher ~~didn't~~ don't think of. They can ask me ~~some indeterminable questions or incomprehensive knowledge~~[3] about things they do not understand and then I can ~~explain~~ answer these questions ~~to~~ for them. I also recommend they watch the film "Hidden fFigures"[4] to know women can be mathematical geniuses and to break that old misconception.

续　表

学生原先的文书	由独立升学顾问修改后
The year I joined my school's robotics club, only two of twenty members were girls. When I became the core member one year later, I suggested to enroll several girls to improve the gender balance. Girls were more out-going than boys, which made us more likely to share our creative ideas. In the past, boys just worked on their own without informing their teammates about what they had been working on. As a result, some robots, though painstakingly designed and carefully built, had a lot of unexpected problems that required constant correction. Besides, girls are good at operating robots due to their carefulness and calmness. Also, I found that the competition officers put more emphasis on girls participating in robot events and even give bonus scores to the teams with girls. I expect that one day a team of all girls will stand on the rostrum as winners of the robotics championship.	The year I joined my school's robotics club, only two of twenty members were girls. When I became the core member one year later, I suggested to ~~enroll~~several girls that they enroll to improve the gender balance. Girls ~~were~~ are more outgoing than boys, which makes ~~made~~us more likely to share our creative ideas. In the past, the boys just worked on their own without informing their teammates about what they had been working on. As a result, some robots, though painstakingly designed and carefully built, had a lot of unexpected problems that required constant correction. Besides, girls are good at operating robots due to their carefulness and calmness. Also, I found that the competition officers put more emphasis on girls participating in robot events and even give bonus scores to the teams with girls. I expect that one day a team of all girls will stand on the rostrum as winners of the robotics championship.
In the future, I believe I will still challenge myself and help others in the science field. I hope that my community will avoid stereotyping the ability of girls in all STEM fields. Science has taught me not to be afraid of things that are new and confusing, which allows me to make more rational and objective decisions. (600 words)	In the future, I believe I will still challenge myself and help others in the science field. I hope that my community will avoid stereotyping the ability of girls in all STEM fields. Science has taught me not to be afraid of things that are new and confusing, which allows me to make more rational and objective decisions.[5] (601 words)

独立升学顾问给学生的建议

1. "to some extent"

你写道:"I thought mathematics would be my answer to some extent"这句话我听起来没有说服力。我将其更改为"I thought mathematics would be an important part of the answer",因为我认为这句话能更准确地反映数学在你生活中的重要性。你同意吗?

2. Opening paragraph

这是一个很好的开篇！有很多有效的细节。

续 表

独立升学顾问给学生的建议	
3. “indeterminable questions or incomprehensive knowledge” 这个短语不成立。也许你的意思是“They can ask me about things they do not understand, and then I can answer their questions”。	
4. “Hidden Figures” 是的！这是一部了不起的电影。很高兴你提到它。它有助于支撑你对数学领域中女性的观点。	
5. Your essay’s closing paragraph 遗憾的是，这是一个无聊的结尾段落。请在下面查看我的评论。	
独立升学顾问的评论	
你对问题提示做出了有效的回应。你的数学老师在你需要时给予你鼓励，这也鼓励你为学习数学有困难的女孩们建立学习小组，并成功招募了更多女孩加入机器人俱乐部。它表明你正在为他人做着数学老师为你所做的事情。我非常喜欢！ 我主要顾虑的一点是你的结尾段落，结尾很无聊。我会敦促你将其替换为与你的开篇段落一样生动有趣的文字。为什么不写一些能使你申请的大学招生委员会更了解你的内容呢？例如，你的开篇段落很有说服力的原因之一是，你通过一些具体示例，展示年轻时激发你想象力(无人机和埃隆·马斯克)的问题。读者可以感受到你是一个充满好奇心的孩子。那么如今成年的你，有没有类似的例子可以激发你的想象力？换句话说，你的文书是从向读者展示科学如何激发了你的童年想象力而开始的，那你也可以通过向读者展示科学如何激发你成年后的想象力来结束。 另一种可能性是在结尾处回到你在上一段中关于创意合作的观点(“Girls are more outgoing than boys, which makes us more likely to share our creative ideas”)也许你可以描述一个与其他学生成功合作的事件，特别是读者可能会认为很有趣的事件。 有了正确的结尾后，你的文书将会非常出色。	
在顾问的建议下，学生重新写了结尾段	
原来的结尾段	**修改后的结尾段**
In the future, I believe I will still challenge myself and help others in the science field. I hope that my community will avoid stereotyping the ability of girls in all STEM fields. Science has taught me not to be afraid of things that are new and confusing, which allows me to make more rational and objective decisions.	Mathematics has taught me not to be afraid of things that are new and confusing, which allows me to make more creative decisions. I started to learn the piano by myself despite my heavy schedule. I also started talking in front of strangers despite my fear of speaking in front of audiences and signed up for volunteer work at a hospital.

我们来比较一下本文的原始版本和最终版本(见表 3.9)。注意观察文书是怎样捕捉到学生故事中几个不同的重要主题：她对数学的热爱，即使在缺乏支持的情况下依然对数学有所追求，自信心的发展以及在帮助他人方面的利他主义。

表 3.9 《数学与科学领域中的女性》原始版本及最终版本

<table>
<tr><th colspan="2">美国大学通用申请系统主文书第三题:“回想一下你曾质疑或挑战某个信念或权威想法的时候,是什么促使你思考? 结果怎么样?”(650 词)的回答。</th></tr>
<tr><th>原始版本</th><th>最终版本</th></tr>
<tr><td>When I was a toddler, I always wanted to know how things worked. I attempted to take apart my father's DJI drone to get a feel why it flies. As got older, I was always wondering about the news about Elon Musk's SpaceX project and asking why this or that was a better way of implementing these or those ideas. Everyone around me was only concerned with things that were practical or had what I call "measurable value." However, this was never good enough for me. I challenge myself not knowing why things mattered, but why things were. I thought mathematics would be my answer to some extent.

There is a common belief that "boys learn science and math easier than girls." Women remain vastly underrepresented in science fields. I believe that girls do not receive the same level of support and encouragement to do well in math and science as boys do.

When I was in primary school, I was even the worst in the calculation test in grade two. After I practiced a lot and learned some mathematical methods beyond just calculations, I worked better on Math. Many mathematic skills can be practiced and memorized for improvement, no matter whether you are a girl or a boy. When I went to middle school, I continued to work better and better because I had more confidence in Math. However, when I entered high school, I again felt dejected by the fact that boys were getting full marks in Math and I was not. My Math teacher smiled and encouraged me instead of criticizing. With her encouragement, I retrieved my original status on the exams. I realized that by continuing to challenge myself I would succeed.</td><td>When I was a toddler, I always wanted to know how things worked. I attempted to take apart my father's DJI drone to get a feel for why it flies. As I got older, I was always wondering about the news about Elon Musk's SpaceX project and asking why this or that was a better way of implementing these or those ideas. Everyone around me was only concerned with things that were practical or had what I call "measurable value." However, this was never good enough for me. I challenged myself to know not why things mattered, but why things were. I thought mathematics would be an important part of the answer.

There is a common belief that "boys learn science and math easier than girls." Women remain vastly underrepresented in science fields. I believe that girls do not receive the same level of support and encouragement to do well in math and science as boys do.

When I was in primary school, I was the worst in the calculation test in grade two. After I practiced a lot and learned some mathematical methods beyond just calculations, I worked better on Math. Many mathematic skills can be practiced and memorized for improvement, no matter whether you are a girl or a boy. When I went to middle school, I continued to work better and better because I had more confidence in Math. However, when I entered high school, I again felt dejected by the fact that boys were getting full marks in Math and I was not. My Math teacher smiled and encouraged me instead of criticizing. With her encouragement, I regained my original status on the exams. I realized that by continuing to challenge myself I would succeed.</td></tr>
</table>

续 表

原始版本	最终版本
Since I regained my confidence, I wanted to empower other women too. I started a study group with several girls in my class who are poor at learning Math and even afraid of Math. Many of them want to give up and they have no confidence. I encourage them, tutor them, and share with them my experience. I believe that women can have more creative thoughts than men. I realize that I can provide some special solutions that other boys and even our teacher didn't think of. They can ask me some indeterminable questions or incomprehensive knowledge, and then I can explain these questions to them. I also recommend they watch the film "Hidden figures" to know women can be mathematic geniuses and to break that old conception.	Since I regained my confidence, I wanted to empower other women too. I started a study group with several girls in my class who are poor at learning Math and even afraid of Math. Many of them want to give up and have no confidence. I encourage them, tutor them, and share with them my experience. I believe that women can have more creative thoughts than men. I realize that I can provide some special solutions that boys and even our teacher don't think of. They can ask me about things they do not understand, and then I can answer their questions. I also recommend they watch the film "Hidden Figures" to know women can be mathematical geniuses and to break that old misconception.
The year I joined my school's robotics club, only two of twenty members were girls. When I became the core member one year later, I suggested to enroll several girls to improve the gender balance. Girls were more out-going than boys, which made us more likely to share our creative ideas. In the past, boys just worked on their own without informing their teammates about what they had been working on. As a result, some robots, though painstakingly designed and carefully built, had a lot of unexpected problems that required constant correction. Besides, girls are good at operating robots due to their carefulness and calmness. Also, I found that the competition officers put more emphasis on girls participating in robot events and even give bonus scores to the teams with girls. I expect that one day a team of all girls will stand on the rostrum as winners of the robotics championship.	The year I joined my school's robotics club, only two of twenty members were girls. When I became the core member one year later, I suggested to several girls that they enroll to improve the gender balance. Girls are more outgoing than boys, which makes us more likely to share our creative ideas. In the past, the boys just worked on their own without informing their teammates about what they had been working on. As a result, some robots, though painstakingly designed and carefully built, had a lot of unexpected problems that required constant correction. Besides, girls are good at operating robots due to their carefulness and calmness. Also, I found that the competition officers put more emphasis on girls participating in robot events and even give bonus scores to the teams with girls. I expect that one day a team of all girls will stand on the rostrum as winners of the robotics championship.

续　表

原始版本	最终版本
In the future, I believe I will still challenge myself and help others in the science field. I hope that my community will avoid stereotyping the ability of girls in all STEM fields. Science has taught me not to be afraid of things that are new and confusing, which allows me to make more rational and objective decisions. (600 words)	Mathematics has taught me not to be afraid of things that are new and confusing, which allows me to make more creative decisions. I started to learn the piano by myself despite my heavy schedule. I also started talking in front of strangers despite my fear of speaking in front of audiences and signed up for volunteer work at a hospital. (629 words)

同样是关于数学主题，我们来看另一篇文书(见表 3.10)。想象一下，这个学生正在申请几所数学、计算机科学和工程学专业领先的顶尖大学。我们来分析一下这篇文书，以更好地了解聪明的学生如何让自己脱颖而出，让招生官们留下深刻印象。

表 3.10　什么样的文书能让人印象深刻？关于分形与分析的文书

美国大学通用申请系统主文书第一题：有些学生的背景、身份、兴趣或才能很值得在申请中分享出来，你可以分享你的故事。(650 词)	
Essay **文书**	**Why is this essay effective?** **为什么这是一篇好的文书？**
Several years ago, while browsing in the science section of a bookstore, I spotted a stack of very old magazines. On top was the 5 May 1967 issue of *Science Magazine*. As I thumbed past articles with titles such as, "Salvage Archeology in the Missouri River Basin" and "Pleistocene Coral Reefs on Barbados," I spotted one with the intriguing title, "How Long Is the Coast of Britain?" It was written by a mathematician whose name I had never heard before: Benoit B. Mandelbrot. Mandelbrot explained that coastlines are never straight. They are jagged. As you measure up and down the jagged edges, the closer you look the more you discover that the sides of those jagged edges are themselves jagged. That's why, paradoxically, Britain's coastline is 2,400 km if you measure it	1. First and foremost: the essay tells an interesting story. 首先最重要的是，这篇文书讲了一个很有趣的故事。 2. It's opening paragraph grabs a reader's attention. But more than that, it shows that even at an early age the writer had an abundant amount of "intellectual curiosity." 文书的开头就引起了读者的注意。不仅如此，也表现了作者在很小的时候就有很强的好奇心。 3. It does a wonderful job of explaining a complex subject. Even readers who are not proficient in math

续 表

Essay 文书	Why is this essay effective? 为什么这是一篇好的文书?
every 200 km, but 3,400 km if you measure it every 50 km. At 50 km there are more jagged edges to measure. Mandelbrot showed how you could enhance estimating the length of coastlines by using a "fractal" known as the Hausdorff dimension. That is when I first read the words "fractals," "self-similarity," and "coastline paradox" and began to explore the mathematics of shapes whose parts look like miniatures of the whole shape. Trees are a common example of a fractal shape. Each limb of a tree looks like it is a smaller tree. Each branch on each limb looks like an even smaller tree, and each twig on each branch of each limb is yet another, even smaller "tree," and each bud on each twig is about to become yet another, even tinier, tree. From there, I explored different kinds of fractal shapes and the mathematical formulas that produced them. Fractal mathematics lets you create an infinite number of designs from snowflakes to designs that look like microscopic organisms, mountain ranges, waves in the ocean, the insides of lungs, the patterns on the walls of Moorish architecture, or an abstract art painting in a museum of modern art. Fractal formulas recreate these patterns, and many are strikingly beautiful. My fascination with fractals and the increasingly complex mathematics needed to create them led to me to teach myself mathematics that I would not normally be learning until several years later in school. It was weird to be sitting in pre-calculus classes when I was already working my way through online courses on differential equations. Fractals also propelled me into learning more computer programming, since complex fractal designs are computer generated. Trial and error produced startling patterns of vibrant, pulsating colors. Friends joked that they sit with me at lunch	can understand why she is fascinated by fractals. 作者很好地解释一个复杂的主题。即使是不精通数学的读者也可以理解为什么她对分形这么着迷。 4. It captures the writer's intellectual journey. It is especially impressive that the writer taught herself so much mathematics and computer programming. 这里记录了作者的"知识之旅"。令人尤为印象深刻的是,作者自学了很多数学和计算机编程的知识。 5. It gives the admissions committee a picture of a student who is driven by a passion for something — in this case the fascination and even beauty of fractals. 在这里,一个对分形格外热爱,并且在不断为之努力的学生形象就跃然纸上了。 6. It mentions sharing images created by fractals with her friends in the lunchroom. From that, readers get a sense that she is a social person. That, too, is important. 这里作者又提到在学校餐厅和朋友分享由分形创建的图像。由此,读者可以感觉到她是一个社交达人。这也是很重要的。 7. It is well-written. 这篇文书整体写得很好。 8. This is an essay that would make a professor want to teach this student and a classmate want to get to know her better.

续 表

Essay 文书	Why is this essay effective? 为什么这是一篇好的文书?
just to see the latest design on my laptop screensaver. Several high schools near me asked me to give talks to their math and AP Computer Science classes on fractals. Last year five students and I entered a national science competition with a project on how fractal mathematics explains natural structures as diverse as fern fronds and the path that lightning takes as it heads to the earth. We won first place. My science friends mostly plan to study engineering in college and see mathematics as merely a tool for solving complex engineering problems. I get that, but I have become enthralled by the tool, itself, and its creative possibilities. So I'm my school's "fractals girl" and it all began from an old magazine in a bookshop.	这篇文书能让教授乐意教这样的学生,能让其他学生希望能去更多地了解她。 9. Finally, the essay gives you the sense that other students on campus would learn a lot from knowing this student. 最后,这篇文书给人的感觉是,学校里的其他学生将从认识这位学生中受益匪浅。

通过案例也足以证明一点:写文书最好是直接的表达——用清晰明了的词句来总结,让招生官更直接地明白其中的含义才是最重要的。

第五节

如何撰写英国大学申请系统的文书

如果你申请的是英国大学，那么你需要使用英国大学申请系统（即英国大学和学院招生服务中心 UCAS）。和美国大学通用申请系统一样，学生需要写一篇主文书。但是，美国大学通用申请系统主文书和英国大学申请系统主文书还是不一样的，如表 3.11 所示。

表 3.11　美国大学通用申请系统主文书与英国大学申请系统主文书区别

	美国大学通用申请系统	英国大学和学院招生服务中心
Length 长度	250～650 words. 250～650 词。	Maximum 4 000 characters (approx. 500 words) and no more than 47 lines. 最多 4 000 个字符（约 500 词），不超过 47 行。
Content 内容	Students respond to one of seven essay prompts, including a prompt that allows them to writing on a topic of their own choice. The topics draw primarily on life experiences and personal accomplishments (e.g. "Discuss an accomplishment, event, or realization that sparked a period of personal growth ...") 学生从 7 个文书题目中选一个来写，其中还有一个开放式的文书题目，学生可以写任何他们感兴趣的主题。 文书题目基本都是关于生活经历和个人成就（例如，"分享一个激发个人成长时期的成就、事件或领悟……"）	It focuses *exclusively* on why you want to pursue a particular field of study. The UCAS website describes it "as a chance for you to articulate why you'd like to study a particular course or subject, and what skills and experience you possess that show your passion for your chosen field." 仅侧重于你为什么要追求特定的研究领域或者专业。 英国大学和学院招生服务中心网站显示"请阐明你为什么要学习特定的领域或专业，以及你的哪些技能和经历能展现出你对所选专业的热爱。"

续 表

	美国大学通用申请系统	英国大学和学院招生服务中心
Activities 活动	Has a section devoted entirely to describing in-school and out-of-school activities 有专门用于描述校内和校外活动的部分。	Does not ask about activities. 不问课内外活动相关的问题。
Admissions Philosophy 录取宗旨	Since American colleges seek entering classes that have a diversity of different talents and life experiences, the Common Application promotes a holistic admission review that assesses not only your academic preparation for college, but also what your life experiences, special talents, and out-of-class accomplishments might contribute to the campus. 美国大学希望录取的学生有多样的才能和生活经历，所以美国大学通用申请系统会整体评估学生的学术水平、生活经历、特殊才能以及课外成就等。 A "holistic" admissions review includes qualities such as "resilience," "overcoming obstacles," "adding diversity to the student body," and talent in such areas as athletics, writing, and the arts. While these can never overcome a weak academic record, strengths in any of these areas can be reasons for choosing you over another applicant with an equally strong academic record. 整体评估会看重一些品质，如韧性、克服障碍的能力、能为学生群体增加多样性，以及在体育、写作和艺术等领域的才华。即便学生学术成绩较差，但如果学生在这些领域发挥出色的话，你同样有可能会被录取。	Universities in the UK are looking to select students who have the best preparation of their chosen field of study and the most convincing and well thought-out reasons for choosing it. 英国的大学希望录取的学生已经为自己将来所选专业做足了充分准备，而且能给出充足的选择理由。 The content of a UCAS Personal Statement, therefore, will be almost wholly focused on why you have chosen your field of study and those academic accomplishments that demonstrate why you are such a strong candidate for it. 所以英国大学和学院招生服务中心文书内容基本都是围绕着你为什么选择申请你感兴趣的专业，你已经获得了哪些学术成就，来展示你是一个强有力的申请者。

我们来看一篇英国大学和学院招生服务中心主文书的示例(见表 3.12)。

表 3.12 申请英国学习艺术史方向的英国大学和学院招生服务中心文书范文

<table>
<tr><td colspan="2">From the UCAS website: "A personal statement supports your application to study at a university or college. It's a chance for you to articulate why you'd like to study a particular course or subject, and what skills and experience you possess that show your passion for your chosen field." Maximum: 4,000 characters (including spaces) and 47 lines.
英国大学和学院招生服务中心官网:"主文书可以帮助你申请大学。对你来说,这是一个阐明为什么你想学习某一特定课程或学科的机会,以及你拥有哪些技能和经验来显示你对所选领域的热情。"最多 4 000 个字符(包括空格)和 47 行。</td></tr>
<tr><th>Essay
文书</th><th>Why is this essay effective?
这篇文书好在哪里?</th></tr>
<tr><td>"Xuan Paper," "Wenfang Sibao," "Provenance," "Pentimento," "Sfumato," "Brushwork," "Conceptual," "Iconography" "Perspective," "Cubism," "Bronze Wares" are just some of the words and phrases that entered my vocabulary when I volunteered at a local art museum the summer before I started grade 10. When I wasn't stuffing brochures into envelopes or smiling at visitors, I encountered these and many other art history terms from the bits of conversation I overheard as docents led their museum tours past my workstation. Unfamiliar terms merged with familiar ones, like the names of the Chinese dynasties I had studied in school or the names of famous kings, emperors, and popes I learned from studying Western history and literature.

Since I love studying history in school, at first my attraction to art was that it helped me better understand the history and culture of the period and country in which it was created. But in time my focus reversed itself, and I found myself more fascinated by the artifacts I was viewing, and history became a way to understand better why they were created. I spent three days a week in the museum during that miraculous summer, and these enthusiastic docents were teaching me how to see.

I found that, as I looked again and again at the same paintings, sculpture, and calligraphy, what I "saw" kept changing and maturing. By the end of the summer, I saw things in each artwork that I had hardly noticed at the start of the summer. I said to myself, "Oh, yes, there's a change in brushstroke here." "The arrangement of figures in the center of the triptych mirrors the composition of the side panels." "What stunning detail on that mountain-shaped,</td><td>The essay is carefully focused on showing:
1. How the student became interested in art history.
2. How the student acquired the necessary background to succeed in this field of study at a university.
3. Relevant coursework — classes in drawing, IB higher level coursework, and an IB Extended Essay in the field.
4. Career goals in the field
5. Most of all: enthusiasm for the field!</td></tr>
</table>

续　表

Essay 文书	Why is this essay effective? 这篇文书好在哪里?
Han Dynasty incense burner!" And my most recurrent thought that summer: "Why hadn't I noticed these things earlier?" It was the most exciting weeks of my life, and that is why I continued to volunteer for the following two summers. It soon followed that my parents let me take classes in drawing. I do not see myself as a professional artist even though a few of my drawings have earned second and third place awards in several art competitions. But I believe that I become a better student of art when I put myself through the rigor of creation. It sharpens my focus. My IB Extended Essay focuses on the Barnes Collection in Philadelphia, Pennsylvania in the United States. Albert C. Barnes build his collection of mostly impressionist art in the early years of the 20th century. One of its most remarkable features is Dr. Barnes's practice of encouraging viewers to look closely by placing specific works of art next to each other so that one work seemed to comment on the other. Next to a Cezanne masterpiece you might see a piece of decorative metalwork. They seem to have nothing in common, and yet, when you look closely, you realize that the shape of a table in the Cezanne painting mirrors the shape of the center of the metalwork. I see my future as being an art historian, a museum curator, or perhaps even as someone who works in art conservation and restoration. Since I know that the last would require, not only a knowledge of art history, but also a strong background in chemistry, I have been careful to include HL Chemistry among my IB courses as well as HL Visual Arts, HL History, and HL Business Management. At the moment, I feel equally drawn to teaching, research, and art restoration. I am not sure which of these will eventually prevail over the others, but I do want my art history curriculum to leave each of these options open to me and prepare me to seek an advanced degree after I complete my undergraduate work. Finally, study in the UK has the great advantage of giving me access not only to outstanding art history programs, but also to a huge array of museums devoted to artwork from all the world's cultures. **(3,823 characters, 47 lines)**	这篇文书重点展现了: 1. 学生是如何对艺术史产生兴趣的。 2. 学生如何获得必要的背景,以保证在大学的这一领域获得成绩。 3. 相关课程-绘画课程,IB高水平课程,以及该领域的IB EE论文。 4. 领域内的职业目标。 5. 最重要的是:对这个领域的热情!

第六节

如何撰写美国加州大学系统的文书

尽管大多数大学是美国大学通用申请系统的成员，有些则不是。加州大学就是一个典型的例子(见表 3.13)。

表 3.13　2020～2021 年申请加州大学文书个人见解问题
(回答以下 8 个问题中的 4 个，每篇最多 350 个单词)

第一题	Describe an example of your leadership experience in which you have positively influenced others, helped resolve disputes, or contributed to group efforts over time. 举例说明你的领导经历，在这个过程中如何积极影响了他人，帮助解决了争端或随着时间的推移为团队做出贡献。	加州大学个人见解问题，旨在确保不论是何背景，每一个申请人都可以找到一个或多个能很好发挥的问题。 加州大学系统招生网站提供详细的问题指导链接，这些指南特别有用。例如，关于第一题，官网指南写道： 需要考虑的因素是一个有领导力的角色可能不仅是一个头衔。你可能是他人的良师益友，是一个任务的负责人，或是一个组织或活动的带领组织者。想一想你的成就以及你从这些经验中学到什么。你肩负了哪些责任？ 你是否带领了一个团队？你的经历如何改变了你对领导他人的看法？你是否在你的学校、教会、社群或组织中帮助解决过争议？你的领导经历不必局限于校内活动。如你是否帮助
第二题	Every person has a creative side, and it can be expressed in many ways: problem solving, original and innovative thinking, and artistically, to name a few. Describe how you express your creative side. 每个人都有创造力，创造力可以用多种方式表达出来，如解决问题、创新的思维或想法，以及艺术性等等。描述你如何表达自己的创造力。	
第三题	What would you say is your greatest talent or skill? How have you developed and demonstrated that talent over time? 你认为你最大的才能或技能是什么？随着时间的推移，你如何发展和展示这种才能？	

续　表

第四题	Describe how you have taken advantage of a significant educational opportunity or worked to overcome an educational barrier you have faced. 描述你是如何把握一个重要的教育机会的，或是如何克服你在教育方面面临的一个困难。	或照顾过你的家人？ 官网指南针对第二题的指导如下： 需要考虑的因素是创造力对你而言意味着什么？你有没有一项对你而言重要的，且发挥创造力的技能？你用这个技能做了些什么？如果你用创造力解决了一个问题，你处理问题的过程中有哪些步骤？你的解决方案是什么？ 你的创造力如何影响着你在课内外所做的决定？你的创造力是否与你的专业或将来的职业有关联？
第五题	Describe the most significant challenge you have faced and the steps you have taken to overcome this challenge. How has this challenge affected your academic achievement? 描述你遇到过的最大的挑战以及为克服挑战所采取的措施。这一挑战如何影响你的学术成就？	
第六题	Think about an academic subject that inspires you. Describe how you have furthered this interest inside and/or outside of the classroom. 想一想启发你的学术学科。描述你是如何在课内外发展这种兴趣的。	
第七题	What have you done to make your school or your community a better place? 你做了哪些使你所在的学校或社区变得更好的事情？	
第八题	Beyond what has already been shared in your application, what do you believe makes you stand out as a strong candidate for admissions to the University of California? 除了申请表中提供的内容之外，你认为还有什么能使你脱颖而出，成为加州大学强有力的录取候选人？	

学生通常可以修改其美国大学通用申请系统里的主文书，来回复加州大学的申请系统必须回答的四个问题。还记得我们刚刚读过的关于中日文化的文书吗？由于美国大学通用申请系统主文书最多允许 650 词，而加州大学的文书仅允许 350 词，学生必须削减其文书。让我们看看他如何巧妙地做到了这一点，如表 3.14 所示。

表 3.14　关于中日文化的文书

University of California response to Personal Insight Question: "Think about an academic subject that inspires you. Describe how you have furthered this interest inside and/or outside of the classroom." (350 words)
加州大学个人见解题："想一想启发你的学术学科。描述你如何在课内外发展这种兴趣。"(350 词)

续　表

学生的美国大学通用申请系统原文	减到350词以下后
"What is this kind of language, it is … Chinese, right?" I can still remember once in my childhood I watched an animation on TV. The subtitle included some Chinese characters I knew well and some foreign letters I had not seen before. I asked my father what they were. "Oh, they are Japanese characters named 'kana', In Japanese kana are used with Chinese characters. You may feel a sense of familiarity, but it is a totally different foreign language from Chinese. " Maybe that was my initial motivation to learn Japanese because it is amazing to find another language that shares Chinese characters but whose usage is different from Chinese, the original language. I wanted to figure out the role the Chinese letters play in Japanese. In Japanese there exists a grammatical system including honorific and modest expression that is used when talking with someone whose status, whether in society, company or at home, are higher, which means one must use another way of expression differing from that used in daily conversation when facing his parents, teachers, bosses, etc., and of course it greatly increases the difficulty for people who are learning Japanese, like me. I doubt the necessity of learning honorific and modest expression, for without it we can still express respect to elders, and it doesn't exist in English, nor in Chinese. "Intriguing idea." My father said, "but remember, every language has its cultural background, since you are learning Japanese, why not learning something more about Japan the country?"	"What is this kind of language, it is … Chinese, right?" I can still remember once in my childhood I watched an animation on TV. The subtitle included some Chinese characters I knew well and some foreign letters I had not seen before. I asked my father what they were. "Oh, they are Japanese characters named 'kana'. In Japanese kana are used with Chinese characters. You may feel a sense of familiarity, but it is a totally different foreign language from Chinese. " I said I wanted to figure out the role the Chinese letters play in Japanese. "Intriguing idea," my father said, "but remember, every language has its cultural background, since you are learning Japanese, why not learn something more about Japan the country?" Actually, I was attracted by Japanese culture, both the modern one and the traditional one. In spring days I was charmed by the beauty of cherry blossoms, whose other name is sakura, the national flower of Japan through which Japanese poets expressed their delightful or pensive emotions in ancient times. Every time I read these poems (of course the translated version), I could also catch the poets' feelings that life comes and goes, like sakura being blown away by winds within a transient lifetime. When China was in a coronavirus crisis, what moved many Chinese people was not only that Japanese people sent us many surgical masks, but also that they wrote an ancient Japanese verse on the package, "Though we're oceans apart, a shared moon connects hearts". 1300 years ago a Japanese

续　表

学生的美国大学通用申请系统原文	减到 350 词以下后
Actually, I was attracted by Japanese culture, both modern one and traditional one. I can still remember the time I sat in front of the television and filled in Japanese animation with joy and laughter, or played Japanese video games like Contra together with my brothers. In spring days I was charmed by the beauty of cherry blossoms, whose another name is sakura, national flower of Japan through which Japanese poets express their delightful or pensive emotions in ancient times. Every time I read these poems (of course the translated version), I could also catch poets' feelings that life comes and goes, like sakura being blown away by winds with a transient lifetime. These poems reminded me of Chinese poems I learned before. It seems like a coincidence that both Chinese and Japanese poets love to leave their thoughts and feelings in natural objects like flowers, mountains, rivers, etc. As we know, kana derives from running style of Chinese calligraphy, and now Japan and China are only two countries that use Chinese letters around the world. When China was in a crisis of coronavirus at the beginning of this year, what made Chinese move was not only that Japanese people sent us many surgical mask, but also that they wrote an ancient Japanese verse on the package, 'Though we're oceans apart, a shared moon connects hearts'. The verse was once created by a Japanese prince in 7th century. Back to 1300 years ago, it was a period that China and Japan were in a good relationship and each was seeking for bilateral communications on politics, culture, religion, etc. Under this background, the Japanese prince sent	prince attached this verse to a letter accompanying thousands of cassocks to Chinese monks as a way to show his respect for the great Tang Dynasty. Over a millennium later, though under a different situation, but with the same verse, we can still show friendliness and care to each other with shared Chinese characters. That is why I am charmed by Japanese, for it is amazing to find a bridge between these two totally different languages through which we can share our emotions, from the ancient time to now. (346 words)

续 表

学生的美国大学通用申请系统原文	减到 350 词以下后
thousands of cassocks to Chinese monks as a way to show his respect for the great Tang Dynasty and his will to study Buddhist dharma from Chinese scholars, with this verse in attached letter. A millennium or so later, though under different situation, but with the same verse, we can still show friendliness and care to each other with shared Chinese characters. That is why I am charmed by Japanese, for it is amazing to find a bridge between these two totally different languages through which we can share our emotions, from the ancient time to now. (623 words)	

通过文书我们可以发现，尽管篇幅缩简，但是该版本仍然抓住了学生学习日本语言和文化的热情，并设法显示它如何"激励"自己。正如许多学生所发现的，写一篇 350 词的文书通常比写一篇 650 词的文书更难，它需要学生对文书更深入的挖掘和筛选，留下最具有闪光点的内容。

下面我们再给大家展示一篇文书（见表 3.15），通过这篇文书大家可以更深入地了解独立升学顾问在文书中寻找闪光点的全过程。

表 3.15 版本 1：加州大学文书——关于手工艺品

University of California response to Personal Insight Question: "What would you say is your greatest talent or skill? How have you developed and demonstrated that talent over time?" (350 words) **加州大学个人见解题：什么才是你的最大的才能或技能？随着时间的推移，你是如何发展和证明这种才能的？(350 词)**	
学生的原始回答	**由独立升学顾问修改后**
Referring my greatest skill, it is making handwork which was developed since my childhood. The making of handcraft curved me to be a considerate and harmonious person. When I was a child, it was very	~~Referring~~ Since childhood, my greatest skill ~~, it is~~ has been making ~~handwork~~ handcrafted objects. ~~which was developed since my childhood.~~ I have tried different types of handwork, including needlework,

续　表

学生的原始回答	由独立升学顾问修改后
hard for me to concentrate on one thing because I was curious about everything. However, after doing the handcraft, I could always concentrate on one thing for long time and not get interrupted by others. Thus, it made me into completing one thing with higher efficiency and quality. One time, I felt annoyed because I had a fight with my friends. Then I chose to do some handcraft. At first, it was still hard for me to calm down. But making handcraft requires concentration because every step is important and some materials are very tiny. I just focused on the needle in my hand and the shape of the cloth. Then I came back to be rational and calmed. I thought it over and fixed the problem with my friends. In order to develop my skill, I tried different types of handwork, including needlework, stamp carving, cellphone-cover making and seal making. All of those works were learned by myself. By the chance of searching for methods of doing those handcrafts, I also learned Chinese traditional culture.[1] As for the preparation, I would find some teaching video or blog to learn; then acquired some materials via Internet. After trying, I made some cellphone-covers for my friends and decorated my table lamp as well. It was difficult for me to finish a piece of fine works at the beginning. Gradually, I learned that the key to success is patience.[2] All in all, I think the skill of making handcraft could make me calm down and be concentrated when encounter problems. (293 words)	stamp carving, cellphone-cover making, and seal making. I learned to create those works by myself. By searching for methods to create those handcrafts, I also learned Chinese traditional culture.[1] I would find some teaching video or blog to teach me and then acquired some materials via the Internet. I made some cellphone-covers for my friends and decorated my table lamp as well. At first, it was difficult for me to finish a piece of fine work. Gradually, I learned that the key to success is patience.[2] ~~The m~~Making ~~of handcraft curved~~ handicraft has also made me ~~to be~~ a considerate and harmonious person. When I was a child, it was very hard for me to concentrate on one thing because I was curious about everything. ~~However, after d~~Doing ~~the handcraft,~~ handicraft ~~I could always~~ taught me to concentrate on one thing for a long time and not get interrupted by others. ~~Thus, it made me into completing one thing with higher efficiency and quality.~~ ~~One time, I felt annoyed because I had a fight with my friends. Then I chose to do some handcraft. At first, it was still hard for me to calm down.~~[3] ~~But making handcraft~~ It requires concentration because every step is important and some materials are very tiny. When I ~~just~~ focused on the needle in my hand and the shape of the cloth ; ~~Then I came back to be~~ I become rational and calmed. ~~I thought it over and fixed the problem with my friends.~~ ~~In order to develop my skill, I tried different types of handwork, including needlework, stamp carving, cellphone-cover making and seal making. All of those works were learned by myself. By the chance of searching for methods of doing those~~

续 表

<table>
<tr><th>学生的原始回答</th><th>由独立升学顾问修改后</th></tr>
<tr><td></td><td>~~handcrafts, I also learned Chinese traditional culture. As for the preparation, I would find some teaching video or blog to learn; then acquired some materials via Internet. After trying, I made some cellphone-covers for my friends and decorated my table lamp as well. It was difficult for me to finish a piece of fine works at the beginning. Gradually, I learned that the key to success is patience.~~

~~All in all, I think the skill of making handcraft could make me calm down and be concentrated when encounter problems.~~</td></tr>
<tr><th colspan="2">独立升学顾问给学生的评论</th></tr>
<tr><td colspan="2">1. “I also learned about Chinese traditional culture”
这很有趣！我认为你可以增加一两句话来描述你对中国文化特别感兴趣的具体例子。</td></tr>
<tr><td colspan="2">2. “In order to develop my skill, I tried different types of handwork … Gradually, I learned that they key to success is patience.”
我将此内容移至你的文书开头，因为我认为它比你原版的开头要有效得多，而且有趣得多。原版的开头关注的是手工艺教会你如何“长时间专注于一件事”。
另一个原因是，由于手工艺品种类繁多，将这段上移有助于读者从一开始就知道你正在谈论的是哪种手工。</td></tr>
<tr><td colspan="2">3. “One time, I felt annoyed because I had a fight with my friends … it was still hard for me to calm down.”
请参阅下面的评论，我解释了为什么在本段中做了删改。</td></tr>
<tr><th colspan="2">独立升学顾问的评论</th></tr>
<tr><td colspan="2">文书最重要的部分是你谈论自学针线活、印章雕刻等。这就是为什么我将这一部分移至文书的开头。
而最薄弱的部分是你与朋友吵架后如何通过制作手工品使自己平静下来的讨论。我担心加州大学招生委员会认为这很琐碎。为什么不多写点更有趣，更重要的主题？例如：
(1) 向你的读者介绍你在自学手工知识的同时学到的中国传统文化。
(2) 你是如何选择自己要制作的物件。
(3) 你多年来如何提高自己的技能和技巧。
(4) 你可以描述一件自己特别引以为傲的作品。

这些都是你可以扩展的点，它们都是可以帮助招生委员会欣赏你的独特才华的主题。由</td></tr>
</table>

续 表

独立升学顾问的评论
于我提出的修改将你文书的字数减少到 191 词，你有足够的空间执行此操作！ 以下是修改后的完整版： Since childhood, my greatest skill has been making handcrafted objects. I have tried different types of handwork, including needlework, stamp carving, cellphone-cover making, and seal making. I learned to create those works by myself. By searching for methods to create those handcrafts, I also learned Chinese traditional culture. I would find some teaching video or blog to teach me and then acquired some materials via the Internet. I made some cellphone-covers for my friends and decorated my table lamp as well. At first, it was difficult for me to finish a piece of fine work. Gradually, I learned that the key to success is patience. Making handicraft has also made me a considerate and harmonious person. When I was a child, it was very hard for me to concentrate on one thing because I was curious about everything. Doing handicraft taught me to concentrate on one thing for a long time and not get interrupted by others. It requires concentration because every step is important and some materials are very tiny. When I focus on the needle in my hand and the shape of the cloth, I become rational and calmed. (191 words)

在独立升学顾问建议后，该学生是如何利用独立升学顾问的建议来改进自己的文书的呢？左边是顾问修改前她的原始版本，右边是她的最终版本。如表 3.16 所示。

表 3.16　版本 2：加州大学文书——关于手工艺品

加州大学文书题目：什么才是你的最大的才能或技能？随着时间的推移，你是如何发展和证明这种才能的？(350 词)	
学生的原始版本 1	学生的最终版本 2
Referring my greatest skill, it is making handwork which was developed since my childhood. The making of handcraft curved me to be a considerate and harmonious person. When I was a child, it was very hard for me to concentrate on one thing because I was curious about everything. However, after doing the handcraft, I could always concentrate on one thing for long time and not get interrupted by others. Thus, it made me into completing one thing with higher efficiency and quality.	Since childhood, my greatest skill has been making handcrafted objects. I have tried different types of handwork, including needlework, stamp carving, cellphone-cover making, and seal making. I learned to create those works by myself. By searching for methods to create those handcrafts, I also learned the Chinese traditional art of paper cutting. The subjects are diverse in figures, flowers, birds, words, kinds of natural sceneries and familiar folk stories and fairy tales. For instance, I made the popular

续 表

学生的原始版本 1	学生的最终版本 2
One time, I felt annoyed because I had a fight with my friends. Then I chose to do some handcraft. At first, it was still hard for me to calm down. But making handcraft requires concentration because every step is important and some materials are very tiny. I just focused on the needle in my hand and the shape of the cloth. Then I came back to be rational and calmed. I thought it over and fixed the problem with my friends. In order to develop my skill, I tried different types of handwork, including needlework, stamp carving, cellphone-cover making and seal making. All of those works were learned by myself. By the chance of searching for methods of doing those handcrafts, I also learned Chinese traditional culture. As for the preparation, I would find some teaching video or blog to learn; then acquired some materials via Internet. After trying, I made some cellphone-covers for my friends and decorated my table lamp as well. It was difficult for me to finish a piece of fine works at the beginning. Gradually, I learned that the key to success is patience. All in all, I think the skill of making handcraft could make me calm down and be concentrated when encounter problems. (293 words)	Chinese Character Fu (happiness) for the Spring festival. As the symbols for good things with its rich cultural associations, paper-cutting is also a popular gift for friends and relatives. I find some teaching video or blog to teach me and then acquire some materials via the Internet. I have made cellphone-covers for my friends and decorated my table lamp as well. At first, it was difficult for me to finish a piece of fine work. Gradually, I learned that the key to success is patience. Making handicraft has also made me a considerate and harmonious person. When I was a child, it was very hard for me to concentrate on one thing because I was curious about everything. Doing handicraft taught me to concentrate on one thing for a long time and not get interrupted by others. It requires concentration because every step is important and some materials are very tiny. When I focus on the needle in my hand and the shape of the cloth, I become rational and calmed. (249 words)
独立升学顾问的评论	
我很高兴你采纳了我的建议，并提供了更多有关你手工制作的详细信息。你所添加的有关剪纸的好处非常有趣！你现在有的是一篇更加连贯的文书，并告诉招生委员会你除了是一名熟练的手工制作者之外，还对艺术持有热情，以及你如何将这份热情分享给他人。	

在加州大学的题目中，还有一个开放式题目(见表 3.17)，让你可以分享更多你认为有助于自己的申请的信息。

表 3.17 加州大学文书——关于冒险

University of California response to Personal Insight Question: "Beyond what has already been shared in your application, what do you believe makes you stand out as a strong candidate for admissions to the University of California?" (350 words)
加州大学个人见解题的回答:"除了你的申请中已经共享的内容之外,你认为是什么可以让你成为被加州大学录取的有力候选人?"(350 词)

学生的原始回答	由独立升学顾问修改后
"Ted, why don't you talk to your girlfriend?" I asked. "She waits for you every day on the way to the dining hall."	"Ted, why don't you talk to your girlfriend?" I asked. "She waits for you every day on the way to the dining hall."
"Emmm ... She is not the best choice for me. She is not beautiful enough. Anyway, I will study aboard, and she will stay here."	"Emmm ... She is not the best choice for me. She is not beautiful enough. Anyway, I will study ~~aboard~~ abroad, and she will stay here."
Ted's girlfriend always wanted to have lunch with him. However, Ted usually ate with his friends, leaving her alone. She was very sad which prompted me to talk to him.	Ted's girlfriend always wanted to have lunch with him. However, Ted usually ate with his friends, leaving her alone. She was very sad which prompted me to talk to him.
I think teenagers should cherish their relationships. Thus I decided to talk about love in our class meeting. Discussing such a sensitive subject was risky because my classmates usually introduced hobbies with PowerPoint.	I think teenagers should cherish their relationships. Thus I decided to talk about love in our class meeting. Discussing such a sensitive subject was risky because my classmates usually introduced hobbies with PowerPoint.
I used to fear taking risks and avoided being at the center of the stage. However, I decided to try. I even volunteered for the opening class meeting, where both students and teachers from my class and other administrators would attend. My teacher was surprised I volunteered for this role because I was not usually willing to speak in front of so many people.	I used to fear taking risks and avoided being at the center of the stage. However, I decided to try. I even volunteered for the opening class meeting, ~~where~~ attended by ~~both~~ students and teachers ~~from my class~~ and other administrators ~~would attend~~. My teacher was surprised I volunteered for this role because I was not usually willing to speak in front of so many people.
To make the class meeting convincing, I created a drama with an exciting piece of music. My favorite song is Canon. Pachelbel[1] composed it to lament the death of his lover. When the son of the mayor deceived her that Pachelbel died in the war,	To make the class meeting convincing, I created a drama with an exciting piece of music ~~.~~, ~~My favorite song is Canon.~~ Pachelbel's Canon in D. I pretended that it was composed[2] ~~it~~ to lament the death of his lover ~~.~~ and that when ~~When~~ the son of the

续 表

学生的原始回答	由独立升学顾问修改后
she killed herself to avoid being forced to marry the son of the mayor. I thought my classmates may learn from this moving story. The script I wrote would last for half an hour, so I added some interesting dialogue and exaggerated action in the foreshadowing part to intrigue the audience. The whole audience was surprised and enjoyed seeing something different.	mayor deceived her that Pachelbel died in the war, she killed herself to avoid being forced to marry him ~~the son of the mayor~~. I thought my classmates ~~may~~ might learn about love from this moving story. The script I wrote ~~would~~ had to last for half an hour, so I added some interesting dialogue and exaggerated action in the foreshadowing part to intrigue the audience. The whole audience was surprised and enjoyed seeing something different.
"Presenting a drama in the class meeting was creative. I hope our students can think differently about how they treat each other, now," my teacher commented. "And I hope you will continue to try new things."	"Presenting a drama in the class meeting was creative. I hope our students can think differently about how they treat each other, now," my teacher commented. "And I hope you will continue to try new things."
Her positive feedback motivated me! I started to learn the piano by myself despite my heavy schedule. I also started talking in front of strangers and signed up for volunteer work at a hospital.	Her positive feedback motivated me! I started to learn the piano by myself despite my heavy schedule. I also started talking in front of strangers and signed up for volunteer work at a hospital.

独立升学顾问给学生的备注

1. "Canon"

通常在英语里，用"Pachelbel's Canon in D"表达。

2. "I pretended that it was composed to lament the death of his lover."

我添加了"I pretended that"一词，以明确表达这个事例是你编的，而不是真实的事件。

独立升学顾问给学生的评论

很好！这篇文书读起来很有趣。它为你应对个人挑战，克服恐惧和扩展才华的能力提供了一些令人信服的观点。我已经提供了一些更改建议，这篇文书可以定稿了。

以下是我修改后的完整文书：

"Ted, why don't you talk to your girlfriend?" I asked. "She waits for you every day on the way to the dining hall."

"Emmm ... She is not the best choice for me. She is not beautiful enough. Anyway, I will study abroad, and she will stay here."

Ted's girlfriend always wanted to have lunch with him. However, Ted usually ate with his friends, leaving her alone. She was very sad which prompted me to talk to him.

I think teenagers should cherish their relationships. Thus I decided to talk about love in our

续　表

独立升学顾问给学生的评论
class meeting. Discussing such a sensitive subject was risky because my classmates usually introduced hobbies with PowerPoint.
I used to fear taking risks and avoided being at the center of the stage. However, I decided to try. I even volunteered for the opening class meeting, attended by students and teachers and other administrators. My teacher was surprised I volunteered for this role because I was not usually willing to speak in front of so many people.
To make the class meeting convincing, I created a drama with an exciting piece of music, Pachelbel's Canon in D. I pretended that it was composed to lament the death of his lover and that when the son of the mayor deceived her that Pachelbel died in the war, she killed herself to avoid being forced to marry him. I thought my classmates might learn about love from this moving story. The script I wrote had to last for half an hour, so I added some interesting dialogue and exaggerated action in the foreshadowing part to intrigue the audience. The whole audience was surprised and enjoyed seeing something different.
"Presenting a drama in the class meeting was creative. I hope our students can think differently about how they treat each other, now," my teacher commented. "And I hope you will continue to try new things."
Her positive feedback motivated me! I started to learn the piano by myself despite my heavy schedule. I also started talking in front of strangers and signed up for volunteer work at a hospital. (348 words)

你可能会思考,一篇关于克服恐惧来创作和表演戏剧的文书是否足以回答这样一个题目。这就取决于学校的招生委员会从这位学生其余的申请材料里看到什么了。委员会从来都不会只阅读这一篇文书。他们只会把文书看作是你高中成绩单、标化考试成绩、课外活动、推荐信,以及其他你提交的文书的锦上添花的部分。例如,你想象一下,如果这份申请材料中的推荐信里有提到,"他创作了一部惊人的剧作,结合了音乐和文字来传递一个凄美的爱情悲剧。它有强大的影响力,不仅对他的同学而言,也对我们这些老师而言",你会怎样看待这份文书?

至少,招生官希望文书能够呈现一位申请者的个性。他们希望可以看见这位学生的模样,感受到他的价值观、自我意识、天赋和梦想。

我们再来看看表 3.18 中这篇文书。

表 3.18　加州大学文书——关于帮助老年人使用科技

University of California response to Personal Insight Question: "What have you done to make your school or your community a better place?" (350 words) **加州大学个人见解题的回答: 为了让学校或社区变得更美好,你做了哪些工作?(350 词)**

续 表

学生的原始回答	由独立升学顾问修改后
As the advancement of technology, most of the facilities around us are getting increasingly complicated to use. When I volunteered at Longhua hospital, my job is to help senior patients who had problem with operating the self-service registration machine. During the process, I noticed that most of the senior citizens had almost no idea on most of the modern electronic facilities. Without the help of volunteers, they could only queue up for a long time to register at the traditional service desk. To address this issue, my classmates and I designed some brochures on specific instructions of the self-service machine so that senior citizens can follow the procedures when they lack assistance. Also, we made a short video to briefly introduce the functions of the self-service machine as well as where patients can get help when they have problem using them. Such cases are quite common. My grandparents never enjoyed the large crowds in the food market, so they were thrilled to know that a supermarket offering all kinds of daily necessities was opening soon. However, it turned out that the supermarket was based on self-service machines with online payment, which my grandparents did not know how to use. As a result, my grandparents could only visit the supermarket when we were with them, and in most cases, they would still have to put up with the lousy condition in the farmer's market. There are also many impoverished and illiterate people who cannot benefit from advanced technologies. They, too, may feel lost in modern society. My experience has made me more aware of the need to develop technologies that can be	~~As~~ With the advancement of technology, most of the facilities around us are getting increasingly complicated to use. When I volunteered at Longhua hospital, my job was ~~is~~ to help senior patients who had problems ~~with~~ operating the self-service registration machine. During the process, I noticed that most of the senior citizens had almost no idea ~~on~~ how to use most of the modern electronic facilities. Without the help of volunteers, they could only queue up for a long time to register at the traditional service desk. To address this issue, my classmates and I designed ~~some~~ brochures on specific instructions of the self-service machine so that senior citizens can follow the procedures when they lack assistance. Also, we made a short video to briefly introduce the functions of the self-service machine ~~as well as where~~ and tell patients where they can get help when they have problem using them. Such cases are quite common. My grandparents never enjoyed ~~the large crowds in the~~ shopping in a large food market, so they were thrilled to know that a supermarket offering all kinds of daily necessities was opening soon. However, it turned out that, because of the large crowds, the supermarket was based on self-service machines with online payment, which my grandparents did not know how to use. As a result, my grandparents could only visit the supermarket when we were with them, ~~and in most cases, they would still have to~~[1] or put up with the lousy conditions in the farmer's market. There are also many impoverished and illiterate people who cannot benefit from advanced technologies.

续 表

学生的原始回答	由独立升学顾问修改后
used by all the citizens. We should do more to help these people to use the current technology better. For example, a more user-friendly system can be developed to help people get a clearer understanding of the machine. We should never leave anyone behind. I intend to get a college education in UC to better exercise my social responsibility by trying my best to help those who have been marginalized by the society in the future. (343 words)	They, too, may feel lost in modern society. My experience has made me more aware of the need to develop technologies that can be used by all the citizens. We should do more to help these people to use the current technology better. For example, a more user-friendly system can be developed to help people get a clearer understanding of the machines. We should never leave anyone behind[2]. I intend to get a college education in UC to better exercise my social responsibility in the future by trying my best to help those who have been marginalized by the society. ~~. In the future.~~ (343 words)
独立升学顾问给学生的备注	
1. "and in more cases, they would still have to" 我删除了该短语以减少文书的总字数。	
2. "We should never leave anyone behind" 非常好的观点!	
独立升学顾问给学生的评论	
这篇文书是对个人见解题很好的回复。只需进行一些修改(如上所述),就可以递交了。以下是根据我的修改后的完整文书: With the advancement of technology, most of the facilities around us are getting increasingly complicated to use. When I volunteered at Longhua hospital, my job was to help senior patients who had problems operating the self-service registration machine. During the process, I noticed that most of the senior citizens had almost no idea how to use most of the modern electronic facilities. Without the help of volunteers, they could only queue up for a long time to register at the traditional service desk. To address this issue, my classmates and I designed brochures on specific instructions of the self-service machine so that senior citizens can follow the procedures when they lack assistance. Also, we made a short video to briefly introduce the functions of the self-service machine and tell patients where they can get help when they have problem using them. Such cases are quite common. My grandparents never enjoyed shopping in a large food market, so they were thrilled to know that a supermarket offering all kinds of daily necessities was opening soon. However, it turned out that, because of the large crowds, the supermarket was based on self-service machines with online payment, which my grandparents did not know how to use. As a result, my grandparents could only visit the	

续 表

独立升学顾问给学生的评论
supermarket when we were with them or put up with the lousy conditions in the farmer's market. There are also many impoverished and illiterate people who cannot benefit from advanced technologies. They, too, may feel lost in modern society. My experience has made me more aware of the need to develop technologies that can be used by all the citizens. We should do more to help these people to use the current technology better. For example, a more user-friendly system can be developed to help people get a clearer understanding of the machines. We should never leave anyone behind. I intend to get a college education in UC to better exercise my social responsibility in the future by trying my best to help those who have been marginalized by the society. (343 words)

第七节

如何应对美国部分大学的辅文书

除了美国大学通用申请系统的文书，你还必须写些什么文书呢？大多数“非常挑剔”的大学会要求写一篇或多篇额外的“辅文书”。这些通常被称为“大学特定”或“大学补充”文书，因为主文书会被你申请的所有大学看到，而这些辅文书只会被提出补充问题的大学看到。

为什么有些大学会要求这些额外的文书呢？

(1) 他们想知道你对上他们的大学有多感兴趣。为什么要把录取通知书浪费在一个不太可能接受录取通知书的学生身上呢？

① 如果学校在你的名单上排名很低，这些额外的问题可能会说服你不要申请，因为你不想花时间回答这些问题。从大学的角度来看，这意味着不写辅文书的学生对这所大学不感兴趣。

② 如果你真的决定申请的话，如果你的答案太笼统以至于可能涉及其他几百所大学，那么大学仍然会认为你不是很感兴趣。例如，告诉纽约大学你喜欢纽约市是可以的，但这最好不是你申请的唯一理由。毕竟，在纽约市及其周边地区还有许多其他大学。

③ ②中的笼统理由只是浮于表面的回答，也不太可能说服招生委员会。例如，“从我小时候起，上贵校就一直是我的梦想”或“大家都知道你有世界上最好的计算机科学课程”。表达你对学校的爱是可以的，但你需要其他更好的回答。

④ 引用相关学院的具体特点并解释为什么它们对你如此重要。这将证明你已经完成了你的调查。它们将向大学展示你对它们的兴趣。

(2) 他们想看到一些主文书里没有呈现的特质，如想象力、创造力、跳出固有思维模式的能力。

(3) 他们把自己的问题看作是向你展示(并给你留下深刻印象)他们所能提供的东西的一种方式。

例如，一所大学可能会有这样的辅文书题目：“*When Nobel Laureate ________ met with students on our campus last year, she said, '________.' Tell us whether you agree with her comment.*” *The message here is*, “*our students get to meet some of the world's most important people!*”

“当诺贝尔奖获得者某某去年在我们的校园里与学生见面时，她说，‘________’。告诉我们你是否同意她的言论。”这里的信息是，“学生在我们大学会遇到一些世界上最重要的人物！”

1. “你为什么要申请这所大学?”文书示例

表 3.19 是一个好的示例和一个较差的示例。

表 3.19 “你为什么要申请这所大学?”文书示例对比

Imagine you are a member of a college admissions committee. **Compare these two responses to the question, “Why are you applying to Podunk College?” 150 words maximum** 假设你是一个大学招生委员会的成员。请比较这两个问题的答案，“你为什么要申请无名学院?”(最多 150 词)		
点　评	**Why Podunk? 回答 1**	**Why Podunk? 回答 2**
It is not hard to see who is the more seriously interested candidate for admission, is it? Response #2 details specific reasons for being attracted to Podunk's Environmental Engineering major. The student has taken the time to visit the campus and to research what it has to offer. Notice, too, that by mentioning badminton, Response #2 shows the admissions	Podunk University has been my dream school since I was a small child. I have always wanted to attend college in California. My family and I love to go hiking and camping in the outdoors, and California's mix of sunny beaches and snow-capped mountains is ideal for me. Podunk also has one of the top-ranked environmental engineering programs in the	Podunk University made a powerful impression on me when I visited your beautiful campus last summer. I toured some of the labs in the Environmental Engineering Department and saw that you have some of the most sophisticated EPA-compliant equipment for measuring air pollutants that I have seen during my college tours. I especially enjoyed talking to Prof. Jermaine Fox, who

续 表

点 评	Why Podunk? 回答 1	Why Podunk? 回答 2
committee that the student sees Podunk not only as an excellent academic fit, but also as an excellent extracurricular fit. 这里不难看出谁更容易被录取。 回答 2 详细说明被无名学院环境工程专业吸引的具体原因。这个学生花时间参观了校园，并研究了它能提供什么。 同样要注意的是，回答 2 通过提到羽毛球俱乐部向招生委员会表明，学生不仅喜欢无名学院的学术氛围，而且喜欢它的课外活动，和自己的兴趣爱好完美匹配。	country. I know that it would inspire me to excel as a student. I am drawn to Podunk's environmental engineering major because I have been very active in my high school's environmental club. Air pollution is a serious problem where I live, and I'd like to use my strengths in science to engineer solutions. I know that Podunk is the place where I can do that and also enjoy the scenic beauty that surrounds your campus. (136 words)	does research in controlling the particulate matter that is emitted from power plants, boilers, and incinerators. Since I am strongly interested in doing undergraduate research, I was glad to see that 75% of Podunk's undergrads participate in your research program. Finally, in my spare time I play badminton. Podunk was one of the few colleges I visited that has an active badminton club. For all of these reasons, I am very eager to become a Podunk "Beaver" this fall. (139 words)

那什么才能帮助你对“你为什么申请本校”这个问题写出令人信服的答案呢？

(1) 参观校园，如果可能的话参加学校组织的参观活动，探访一两个你感兴趣的系（通常大学的招生办公室可以为你安排到各系的访问）。

(2) 像 Why Podunk? 回答 2 的作者一样，记下访问期间给你留下深刻印象的一切事物。

(3) 花时间浏览学校官网。请务必访问以下网页。

① 本科招生。这里通常会提醒你一些学校自认为与众不同、值得夸耀的事情。

② 提供你感兴趣的专业的系。看看各种各样能吸引你眼球的课程选择。查看课程描述和教师履历（包括他们的研究和教学兴趣），寻找你特别感兴趣的

东西。

③ 在大学的学生生活网页中，会讨论学生组织和活动、职业指导以及实习机会。

④ 在这里，还要记下让你兴奋的一切，尤其是对于这所学院来说独特的或近乎独特的事物。

如果你按照我们的方式进行调查，你就会获得一篇文书的材料，这样的文书将向招生委员会显示你已花时间了解大学能为你提供什么，并了解为什么这个学校适合你。

2. 其他学校的辅助题目

正如我们指出的那样，许多大学也对性格特征的评估（从你对美国大学通用申请系统的文书的回答中可能看不到的特征）感兴趣。除了回答美国大学通用申请系统申请的文书外，我们来看一些其他美国大学希望你回答的问题（见表 3.20）。

表 3.20 哥伦比亚大学 2020～2021 年本科申请

哥伦比亚大学要求申请人回答以下每一个问题	
第一题	List the titles of the required readings from academic courses that you enjoyed most during secondary/high school. (150 words or fewer) 列出你在高中最喜欢的课内必读书目。(150 词以内)
第二题	List the titles of the books, essays, poetry, short stories or plays you read outside of academic courses that you enjoyed most during secondary/high school. (150 words or fewer) 列出你在高中课外最喜欢的书目、散文、诗歌、故事或剧作。(150 词以内)
第三题	List the titles of the print or digital publications, websites, journals, podcasts or other content with which you regularly engage. (150 words or fewer) 列出你平时经常接触的纸质或电子刊物、网站、期刊、博客或是其他内容。(150 词以内)
第四题	List the titles of the films, concerts, shows, exhibits, lectures and other entertainments you enjoyed most during secondary/high school (in person or online). (150 words or fewer) 列出你在高中最喜欢的电影、音乐会、演出、展览、讲座和其他娱乐活动的名字。(150 词以内)
第五题	Why are you interested in attending Columbia University? (200 words or fewer) 你为什么想要就读哥伦比亚大学？(200 词以内)

续　表

第六题	Columbia students take an active role in improving their community, whether in their residence hall, classes or throughout New York City. Their actions, small or large, work to positively impact the lives of others. Share one contribution that you have made to your family, school, friend group or another community that surrounds you. (200 words or fewer) 哥伦比亚的学生在社区提升这方面扮演着积极的角色，不论是在宿舍、课堂还是整个纽约市内。他们或大或小的行动都致力于对他人的生活产生正面影响。请与我们分享一个你对你的家庭、学校、朋友圈或其他你所在的社区所做出的贡献。(200词以内)
第七题	**For applicants to Columbia College,** please tell us what from your current and past experiences (either academic or personal) attracts you specifically to the areas of study that you previously noted in the application. (200 words or fewer) ***Or*** **If you are applying to the Fu Foundation School of Engineering and Applied Science,** please tell us what from your current and past experiences (either academic or personal) attracts you specifically to the areas of study that you previously noted in the application. (200 words or fewer) **对于哥伦比亚学院的申请者：**请告诉我们你目前和过去的哪些经验(学术或个人经验)使你对你在申请中已经提到的研究领域产生兴趣。(不超过200词)。 **对于工程与应用科学学院的申请者：**请告诉我们你现在和过去的哪些经验(学术或个人经验)使你对你在申请中已经提到的研究领域产生兴趣。(不超过200词)。

如果我们问自己，什么样的学生会更好地回答哥伦比亚大学的问题，答案如下所示。

(1) 不仅在学校而且在校外读书的很多学生(请参阅前三个问题)。顺便说一句，不要试图通过列出从未读过的书来打动一所大学。他们可能会感觉你在说谎。更糟糕的是，如果你是在现场或在线面试，他们可能会要求你谈论这些书。

(2) 重视某种形式文化的学生(“列出电影、音乐会、表演、展览、演讲和其他娱乐活动的标题……”)。请注意，无论你想在哥伦比亚大学攻读哪个专业，哥伦比亚大学都需要你回答这个问题。

(3) 有充分理由申请哥伦比亚大学的学生。

(4) 关心帮助他人的学生(“分享你对家人、学校、朋友团体或你周围的另一个社区的贡献……”)

(5) 曾经考虑过要在大学学习什么专业的学生，可以引用特定的经历来解释为什么选择他们的专业。

让我们将哥伦比亚大学的问题与芝加哥大学对申请人提出的问题进行对比，会很有启发性的。芝加哥大学的文书题目是充满创造性想象力的文书的杰出典范(见表 3.21)。你会发现题目是由现在和以前的芝加哥大学学生提交的。他们的招生委员会指出：“每年我们都会通过电子邮件向新招收的和在读的大学生发送邮件，并要求他们提出文书主题。我们会收到数百个回复，其中许多都是动人的、有趣的或非常奇怪的主题。”

表 3.21　芝加哥大学 2020～2021 年本科申请

<table>
<tr><td colspan="2">Question 1 (Required). Upload a file. Max file size: 2000 KB.
How does the University of Chicago, as you know it now, satisfy your desire for a particular kind of learning, community, and future? Please address with some specificity your own wishes and how they relate to UChicago.
问题 1(必填)。上传一个文件。文件大小上限：2 000 KB。
你现在所了解的芝加哥大学如何满足你对学习、社区和未来的渴望？请具体说明你自己的期许以及它们与芝加哥大学的关系。</td></tr>
<tr><td colspan="2">Question 2: Extended Essay (Required; Choose one). Upload a file. Max file size: 2000 KB.
问题 2：扩展文书(必填；选择以下题目中的一个)。上传一个文件。文件大小上限：2 000 KB。</td></tr>
<tr><td>Essay Option 1
选择 1</td><td>Who does Sally sell her seashells to? How much wood can a woodchuck really chuck if a woodchuck could chuck wood? Pick a favorite tongue twister (either originally in English or translated from another language) and consider a resolution to its conundrum using the method of your choice. Math, philosophy, linguistics ... it's all up to you (or your woodchuck).
萨利将贝壳卖给谁？如果土拨鼠能夹住木头，那么土拨鼠能真正夹住多少木头？选择最喜欢的绕口令(最初是英语或从其他语言翻译而来的)，并使用你选择的方法考虑其难题的解决方案。数学，哲学，语言学，等等。一切都取决于你(或土拨鼠)。
——由 2020 级 Blessing Nnate 提供</td></tr>
<tr><td>Essay Option 2
选择 2</td><td>What can actually be divided by zero?
什么可以真的被零整除？
——由 2020 级 Mai Vu 提供</td></tr>
</table>

续　表

Essay Option 3 **选择 3**	The seven liberal arts in antiquity consisted of the Quadrivium — astronomy, mathematics, geometry, and music — and the Trivium — rhetoric, grammar, and logic. Describe your own take on the Quadrivium or the Trivium. What do you think is essential for everyone to know? 古时的七门文科包括“四艺”——天文学、数学、几何学和音乐，以及“三艺”——修辞学、语法和逻辑学。描述你对“四艺”或“三艺”的看法。你认为每个人都必须知道些什么？ ——由 2018 级 Peter Wang 提供
Essay Option 4 **选择 4**	Subway maps, evolutionary trees, Lewis diagrams. Each of these schematics tells the relationships and stories of their component parts. Reimagine a map, diagram, or chart. If your work is largely or exclusively visual, please include a cartographer's key of at least 300 words to help us best understand your creation. 地铁图，进化树，刘易斯表格。这些示意图中的每一个都讲述了其组成部分的关系和故事。重新构想地图，图表或表格。如果你的作品大部分是视觉作品，请提供至少 300 词的制图师的关键词，以帮助我们更好地了解你的创作。 ——由 2016 级 Maximilian Site 提供
Essay Option 5 **选择 5**	“Do you feel lucky? Well, do ya, punk?” — Eleanor Roosevelt. Misattribute a famous quote and explore the implications of doing so. “你感到幸运吗？你真觉得吗？你这个流氓。”——埃莉诺·罗斯福。像这样错误地使用一则名言，并探讨这样做的含义。 ——由 2013 届校友 Chris Davey 提供
Essay Option 6 **选择 6**	Engineer George de Mestral got frustrated with burrs stuck to his dog's fur and applied the same mechanic to create Velcro. Scientist Percy Lebaron Spencer found a melted chocolate bar in his magnetron lab and discovered microwave cooking. Dye-works owner Jean Baptiste Jolly found his tablecloth clean after a kerosene lamp was knocked over on it, consequently shaping the future of dry cleaning. Describe a creative or interesting solution, and then find the problem that it solves. 工程师乔治·德·梅斯特拉对狗的皮毛上粘有毛刺而感到沮丧，并采用了这种机制制作了魔术贴。科学家珀西·勒巴伦·斯宾塞在他的磁控管实验室发现了一块融化的巧克力棒，并发现了微波烹饪方法。染厂的老板让·巴蒂斯特·乔利在用煤油灯敲打后发现桌布很干净，因此塑造了干洗的未来。描述一个创造性的或有趣的解决方案，然后找到它可以解决的问题。 ——由 2019 届校友 Steve Berkowitz 和 2020 级 Neeharika Venuturupalli 提供

续 表

Essay Option 7 **选择 7**	In the spirit of adventurous inquiry (and with the encouragement of one of our current students!) choose one of our past prompts (or create a question of your own). Be original, creative, thought provoking. Draw on your best qualities as a writer, thinker, visionary, social critic, sage, citizen of the world, or future citizen of the University of Chicago; take a little risk, and have fun! 本着冒险的精神(在我们学生的鼓励下),请选择我们过去的提示之一(或提出你自己的问题)。要有原创性和创造力,有深度。发挥你身上作家、思想家、社会评论家、贤哲、世界公民或芝加哥大学未来公民的最佳品质,敢于冒险,玩得开心。

芝加哥大学的问题针对的是富有创造力和对世界充满好奇的学生,尤其是那些喜欢发挥想象力,沉迷于冒险或表现出聪明、机智甚至一点点幽默的学生。

即使是芝加哥大学的第 7 个选项(允许你设计自己的问题),也仍然清楚地表明,创意和冒险精神是他们想看到的。

芝加哥大学不会担心因为提出棘手的问题而吓退申请人。甚至还会询问申请人“为什么要选择芝加哥大学?”他们希望你展示出芝加哥大学将如何“满足你对特定学习方式,社区和未来的渴望”。“一种特殊的学习方式,社区和未来”一词迫使你思考自己想要什么样的学习环境和同学,以及芝加哥大学的教育如何与你的未来计划联系在一起。

与芝加哥大学一样,维克森林大学也提出了开放性的问题(见表 3.22),这些问题可以通过许多不同的方式来解答。

表 3.22 维克森林大学 2019～2020 年本科申请

维克森林大学写道:“通过简短回答以下问题,帮助我们更好地了解你。发挥你的创造力,享受这一过程!” **“Help us to get to know you better by responding briefly to these questions. Be creative, and enjoy the process!”**	
第一题	In brief: 1a. List five books you have read that intrigued you (title, author, whether required for a class) 1b. Explain how a book you've read has helped you to understand the world's complexity. (150 words)

续　表

第一题	简答： 1a. 列举 5 本你阅读过且吸引你的书(标题、作者,以及是否是课内的必读书目) 1b. 你读过的一本书是如何帮助你理解了这个世界的复杂性。(150 词)
第二题	Tell us more about the topic that most engages your intellectual curiosity. (150 words) 与我们分享一个引起你思维探索的话题。(150 词)
第三题	Describe a community that is important to you. How has that community prepared you to engage with, change, or even build the Wake Forest community? (150 words) 描述一个对你重要的社群。这个社群是如何帮助你准备参与、改变甚至建设维克森林的社区的?(150 词)
第四题	Give us your top ten list (pick a theme) 给我们你的前十名列表(自选一个主题)
第五题	How did you become interested in Wake Forest University? Feel free to tell us about any contact that you had with Wake Forest that was important to you. (150 words) 你是如何对维克森林大学产生兴趣的?告诉我们任何对你而言重要的与维克森林大学的联系。(150 词)

与芝加哥大学一样,维克森林大学希望看到你的创造力。最有趣的是第四个问题,询问你的“前十名”。哪些前十名?这就取决于你了。正如维克森林大学所说,选择一个主题。主题可能是很严肃的事情,例如,我一生中想完成的十件事,也可能是古怪的事情。你选择的主题将与你提供的答案一样表达出你的个性。

你可以从大学所提出的问题中获得一些其他信息,他们知道一些学生是完全“被动的”,只学习(或背诵)被告知要学习的内容,有些人从未想过为使世界变得更美好该做些什么。你会发现许多问题都是大学为了淘汰这些学生而设计的,他们希望学生在生活中能积极提出问题和寻求答案,或者积极应对他们需要完成的事情。让我们研究这些大学所提出的问题(见表 3.23),更好地了解这些大学希望招收的学生类型。

表 3.23 其他例子

Questions from 2020～2021 Application **2020～2021 年提出的问题**	**What can we infer from these questions?** **从这些问题中我们可以推断出什么？**
Washington University, St. Louis, Missouri **圣路易斯华盛顿大学** "Tell us about something that really sparks your intellectual interest and curiosity and compels you to explore more. It could be an idea, book, project, cultural activity, work of art, start-up, music, movie, research, innovation, question, or other pursuit. (250 words)" 告诉我们一些能激发你兴趣和好奇心并迫使你进行更多探索的事情，可以是想法、书籍、项目、文化活动、艺术创造、创业项目、音乐、电影、研究、革新、问题或其他追求。(250 词)	Notice how Wash U's question weeds out applicants who have been "wholly passive" and attracts those who "actively curious" about the world. 圣路易斯华盛顿大学的问题淘汰了那些"完全被动"的申请者，并吸引那些"积极好奇"的申请者。
University of North Carolina at Chapel Hill **北卡罗来纳大学教堂山分校** Short Answer Questions. In addition to the essay you provided with your Common Application, please choose two of the prompts below and respond to each in 200 - 250 words. Your essay responses below should be different from your common app essay response. 简答题：除了你美国大学通用申请系统中提供的文书外，请从以下任选两个问题，并以 200～250 词回答，你的回答应与美国大学通用申请系统中的论述不同。 Carolina aspires to build a diverse and inclusive community. We believe that students can only achieve their best when they learn alongside students from different backgrounds. In reading your responses, we hope to learn what being a member of such a community would mean to you. 北卡罗来纳大学渴望建立一个多元化的包容的社区，我们相信，只有与来自不同背景的学生一起学习，才能取得最佳成绩。我们希望从你的回答中，了解成为这个社区的一	Notice how UNC frames its short answer questions by asking you to show how your identity, background, and values would contribute to building "a diverse and inclusive community" on campus. 北卡罗来纳大学教堂山分校通过你对自己身份、背景和价值观的简要回答，判断你是否有助于在大学建立"多元化和包容性社区"。 In its "Activity" section of the Common Application, UNC offers the following guidance. 在申请程序的"活动"部分，北卡罗来纳大学教堂山分校提供以下指导。 **We think it is excellent advice no matter where you are applying for college:** **无论你在哪里申请大学，我们都认为这是一个极好的建议：** "We hope you'll share with us the activities that you've found especially worthwhile. We also hope you won't feel compelled to tell us everything you've ever done or, worse yet, to do things that mean little to you just

续　表

Questions from 2020～2021 Application 2020～2021 年提出的问题	What can we infer from these questions? 从这些问题中我们可以推断出什么?
员对你意味着什么。 1. Expand on an aspect of your identity (for example, your religion, culture, race, sexual or gender identity, affinity group, etc.). How has this aspect of your identity shaped your life experiences thus far? 请展开谈谈你身份的一个方面(如你的宗教、文化、种族、性别或性取向、朋友圈等),到目前为止,你的这些身份如何影响了你的生活? 2. If you could change one thing about where you live, what would it be and why? 如果你可以改变有关你住所的一件事,那会是什么,为什么? 3. Describe someone who you see as a community builder. What actions has that person taken? How has their work made a difference in your life? 描述一个你认为的社区建设者,他们采取了什么行动? 他们的工作对你的生活有何改变?	because you think we expect them. Low-profile pursuits can be just as meaningful as ones that draw more attention, and fewer activities can be just as good, and sometimes even better, than more activities. For example, although starting a new club can be a great experience and helpful to others, so can caring for siblings, parents, or grandparents, working outside the home to put food on the table, or being a good and caring friend. For these reasons, although we're glad to receive complete résumés, we don't require or encourage them. Instead, if you choose to submit something that goes beyond what you're providing through your Common Application, keep it brief; focus less on including everything and more on choosing and explaining the things that have meant the most to you; and upload it here." 我们希望你能分享你认为特别有价值的活动,我们也希望你不是被迫去告诉我们你曾经做的每件事情,或者更糟糕的,仅仅因为你认为要满足我们的期望,而做对你没有意义的事情。一些并不宏大的追求可以同那些更惹人眼球的事情一样充满意义,更少的活动可以与更多的活动一样好,有时甚至更好。例如,尽管成立一个新的俱乐部可能是很好的经历,并且对其他人有帮助,但是照料兄弟姐妹、父母或祖父母,为了食物而出去工作,或者做一位有爱心的朋友同样有意义。出于这些原因,尽管我们很高兴收到完整的简历,但我们并不需要或鼓励这样做。相反,如果你要通过美国大学通用申请系统提供更多的内容,请简短些,不必呈现所有事情,而是更多地选择对你更有意义的事情,并在这里上传。
Emory University, Atlanta, Georgia **埃默里大学** In addition to your Personal Statement,	These questions make it clear that Emory seeks applicants who have thought about what their life experiences mean, how they

续 表

Questions from 2020～2021 Application 2020～2021 年提出的问题	What can we infer from these questions? 从这些问题中我们可以推断出什么?
please answer two (2) of the prompts below. Choose one prompt from the "Reflections" category and one prompt from the "Tell us about you" category. 除了你的文书外,请回答以下问题中的两个,从"思考"类中选择一个问题,从"介绍自己"类中选择一个问题。 We encourage you to be thoughtful and not stress about what the right answer might be. We simply want to get to know you better. Each response should be no more than 150 words. 我们鼓励你全面思考,但不要担心什么才是正确的答案,我们只是想更好地了解你。每个回答不超过 150 词。 **"Reflections" Category: Respond to one of the following.** **"思考"类:从以下选一题回答。** 1. Share about a time when you questioned something that you believed to be true. 分享一次质疑自己以为是正确事情的时刻。 2. If you could go back in time, what advice would you offer yourself at the beginning of secondary/high school? 如果可以回到过去,那么在初中/高中开始时你会给自己提供什么建议? 3. Reflect on a personal experience where you intentionally expanded your cultural awareness. 回想一次有意识地扩大文化意识的个人经历。 **"Tell us about you" Category: Respond to one of the following.** **"介绍自己"类:从以下选一题回答。** 1. Which book, character, song, or piece of work (fiction or non-fiction) represents you, and why? 哪本书、角色、歌曲或作品(虚构或非虚构)可以代表你自己,为什么? 2. If you could witness a historic event first-hand, what would it be, and why?	have shaped them, and what kind of human being they are. 这些问题清楚地说明,埃默里大学正在寻找那些认真考虑过自己的生活经历以及他们是什么样的人的申请者。

续　表

Questions from 2020～2021 Application 2020～2021 年提出的问题	What can we infer from these questions? 从这些问题中我们可以推断出什么？
如果你可以目睹历史事件，那会是什么，为什么？ 3. Introduce yourself to your first-year Emory University roommate. 将自己介绍给埃默里大学的大一室友。	
College of William and Mary, Williamsburg, Virginia **威廉和玛丽学院** In addition to the Personal Statement, one "optional" essay: 除文书外，还有一个"备选"题： Beyond your impressive academic credentials and extracurricular accomplishments, what else makes you unique and colorful? We know nobody fits neatly into 500 words or less, but you can provide us with some suggestion of the type of person you are. Anything goes! Inspire us, impress us, or just make us laugh. Think of this optional opportunity as show and tell by proxy and with an attitude. 除了令人印象深刻的学历和课外经历，还有什么让你与众不同？请用不超过 500 词，向我们介绍一些有关你是个什么样的人的事情。什么都可以！启发我们，给我们留下深刻的印象，搞笑也行，可以以第三人的方式来展示和讲述这个备选题。	Although The College of William and Mary says that this question is optional, it would be a mistake not to answer it. Answering optional questions lets an admissions committee know that you are serious enough about their college that you want to take every opportunity to show them what you have to offer. 尽管威廉和玛丽学院说这个问题是可选的，但不回答是一个错误。回答可选问题可使招生委员会知道你对他们的大学足够重视，因此你会想要抓住一切机会向他们展示你自己。 The question is wide open. It allows you to write about anything you want, and in many ways, that is what makes it such a difficult question to answer. It is an invitation to find a story among your many life experiences that best captures the kind of person you are. 这是个开放题，你可以以任何形式写自己想写的任何东西，这使问题变得难以回答。你可以从你的许多生活经历中选择一个最能反映你自己的故事。

第八节

如何应对“候补名单”

1. 什么是候补名单？为什么大学有候补名单？

当大学将你列入候补名单时，他们是在告诉你他们还没有录取你，但如果在学期开始之前有空位，也许可以录取你，希望被录取的候补生通常会被要求通过线上回复来告知学校。

为什么大学有候补名单？由于许多学生不止申请一所大学，因此没有一所大学能 100%招收所录取的学生（哈佛大学或斯坦福大学也不能）。实际接受录取通知书的百分比称为“接受率”，大学采用前几年的接受率来估算需要录取多少学生才能达到他们所需的入学人数，但是由于接受率可能会在一年之间变化，因此如果接受率下降，一所大学的学生人数可能会少于预期。

这时候补名单就发挥作用了，如果接受录取通知的学生少于预期的学生，那么将有一定名额用于录取候补名单中的申请人。

有时，一所大学会令你大吃一惊，甚至在 5 月 1 日之前就开始将学生从候补名单中“解放”出来，因为他们发现与上一年相比，他们的入学人数明显减少。

2. 如果你被列入候补名单，你应该如何回应？

从大学的角度看：大多数大学，尤其是最挑剔的大学，都告诉录取的学生，5 月 1 日是接受或拒绝录取通知书的截止日期。过了 5 月 1 日，大学发现尚未完成招生名额，他们便希望尽快补上这个空缺。最有效的方法是联系那些最愿意接受录取通知书的候补学生。

现在是你对候补的回应起关键性作用的时候了。这些回复通常被称为“情书”，因为它们重申你仍然非常渴望入学，如果这所大学仍然是你的首选，那么在你的回信中说明这一点很重要。以下是你的回复应该涵盖的内容。

(1) 让大学知道你仍然渴望被录取。

(2) 更新原申请，使用之前未包含的任何新信息，“新信息”可以包括你最近的成绩，获得的新奖项或荣誉，新的课外活动或志愿者活动等。

(3) 如果你在被列入候补名单后访问了大学，也请提到这一点，并提及你访问期间发生的令人难忘的事情。

(4) 不要重复他们已经拥有的信息！大多数招生委员会都觉得这很烦人，因为这浪费了他们的时间。

(5) 一些大学会给他们的候选者发送邮件，询问他们是否仍然愿意被考虑。随着 5 月 1 日的临近，这种情况极有可能发生。一定要经常查看邮件，并及时回复。

(6) 最好的“情书”是那些能清楚表明如果你从候补名单上被录取，你有很大的可能会接受这个录取。

3. 你的期望要现实一点。

越是挑剔的大学，提供给候补学生的名额就越少。另外，即便会有候选名额，也可能不是你想就读的专业。

由于从候选者名单中被录取的可能性很小，你也应该关注那些已经录取你的大学，并确保在截止日期(通常是 5 月 1 日)之前向其中一所大学缴纳注册保证金。

最重要的是保持开放的心态。有很多大一新生并没有去到最初他们的“第一选择”或者“梦想的学校”。然而他们通常在入学几周内或者几天内，就可能发现自己比预期更快乐，甚至可能会比进入他们“梦想的学校”更开心。

第九节 总结

最后，我们再重新回顾一下关于文书的几点重要信息。

1. 什么样学生的大学申请文书特别重要

（1）所有申请"极度挑剔"学校的人——尤其是排名前 50 名的大学。

（2）申请"非常挑剔的"大学的人，特别是成绩和考试分数不在大学入学新生的前四分之一的申请人。

（3）任何申请"比较挑剔的"大学的人，如果他们的学术成绩参差不齐，或考试成绩低于学院的中位数，或有特殊情况影响了他们的成绩(如疾病、家人去世、转学等)。

2. 写大学申请文书时应该问自己的问题

（1）当回顾自己所有生活经历和成就时，哪些经历和成就对自己成年的影响最大？

（2）自己的文书讲了一个故事吗？

（3）自己的故事是否从正确位置开始叙述？我的开篇句子是否使招生官渴望继续阅读？

（4）自己的故事是否包含生动的细节和真实的事件？

（5）自己的句子怎么样？是否可以通过包含以"since""although""because""when"等词开头的句子来使它们更有效？

（6）自己可以利用"少即是多"的原则吗？是否有删除之后仍能读清内容的单词、短语或句子？当使用尽可能少的单词时，写作将变得更好。

(7) 文书题目询问申请者为什么要申请特定的大学或特定的专业，是向招生委员会展示自己对这个大学所做的研究。自己的回答证明这一点了吗？

(8) 招生官会认为自己是一个考虑过自己会对世界产生影响，以及考虑过如何帮助他人的人吗？

(9) 招生委员会希望选出能通过相识而丰富彼此人生的学生，以及教授们会乐于教导的学生。通过阅读自己的文书，人们会判断自己是这样的学生吗？

3. 如果你收到了与自己大学申请文书相矛盾的建议的时候应该怎么办

在你的一生中，你会在做出重大决定之前寻求建议。当它让你意识到你可能没有考虑到的一些事情时，建议是有价值的。例如，如果一个招生官告诉你，他们不明白你在文书中说的一些东西，请你试着更清楚地解释它。或者当你询问他们，你文书的哪一部分给他们留下了最深刻的印象，哪一部分给他们留下了负面的印象。当他们指出语法、拼写和标点符号错误时，请你仔细地考虑。

但是，对于那些仅仅反映了个人品位或试图强加建议者自己个性和价值观的建议时要持怀疑态度。如果你不持有这些价值观，或者他们想让你写的东西让你感到不舒服，或者想让你说："但这听起来不像我"时，也请你保持怀疑的态度。

也要注意给你建议的人的背景。他们是否曾在大学招生部门工作过，询问他们是否目睹过招生委员会是如何谈论学生文书的？他们是否给许多准备上大学的学生提供了建议，并与大学招生官员进行了大量讨论？如果是这样，那么他们的建议就相对比较正确。即使这样，也要永远记住，这是你的文书，不是别人的。你必须对它感到舒服，并为此感到自豪。

同样要记住的是，招生官自己对一篇文书往往有不同的意见，而招生委员会对录取、候补名单、拒绝申请人的投票往往也会不一致。

4. 父母的建议

因为他们比任何人都了解你，所以也请向你的父母寻求建议。他们可以帮助你想起生活中的关键事件，帮助招生委员会了解你的独特性。

但有时你可能不得不拒绝父母的建议。招生委员会审查数千份申请资料，那些在家长眼中看起来很特别的东西在招生官眼里可能就显得很普通、很无趣。

一些糟糕的大学申请文书往往是学生简单地重复他们简历上的奖项和荣

誉。通常情况下,这种情况的发生是因为家长让学生把这些东西都写上。这会使招生委员会反感,因为这浪费了他们的时间。

5. 不要忘记

虽然文书和课外活动很重要,但它们永远不会像优秀的成绩和选择高难度的学术课那样重要。如果你认为一篇优秀的大学申请文书或一次令人印象深刻的活动可以弥补平庸的学习成绩,那你是在欺骗自己。

你有时会看到这样的文书:这样或那样的大学申请文书可以"让一个学生被常春藤大学或美国排名前 30 的名校录取",这是无稽之谈。其实比较真实的情况是一篇非常糟糕的文书会阻碍你被梦想的大学录取,但录取本身是一个两步的过程:首先你必须先证明你的选课难度和优异的成绩让你在申请时有竞争力,也只有到那一步时,你的文书和活动才会作为"决胜因素"使你领先于其他有很强学术能力的申请者。更准确地说,你优异的学习成绩使你在美国大学申请中具有竞争力,而你的文书和课内外活动等则是帮助你越过终点线的力量。

第四章 获得美国顶尖大学录取的“牛娃”的文书赏析

前文介绍了关于文书的主要信息，包括美国大学的基本情况、文书的重要性、如何发掘材料、撰写各类文书等。接下来，我们将聚焦已获得美国顶尖大学录取通知书的“牛娃”们，看看他们的文书是怎样写的——究竟什么样的文书获得了名校的青睐？在进入正文之前，需要先解释一下，由于这些文书都来自我们热心的优秀学员，所以我们尊重他们本人的选择，仅有部分文书被翻译成中文。剩余的文书因为作者本人认为中文并不能呈现同样好的效果，所以未被翻译。

对于各个申请系统的各类文书题目，牛娃们都作了怎样的应答呢？下面我们一起来看看吧。

第一节 美国大学通用申请系统主文书鉴赏

1. 文书题目：**Some students have a background，identity，interest，or talent that is so meaningful they believe their application would be incomplete without it. If this sounds like you，then please share your story.**

有些学生有着出色的背景、身份、兴趣或才能，以至于如果没有这些他们的申请就称不上完整。如果这正是你的情况，请和我们分享你的故事。

范文作者：Bambi，被斯坦福大学录取

"Why are you staring at the ground again? Did you find a piece of gold?" mom jokes. She never understands why ten-year-old me loves squatting to observe bugs. "Never mind，" I tell myself，"Adults have no idea of my magic."

Zoom in，then out. That's my magic trick. See that beetle crawling along the blade of grass? Zooming in，I imagine I'm just about its size and the beetle becomes king of his kind. The wildflower corona is his palace，and his wings stir the air，which blows a breeze that ruins his ant friends' party. Then zoom out：my mind speeds free from gravity and into outer space. I realize I'm diminutive，just like the little beetle. Mom's voice vanishes；Beijing vanishes，too. Isolated in the grand universe，I feel as if I'm in the middle of nowhere. But there's beauty in this empty wholeness，or "Kong" as Chinese philosopher Laozi called it，which incorporates the immensely big and infinitely small. Years before I wrote my first stanza, these images were my poetry.

As I've grown up, my "zooming" magic faded into childhood memories. "Those silly mind games," my seventeen-year-old self murmurs. Goethe's protagonist Faust turned to magic when he thought he'd mastered science. I've done the opposite. Reading Quantum Physics for Poets, designing Space Stations for a competition, and analyzing how beans pop out from pods captivated me. I relinquished my magic and chose to decipher the world's wonders with science.

Last year, I won a plant physiology research opportunity in Peking University. I aimed to investigate the biomechanics of cucumber plant's spring-like tendrils and why they twist and climb. I needed freshly plucked tendrils for experiments, so I wrote a proposal and was thrilled when the administration allowed me to cultivate the school garden. Then summer came and the cucumbers went wild. Tendrils twirl and swirl, holding on to anything within their reach.

Kneeling in a muddy plot, I delicately harvested tendrils of different lengths. Then I witnessed the green tendrils turn pale after several days in a chemical bath of dimethylbenzene. After immersing the dehydrated samples in bubbling half-liquid-half-gas carbon dioxide to drive out impurities, I finally put them under the scanning electron microscope.

The black-and-white images on the computer screen astonished me. A world invisible to human eyes revealed itself. Fluffy tendrils became thorny tentacles, as terrifying as the giant octopus that haunted the Nautilus. Stomata (air holes) looked like the wide-open blowhole of Moby Dick. Cells formed a dense surface, just like Robinson Crusoe's stone fort, protecting functioning cells from being disturbed.

Science unraveled a world more magical than fiction and reactivated my childhood magic. Zooming-in, I think of the constantly recombining double-helix DNA behind cucumber tendrils. Zooming-out, I think of how, as Darwinians argued, gene mutation makes natural selection possible. These tendrils, though teeny-tiny, epitomize nature's flawed failures and heroic victories over millennia.

In my childhood, zooming felt like poetry. Now that I regularly write poems, I find zooming sparks my ideas. With the tip of my nose against a glass teacup, I watch bubbles burst then reappear, and think how they signify life and death overlapping. Once I spotted a bare ancient tree standing proud in an abandoned alley, and imagined how its flourishing companions must have been cut down in their prime. Pulling out my iPhone, I tapped away to compose an ode about how we never know what our futures hold. Zooming inspires me to see poetry and philosophy in everyday scenes. I see the large from the small, the eternal from the ephemeral, the universal from the particular.

Ancient Chinese philosopher Zhuangzi described people's attempt to look into the universe as "the very small trying to comprehend the very large." I know I'm tiny. Still, I'm eager to explore whether it's with microscopes or my imagination. My "zoom lens" is ready. It's time to perform my magic tricks again.

范文作者：Nijedan，被乔治城大学录取

My friend Ramon and I always had fights when we ordered pizza together.

I'm a thin-crust person: crispy, crunchy. He's a thick-crust guy: calories, fulfilling.

As for music, we have our differences as well. He loves hip-hop and rapping: fast-paced, exciting, contemporary. I prefer country: picturesque, soothing, nostalgic.

When the plate of pizzas lay empty and the sound of music cut off, we got to more talking. I learned that he grew up in Brooklyn and I told him I was born on the other side of the world. He had many siblings and I'm the only child. I went to a middle school where the instructors lectured in front and the rest sat in silence, and he used to attend an institution where everyone was able to voice their opinions or share their insights.

Suddenly, the century-long debate about thin or thick crust became the slightest of our distinctions — sometimes, I felt we were dimensions apart from each other, disconnected.

Growing up in two cultures and educated in two school systems that were oftentimes at odds with each other, I've talked to many people and looked at things from discrete angles, traversing the boundaries of identities and always searching for common grounds that linked myself with others.

Sitting in front of my desk, I close my laptop and take a short break from translating Tony Horwitz's A Voyage Long and Strange, a book I loved endearingly and was eager to introduce to an overseas audience. The author mentioned Viking settlers had described indigenous residents of the Americas as "Skraelings," a Nordic word for "ugly" or "wretches." Interestingly, the Mi'kmaq people recorded that Europeans were pale like "dried sea-salt" and their beards looked like seaweeds dangling from their faces.

Since the first encounter between Europeans and American natives, a millennium had already passed. However, in our contemporary world where communications became instant and accessible, history still repeats itself in many other occasions and places. I remembered listening to a speech by Senator Jeff Flake. A Republican himself, he warned of the danger of divisive politics and the emergence of radical, polarizing factions that began garnering strength within his party. In Just Mercy, Bryan Stevenson exposed the sharp racial divisions persisting in today's criminal justice system.

If only there was a keen observer who could comprehend the perspectives of both parties impartially, and bridge the gap that was pulling them apart and towards animosity.

Earlier this year, I co-founded HOPE humanities platform with a few friends while entrapped at home by covid - 19. HOPE stands for "Humanities Online Platform for Everyone" — Everyone builds from scratches, everyone shares their values and worldviews, everyone takes a bit home.

Every day, I get to meet someone with a perspective and cultural background so distinct and different from mine, sharing my insights and learning something new in return. I could only wish that our efforts would amend and close down the sharp division lines in this world — of nation-states, religions, ideologies — little by little.

After finishing up our not-always-satisfying pizza dinner, Ramon and I would occasionally talk about lives back home, exchange our thoughts on the breaking news, or discuss what we might want to do in the future. Our tiny "classroom" had no classes, nor doors, nor professors: just the two of us debating, reconciling, different voices and perspectives colliding in the air and sparking the fire of connections, taking a part of each other back to our own perceptions and cultures, and turning into something new.

Occasionally, Ramon would put on a Kenny Chesney or Willie Nelson song, and I would try his playlist stacked with Post Malone and Travis Scott. Sometimes, he would sing a tribute to my thin-crust pizza, and I would compliment his.

Thin or thick crust, we still love a nice slice of hot, cheesy pizza on a Saturday night.

2. 文书题目: The lessons we take from obstacles we encounter can be fundamental to later success. Recount a time when you faced a challenge, setback, or failure. How did it affect you, and what did you learn from the experience?

我们从挫折中吸取的教训将会是今后成功的基础。讲述你的一次挑战、挫折或失败的经历,并说明它对你的影响,你从这次经历中学到了什么?

范文作者: Louisa,被范德堡大学录取

"No, this is not going to work. You are too young to know what you're talking about or understand what this is," my supervisor barked. Then he asked me to sit down and he went on listening to others.

I was interning at an e-commerce company and was put in charge of a team launching a new t-shirt for a famous sports brand. After spending countless hours on the project, my supervisor interrupted my presentation and quickly dismissed the strategy I had conceived and knew could be effective.

As I sat in the corner of the conference room listening to others pitching their plans, I was unable to focus on what they were saying. I remembered being the only Asian girl on my school's basketball team, and the coach refusing to let me play because, he said, "Asians can't play basketball." I didn't know it then, but as I sat in the corner I realized it had been the first time my actions were limited because of someone else's idea of me. At that moment, I vowed that it would never happen again.

Yes, I was just a seventeen-year-old intern, the youngest working with a group of people who each had over ten years of experience in the field. But, that is not a reason for him to be dismissive. If he had let me finish, I am confident that he would have seen the valid points in my plan. Without hesitating, I delved back into research to improve my plan. I analyzed each of the "flaws" in my plan and tackled them one by one. Time and again I was told by my supervisor to give up, that somebody else could take over, and I should go back to helping them translate documents. But, I had more to offer than my language abilities.

I figured that the people who would best understand my methodology were the executives, but it took weeks to get through to them When I tried to talk with the marketing consultants, they were reluctant to help because my project was irrelevant to anything they were working on. I even tried to book an appointment with the COO of the company. Since he was extremely occupied with meetings, it took some time for him to agree to meet with me. Eventually he did and was very helpful, patiently giving me advice.

As I handed in my revised report to my supervisor, I listened humbly as he went through my ideas and asked pointed questions. I was able to answer every one of his questions because of my thorough research! In fact, a week later I received an email saying my plan was utilized and had proved to be extremely successful.

This summer I returned to the same company for another internship with the same supervisor. This time, I received the even harder task of developing this brand on another platform. Like last time, I spent countless days and nights working on my proposal. However, this time during my presentation, my supervisor was silent. He didn't interrupt me. Instead, he proudly announced to the entire office that my plan would be the one they implement.

3. 文书题目：Describe a problem you've solved or a problem you'd like to solve. It can be an intellectual challenge, a research query, an ethical dilemma — anything that is of personal importance, no matter the scale. Explain its significance to you and what steps you took or could be taken to identify a solution.

描述一个你已经解决或想要解决的问题。可以是智力挑战，研究调查，道德困境——任何对你个人来说非常重要的都可以，不需要考虑它的大小。解释它对你的重要性，以及你是如何一步步找到解决办法的。

范文作者：Frank，被斯坦福大学录取

I've been in love for 10 years.

Most don't understand why I've pursued her when she's demanding, constantly shifting, and endlessly needy. My growing love for her has led to much critical thinking and moments of self-revelation. This love expands me in ways I hope will be with me to the fourth dimension and beyond.

2009.

Squeezed into a classroom with nine not-so-typical students, our teacher waved her hand and scribbled on the blackboard. Random Greek letters danced alongside straight lines, curves, and stereographic sketches.

Then, she said: "When we place n points onto a single line, we can break the line into a maximum of n+1 segments." Her words were like songs of the Sirens.

"But of course, the problem can extend further ..." Using n lines to cut a plane wasn't too difficult; we quickly found the pattern: one, two, four, seven, eleven ... Each number popped out of the draft paper and linked together. "The differences between consecutive terms are one, two, three, four ..." I added.

"Now, what about a 3-dimensional object like a cake?"

If we cut a cake once, we get two pieces. Twice, four; thrice, eight. And four cuts? Sixteen?

I visualised cakes from friends' birthdays and the numbers didn't add up. "OH! OH! OH! Of course," my friend yelled from the other side of the room. "With four cuts you can only get a maximum of fifteen pieces."

From a top-down perspective, cutting 3 times, we cut it horizontally, vertically, and across the height to obtain 8 pieces. Then, what if we cut it again diagonally? It turns out that we can only cut through 7 of them, hence 7+8=15 pieces.

Sound complicated? Not to me. "The differences between them are one, two, four, seven, eleven ... exactly the same as lines cutting a plane!" Everything clicked. At that instant, my mind was filled with a sense of awe, and yes, love.

2019.

After years of Olympiad training and completing many books of mathematical problems, fate intervened. I stumbled across the cake-cutting problem again. Except this time, I took it further.

Not satisfied with real cakes, I began to dream in hypercakes — cakes in higher dimensions. The problems I investigated before were contained within the first three dimensions, but what if we use 3D spaces to cut a 4D space? And 4D cutting 5D? Better still, is there a general pattern?

Suppose the recursive pattern I discovered ten years ago holds true in higher dimensions? I quickly worked out the general formula for 3D spaces cutting a 4D space — a rather ugly-looking polynomial with quartic power. At that point, my intuition was nudging me toward the idea that maybe those polynomials were somehow connected to combinations.

After getting nowhere for several days, fate again intervened. While browsing math videos on YouTube, I saw a video titled "a curious pattern indeed". I hit play. The video focuses on a completely unrelated puzzle called the circle division problem. As the video unfolded, the narrator detailed how the problem involved an unexpected yet neat pattern. I sat stock still.

The pattern looked EXACTLY like the 3D-spaces-cutting-4D-space pattern.

I paused the video, stood up, walked around, and took a deep breath. The video used Euler's Characteristics to derive a combinatorial formula for the pattern. This was my Eureka moment.

When the video ended, I grabbed a pencil and paper. I worked backward and found the combinatorial formulas for the smaller dimensional cases, then generalized to all dimensions. The initial infinite number of long and complicated polynomials were all condensed into one short line of equation. It appeared so neat and elegant that I just sat there in disbelief.

After pushing my way through the complications of exceptionally high-level mathematics, I discovered that elegance and simplicity are the fundamental principles of both science and math. I am far from a Newton or Einstein ...

But I dare to dream big.

4. 文书题目: Discuss an accomplishment, event, or realization that sparked a period of personal growth and a new understanding of yourself or others.

讨论激发你某段时期个人成长和赋予你自己或他人新认识的成就或事件。

范文作者: LXJ,被宾夕法尼亚大学录取

Reflecting on myself in primary school, I saw a boy who was shy and introverted. I was an avid reader and was considered nerdy since, I had few interactions with classmates. Regardless of how hard I tried, I always felt like an outcast. My attempts to fit in left me empty.

I was envious of those with things to share and regarded acceptance from others as the highest pursuit in my life. I did everything I could to fit in and to find common interests with my classmates. If a new cartoon came out, then I went to watch the cartoon. If a new toy model was popular then I went to my mom begging her to buy it. My interest in these things was only an excuse to befriend my classmates. After the initial excitement wore off, I would toss them in the corner and forget about them.

This was truly a dilemma for me. On one hand, I wanted to be like the other kids, yet, I also wanted to forge my own path and create a separate identity that was not dependent on the approval of others.

Following others and trying to develop genuine friendships was exhausting, since I only pretended to share common interests with my classmates. Pursing my own interests, like reading, came at the cost of social interactions which only furthered my sense of isolation. On the surface things were fine. I was still a good student, and socialized with others, but inside I knew something was off.

Things began to change after I decided to pursue higher education abroad. Instead of getting lost in textbooks and preparing for countless exams, I had more freedom to explore personal interests outside the classroom.

Picking up reading again, I became enchanted with the study of history. I enjoyed the process of discovering new stories and devising my own interpretation of past events. Sharing stories with my classmates gave me a sense of happiness that had been missing. I discovered that many of my classmates shared a passion for history, even though preparing for tests had long been their daily routines.

Together we founded the history club, binding us together for further studies. The discussions were lively, and instead of seeking others' approval and agreeing with their opinions in order to avoid conflict, which I would do before, I began to contribute more original ideas to club discussions and my self-image began to change.

Moreover, club members began to positively influence our history classes. In contrast to the standard dull lectures, my history classes had more discussions with students willing to speak up and challenge mainstream interpretations. Even if we had different opinions, I felt more connected to my classmates when all of us would freely express our own opinions. I felt proud with a sense of belonging when I made contributions to class discussions.

Reflecting on my own development the irony is that by trying so hard to be liked, I was not being genuine to myself or others, and as a result I did not connect with my peers. It was only after I learned to speak out for myself, and contributed my own individual value to the community did I find greater acceptance. Even more valuable than acceptance was personal fulfillment.

When I was a boy, I believed that only those who worked hard to gain acceptance from others would be popular and admired. Now I realize that this has never been a binary choice. By collaborating with others I need not sacrifice my own personal exploration. From my experience, admiration from others is for those complete individuals who remain true to their values. They experience a genuine joy which those who blindly follow or comply with others never find. I feel proud to have found this kind of joy despite years of pursuing the "wrong" path.

5. 文书题目：Share an essay on any topic of your choice. It can be one you've already written, one that responds to a different prompt, or one of your own design.

任选主题写一篇短文。它可以是一篇你过去所写的文书，文书题目不限，也可自行构思。

范文作者：奥特曼，被康奈尔大学录取

"I don't think I can do it."

"Just do exactly what I did. It's not that hard."

She blushed and reluctantly picked up her bow. After grinding through a few notes, she froze while the other cellists stared at her.

Amy reminded me of myself when I first started rehearsing with an orchestra in China. Back then, I, too, was the youngest and most inexperienced, and my teacher singled me out every time. In front of my peers, I felt embarrassed. I had a hard time following instructions under harsh criticism and pressure. However, persisting made me a stronger, more determined cellist. Although I understood Amy's pain, I believed that she could improve faster by playing under pressure and insisted she go on, "Amy, try again."

As I pointed to the measure, she broke into tears.

"Amy, you feeling okay?"

She wouldn't look at me.

"Amy, do you need a break?" I offered her a few tissues, but she refused. Instead she turned around and sobbed.

I had no idea what to do. When Amy's mother arrived, I repeatedly apologized, but she told me not to worry. Why did this strict method, which helped me improve, not work for her? I thought it was fine to teach the way I was taught. But, I felt awful; flashes of Amy's tears haunted me. I knew I had taken something from her. What if her passion and love for music were gone because of me? I couldn't allow that. I had volunteered to inspire young musicians.

When I encounter problems, my first resource is my companions, so I observed my cellist friend Ethan's tutoring session. I noticed he frequently encouraged his student, James. Although from my perspective, James needed to add left-hand shifts, Ethan perfectly imitated James's style and told him he could play just like him with a little practice. I thought Ethan needed to show James a better way, but I saw a developing enthusiasm on James' face. Isn't this what I wanted for my students? I decided to try something different with my next student.

"Hey Paul, want to work on this part of The Happy Farmer a little more?"

He nodded nervously.

As I started to correct his mistakes, he looked at me with the same emptiness Amy had. I thought of James' delight and knew it was time to change.

"Can you show me what you did before?"

Awkwardly, Paul played again.

"Paul, I love your enthusiasm! Your fingerings were perfect; you just need to adjust your bowing a little." Using his fingerings, I made a few demonstrations, "If you start with up bow here and end with down bow like I showed you, you'll sound even better. You're doing great!"

Tentatively, he played the same line again. After he made the adjustments and practiced a few more times, he looked at me and shouted, "I got it! I think I finally got it!" With immense pride, he performed the Happy Farmer which had once been his biggest fear. Finally I could see in him, an enthusiastic cellist truly connected to his instrument.

Since then, I always keep a copy of The Happy Farmer with me. It's a reminder to balance earnestness and flexibility. There are other reminders too.

Now, others are more willing to come to me not only for cello help but also for math and history and even emotional dilemmas. Recently, a friend asked what carrying an easy piece like The Happy Farmer could possibly teach me. "A lot," I smiled. " An open mind, and a simple touch of heart."

范文作者：Jerry，被康奈尔大学录取

In the rattling noises of screws, I, still a 5-year-old boy, saw the interior structure of the piano when the instrument was being tuned. Despite its simple exterior look, the interior was intricately organized with strings, hammers and a large sound board. Immediately, I asked why it was designed in this way and how those complex structures could produce sound. I was only told that I would learn those things when I took physics lessons later. It was the first time I confirmed that there is a way to explain how the world works, a magical possibility still captures my imagination.

The question of sound production no longer confused me after I learned basic science in Grade 1. But more and more questions began to fill my head. What does matter consist of? Why can fields of one mass project force on another substance? How does the universe work? They drove me to read some sophisticated reports in magazines and books.

But those complex things were just too hard for me to understand. The theory of relativity broke my view of time and space; quantum mechanics was just like spells from the future; and the scientists kept releasing new theories and arguments, making me even more confused. (Even the theory that actually sounded like a musical instrument, string theory, baffled me, though I thought that I might be able to understand it like a piano score at first.) The confusion brought a sense of failure, which strangely made me even more anxious and curious. I wanted to discover the world's ultimate secrets. Gradually, I came to view physics as the most important subject in the world because by developing basic theories, we can design new machines, use energy more efficiently and find more powerful energy resources, therefore improving our technology, economy, politics, and ultimately people's lives. I wanted to contribute a little to this progression. I knew it would be hard, but I like challenges, and I want the answers for the world's wonders.

However, the young boy was just like a piano player without discipline. I read A Brief History of Time, but could not understand the most complicated part. I vainly spent many hours on something I could not handle at that time, not realizing what I really needed to do.

Fortunately, I still had another subject for inspiration. My breakthrough came from the advice of my piano teacher. After one performance, he said to me, "You have some personal style, but still lack some basic skills. You will do far better if you practice more Cherny." He was right: besides imagination, it is regular practice that makes people into pianists. Imagination and practice together hone people's skills, sharpen their minds and make them pianists, physicists, engineers ...

I then improved myself by paying more attention in math and physics lessons. I practiced writing and reading to gain knowledge and express my thoughts better. I attended the FIRST Robotic Competition, the biggest and most challenging robotic competition in the world, and started my personal bridge construction project to learn to work like a professional, mastering modeling and experimenting skills. Through those activities, I gradually equipped myself with basic skills and knowledge and saw the beauty of scientific research and innovation.

In the past, I tangled with the problem of sound production; in the future, I will go further to deal with more fundamental questions. The similarity between the past and future is my desire to understand how the world works, a desire that stems from the qualities of human beings: curiosity, the instinct to survive, the ability to form and communicate complex ideas and the responsibility to help each other and contribute to our society.

Perhaps one day I can explain the deepest secrets in my piano.

5岁时，伴随着螺栓嘎吱嘎吱的声响，我看到了正在被调律的钢琴的内部构造。尽管它的外观简洁，但内部却由弦、锤子和音板组成。我立刻问调音师为什么要用这种方式设计，以及那些复杂的结构如何产生声音。直到后来在物理课上我才知道其中的奥妙。这是我第一次认识到有一种方法可以解释世界的运作方式，这神奇的可能性仍然吸引着我。

在我读完1年级的基础自然科学后，钢琴如何发声的问题不再让我感到困惑，但是越来越多的问题开始困扰我。物质到底是什么构成的？为什么物质之间可以用场互相作用？宇宙如何运作？这些驱使我阅读杂志和书籍。

但是那些复杂的事情对我来说太难理解了。相对论打破了我的时空观。量子力学就像来自未来的法术。科学家们不断发布新的理论和论据，使我更加困惑。类似的，有一个听起来像是与音乐相关的理论叫弦理论，尽管我认为一开始可能像读钢琴乐谱一样理解它，但实际上是难以理解的。这种困惑带来了失败感，但奇怪的是，我甚至更加焦虑和好奇。我想发现世界上的终极秘密。渐渐地，我开始将物理学视为世界上最重要的学科，因为我们可以应用它们来创造新的技术，更有效地利用能源，或找到更强大的能源，从而改善我们的技术、经济、政治和生活，最终改善人们的生活水平。我想为此做出一点贡献。我知道这很困难，但我喜欢挑战，我想为世界的奇迹找到答案。

但是，无知的小男孩学物理就像没有章法的钢琴演奏者。在业余时间，我读了《时间简史》，但完全看不懂最复杂的部分，因而白白浪费了很多时间来做我当时无法处理的事情，没有意识到我真正需要做的事情是什么。

幸运的是，有其他人给我带来启发。出乎意料的，钢琴老师的一句话为我找到了突破口。在一次课后，他对我说："你有一些个人风格，但仍然缺乏一些基本技能。如果练习更多的车尔尼的练习曲，你会做得更好。"他是对的、除了想象力之外，一个人需要训练基本功来成为钢琴家。想象力和实践力一起磨炼人们的技能，拓宽他们的思维，使他们成为钢琴家、物理学家、工程师等。

然后，我通过更多地关注数学和物理课程来提高自己。我练习写作和阅读以获取知识并更好地表达自己的想法。我参加了国际青少年机器人挑战赛——

世界上最大、最具挑战性的机器人竞赛，并开始了我的独立桥梁工程项目，学习如何像专业人士一样工作，掌握建模和实验技能。通过这些活动，我逐渐掌握了一些基本技能和知识，并体验到了科学研究和创新的美。

过去，我纠结于声音是如何产生的问题；将来，我将进一步处理更基本的问题。过去和未来之间的相似是我渴望了解世界的运作方式；这种渴望源于人类的特质：好奇心，生存本能，形成和传达复杂思想的能力，以及互相帮助、希望为社会做出贡献的责任感。在这样的驱动力下，也许有一天，我可以解释钢琴键盘下最深层的秘密。

范文作者：M，被纽约大学录取

“Leaning Forward” is more than just a Silicon Valley cliché.

2 years ago, standing on the shoulders of my classmate's father, unsteadily, leaning forward. Hands on the top of the wall, elongating my neck, nearly falling. Inside: a bald man sitting on a bamboo armchair, looking at this intruder with amazement.

I saw the neglected shrine of the temple standing, surrounded by weeds.

“How old are you? Why do you want to buy these books?” the shop assistant asked. Looking back, I'm not surprised: a small, skinny girl who couldn't reach the top of the cashier desk even on tiptoe. “Because ... because I want to find out our history!”

Unlike people who look ahead as soothsayers, I immerse myself in the past where many mysteries remain submerged in the river of time. Leaning into the river of history can both satisfy my curiosity and uncover hidden truths: a historical subject, like a grain of sand, represents a fragment of time.

Winter 2018. My school assigns us to write an essay on the book “Legend of the Three Kingdoms”, based on Chinese history from 220 C.E. to 280 C.E. Subsequent films have made this a “hot” topic in China. Sichuan Province was then part of the “Shu” Kingdom; now, it is a province full of historical sites and traditions. My school partner and I decided to travel to Sichuan to investigate the protection of historical spots associated with the book.

We sought out a town that claimed to have the temple that commemorated my favorite general, Zhao Yun. Because the temple was converted into a school in the 1950s, most of its buildings have been destroyed. Then during the Cultural Revolution, the statue in the audience hall was destroyed — we will never see the statue whose eyes were described as almost alive by locals. Prior to our excursion, I'd searched online and knew that the local Culture Bureau had gained 4.6 million Yuan to renovate the temple; nevertheless, the temple was still desolate except for the man's room who guarded the site from prying eyes.

We then went to Jinghui Park, just blocks from the run-down temple which had a commemorative memorial for this same general, but was open to tourists. When we got there, my sorrow had no bounds.

How long since it had been swept? Dirt and trash everywhere — broken bottles, and grime on the statues. No one cleaned, only ashes from burnt incense. Only during festivals would people come with flowers and incense; it's inhabited by ghosts awaiting notice.

No advertising campaigns, no tour-guides, no tickets except a ten-yuan entrance-fee for the Park. The chance to commemorate national heroes does not belong to the elites; every man on earth could be a carrier of the memory. So is it a kind of sacrifice? Maintaining the memorial open to the public by this slender income, while discarding the temple and leaving it in this poor condition.

Should its shabby state be preserved or restored? I ask myself when I compare the Parthenon to the Summer Palace with its renovated buildings updated to recent tastes: new pigments tourists prefer, an all too modern interpretation of the past.

We don't want cultural destruction to happen again. Should these places, desecrated during that time, be restored or left as a lesson to future generations? Or should new generations enjoy the Disney-like magical kingdoms, while forgetting or burying dark periods of history? "To articulate the past historically", Walter Benjamin once remarked, "means to seize hold of a memory as it flashes up at a moment of danger." I hope one day there will be a long-lasting balance between historical education and the commercial and ideological nature behind these restorations. I plan to devote myself to making sure both things happen in ways that will preserve culture, but also provide jobs and income for thousands. I will always lean forward, unafraid to fall.

范文作者：邵文奕，被埃默里大学录取

The hours at the airport were long and exhausting. After a fourteen-hour flight, my body ached. I longed for a soft bed. But there was no bed, only hard, steel benches. It was freezing. I knew the ads in TV played in order, for I heard the words "Shanghai" and "London" in the same tone many times, and each time they grew more annoying.

I was the only passenger at the gate. The jet lag confused my circadian cycle. As a result, my body struggled to remain energetic, while there wasn't much energy left. I couldn't rest or concentrate, and there was still eight hours till my departure. Eventually I decided to sit up. Staring at the spotless French windows, I saw a desperate girl cringing in a thin, teal blanket.

Suddenly a thought occurred to me. What if I could view this whole experience as part of the long movie I've been watching the past seventeen years? My spirit was somehow lifted up. I always felt that life is like watching a movie, with some repeating plots, and the rest continuously changing. The setting is my surrounding and the camera is my eyes. Mostly, I watch; sometimes, I'm the actor in the scenes. Now, what did I see? I saw lines of benches surrounding the TV in the middle of the gate. Outside, several planes stood motionlessly. The only other person here was a dustman vacuuming the carpets. What did I hear? I heard the vacuuming and the TV, of course, and sharp noises from the air conditioner.

Wondering what the airport terminal was like at three o'clock in the morning, I gathered my belongings and started walking. The walkways, usually crowded by people, had not a single soul in sight. I almost felt like the last human being walking amongst the remnants of human civilization. Costly perfume and leather bags sat silently in the flickering light of glass cases, and water dripped slowly from the restrooms blocked by cleaning carts. Only the escalator leading to the Skytrain worked, reminding me that I wasn't alone.

But was I? What if, as I was walking, I entered a parallel universe of another dimension, where I actually became the last human on earth? The thought scared me. So many times I read about the end of world and the consequent question: what would one do if he/she were among the very last humans? While most people may choose to seek mundane pleasure, I would strive to preserve something for humanity. In this way, I could extend the civilization beyond its creator, and more importantly, to share the thoughts with the species — whatever it would be — that discovers the remnants of ours.

It's all about the mind. Preserving would be the last move I know to seek for understanding. So long as two thoughts resonate, the two minds connect. Then, they fuse, sublime, and mingle with more minds.

I have been living my life as if I were watching a long movie, but I am not only an observer. The things I see and hear turn into miscellaneous material as I write my stories. I always enjoyed writing, yet I never realized why. Now I do. When my stories receive an audience, their minds and mine are weaved into one. This resonance was what attracted me all along.

Immersed in thoughts, I roamed near the security checkpoint unawares. There, I finally saw another passenger staying overnight. Wrapped in a thick blanket, he was lying comfortably in one of the long sofas. The 7-Eleven ten meters away was selling blankets! I almost wanted to throw my arms into the air, but finally decided not to. There is a camera above my head. I didn't want to look weird.

第二节

美国加州大学辅文书鉴赏

1. 文书题目：**Describe an example of your leadership experience in which you have positively influenced others, helped resolve disputes or contributed to group efforts over time.**

描述你的领导经历，期间你是如何积极影响他人，帮助解决问题，并为团队做出贡献的。

范文作者：Frank，被加州大学洛杉矶分校录取

For me, exploring mathematics has never been a solidary experience. Ever since gifted classes in primary school, there have been bright and enthusiastic friends around me. Admittedly, figuring out a problem is a pleasure in itself. But it is the sharing afterwards that makes ideas spark and makes the process exhilarating. Knowing that there are people who have gone before me and who are working beside me is what makes me fearless in the uncertain process of discovering new knowledge.

However, not many people appreciate mathematics nowadays. Many students dropped out of mathematics altogether when it was no longer compulsory. I wanted to support anyone who was struggling and show them that math can be elegant and fun. That's why I started a peer-run math club in year 10.

Getting the momentum started was not easy. I recruited some high-achieving students, put up posters around the campus, and advertised the club in assembly. The first session was an absolute nightmare — no one showed up. Then the second session in the same week was the exact opposite — nearly thirty students came, filling up the whole classroom. Ever since then, there has been consistent attendance.

The club has grown throughout the three-year period. Now, I have gathered more than ten tutors rostering four days a week and students can even book appointments. It has evolved to a stage where the club will continue as a legacy when I graduate.

Apart from helping others with mathematics, the most important aspect is recognizing the benefits of collaborative problem solving. I have received comments such as "that makes so much sense, you explained it better than my teacher", which always inspires me. I also try to innovate by putting up mathematical puzzles on the board. What the club does influences students' perceptions surrounding mathematics and brings out the best in them. Hopefully it provides the confidence for them to pursue further in the subject, just like the way my fellow mathematicians provide me with the necessary motivation.

I hope to inspire. But the pragmatic goal is to promote the true foundation of knowledge — mathematics.

范文作者：Bambi，被加州大学伯克利分校录取

Things to consider: A leadership role can mean more than just a title. It can mean being a mentor to others, acting as the person in charge of a specific task, or a taking lead role in organizing an event or project. Think about your accomplishments and what you learned from the experience. What were your responsibilities?

Did you lead a team? How did your experience change your perspective on leading others? Did you help to resolve an important dispute at your school, church in your community or an organization? And your leadership role doesn't necessarily have to be limited to school activities. For example, do you help out or take care of your family?

Leadership.

"What is leadership? Can you show it in a picture?" I gathered my students around me and threw these questions out there. Twenty minutes later, I watched them pasting their work on the blackboard. One group portrayed Harry Potter. Another group sketched Barack Obama. "Interesting answers," I thought, "what feedback should I give them?"

Serving for two weeks as a teaching assistant for Student Global Leadership Institute program in India, I led eighteen high school sophomores, six from the U.S. and twelve Hyderabad locals, to explore Hyderabad and generate ideas for a future projects in their communities. What new insights into leadership would my students gain? Pondering the students' answers, I reexamined these questions myself.

From the very beginning, it was a culture shock for all of us. On our first day the two groups met, my students were paralyzed by the huge cultural gap, too nervous about offending or embarrassing each other to reach out. That awkward silence lasted for minutes, until I asked: "Anyone up for some Bollywood dance?" More than ten pairs of hands were waving in the air, and an Indian boy volunteered to teach. Soon heated conversations started off, covering topics from Hindi dinner table rituals to Beyoncé's hit songs. This is wonderful.

Standing outside the boundaries of Indian and American cultures, I was, nevertheless, a successful "third party". I organized a scavenger hunt, encouraging students proficient in English, Telugu, and Hindi to talk to local vendors and shopkeepers along the dusty alleys. Drawing on my knowledge of the Silk Road's impact in Chinese history, I invited them to visit Koti Sultan

Bazar, a market with 200 years' history, and challenged them to think about how the British Raj changed Hyderabad's local trades. Using my knowledge about Chinese herbs, I mentored a group of students interested in growing traditional Polynesian herbs to preserve ancient medications.

Now I have my answer: A leader fits in any team. As mentor for these students, instead of a dominating head, I saw myself as a communicator. I accelerated the intersection of cultures because I believe the clash of cultures sparks great ideas.

范文作者: Jerry,被加州大学洛杉矶分校录取

When my class first established a musical team to compete in the school musical contest, the whole group was unprepared. Everyone had his/her own idea and strong urge to win, but none of us actually knew what to do in the next 2 months. I, as the most seasoned musical fanon the team, thought that I could lead them, because I had watched more shows and read more musical reviews than they had. I volunteered to be the team leader for the preparation and presented my plan. I developed a timeline which listed every single task we needed to accomplish by a specific deadline. When I found nobody was qualified for the role of producer or piano accompanist, I volunteered again.

I was lucky to be accepted as the team leader. However, it was really hard to lead. The actors did not know how to act, the chorus could not sing to the keys, and even the prop production stopped for days due to their inexperience. I had to provide stage movement and directions of each performer and help the stage crew to build props. I also slightly changed some people's tasks according to their needs and the necessary team balance. Some people complained that their work was too 'unnoticed' and 'trivial', while the others found the heavy workload stressful.

I needed to do something. So, after every rehearsal, I met with complaining members and had a heartfelt talk with them. I tried to understand their complaints first, and then convince them that everyone was an indispensable part of the final show, no matter if he/she was the leading role or just a stand-by script reminder. By and by, we cooperated well and each one seemed to be happy and contributing in his/her role.

During the competition, the whole cast performed as fabulously as we could imagine and we won the best drama award. The judges said we looked so professional that we surpassed other teams unquestionably. I felt content and fulfilled for working with those talented teammates and made a hit.

当我的班级第一次组建一支团队参加学校的音乐剧比赛时,整个团队都没有做好准备。每个人都有自己的想法和赢得胜利的强烈渴望,但实际上我们每个人都不知道接下来的两个月该做什么。作为团队中经验最丰富的音乐剧迷,我认为我可以带领我们团队,因为与其他人相比,我观看了更多的演出并阅读了更多的戏剧评论。我自荐成了团队的负责人,提出了我的计划并制定了一个时间表,列出了在截止日期之前我们需要完成的每一项任务。同时,我发现没有人可以胜任制片人或钢琴伴奏者,于是只能再兼任一职。

我很幸运被大家接受。但是,带领团队比我想象的困难。演员们不知道该怎么做,合唱团不能合着伴奏演唱,由于缺乏经验,道具制作也停了好几天。我不得不为每个表演者提供舞台指导,并帮助舞台剧组搭建道具。我还根据他们的需求和团队利益而改变了一些人的任务。有些人抱怨说他们的工作太“不起眼”和“琐碎”,而有一些人则认为工作压力很大。

我需要做点事。因此,在每次排练之后,我都找到对自己表现不满意的成员,并与他们进行了由衷地交谈。我试图先了解他们的抱怨,然后再说服他们,无论是主角还是候补人员,每个人都是最终演出必不可少的部分。渐渐地,我们合作得很好,每个人似乎都很高兴并做出了自己的贡献。

在比赛中,整个团队的表现异常出色,并获得了最佳戏剧奖。评委们说,我们看起来是如此专业,以至于我们毫无悬念地超越了其他团队。与这些才华横溢的队友一起工作时,我感到满足。

范文作者：LXJ，被加州大学伯克利分校录取

As a robotics enthusiast, I had been dedicated to pursuing the hobby through competitions. After entering high school, I developed a strong interest in the First Robotics Competition (FRC). Without an FRC team on campus, I, together with several other like-minded peers, decided to found one. Recruiting members and building up a united team became the first challenge. We finally formed a team composed of three groups: the business group, the mechanics group and the programming group.

In order to achieve the final robotics design, the three groups needed to collaborate throughout the whole preparation process. The business group needed to keep in contact with the mechanics group in order to make a complete list of what materials were needed; the mechanics group needed to collaborate with the programming group in order to operate different parts of the robot. However, during competitions, we frequently experienced communication breakdowns. As leader, I took charge of coordinating the groups, monitoring our progress and pushing the project forward.

I began to enforce higher standards to ensure that everyone on the team was not only familiar with their own obligations, but also the team's overall direction. I organized quizzes to test members' knowledge of the competition rules. Some members disagreed with my strict approach but there was no denying that the project progressed more quickly and with fewer disagreements after I emerged as the leader. I have always considered myself a friendly and soft-hearted person, but I soon realized that I had the capacity to deal with criticism and to focus on my task while also helping others complete their assignments.

Leadership does not simply mean giving instructions to others. A good leader guides a team towards the final goal with ideas and inspirations and fully exploits the talents of each member. Moreover, a leader has a lasting impact on those around him when he fully demonstrates his passion and his ability to make wise decisions and interconnect team members. Through this experience I was proud to witness the positive influence I had on the robotics team, and also my own personal growth.

作为一个机器人爱好者，我经常参加机器人比赛。进入高中之后，我对国际青少年机器人挑战赛产生了浓厚的兴趣。在校内没有机器人队伍的情况下，我和其他几个志同道合的朋友决定创建，而招募队员、团队建设就成了我们遇到的第一个挑战。经过种种困难，最终，我们成立了一支由商务组、机械组、编程组组成的队伍。

为了完成最终的机器人设计，三个小组在整个比赛准备过程中要密切沟通合作来完成目标。商务组需要与机械组保持联系来确认所有需要购买的设备、材料；机械组需要与编程组保持合作来保证我们能顺利运转、操控机器人的不同部分。然而，我们在比赛中经常遇到沟通上的问题。作为团队负责人之一，我承担了协调不同小组的工作，确保团队进展顺利。

为了确保每个团队成员既了解自己小组里的职责和工作又能清楚地看到整个团队的大方向，我开始施行高标准、高要求的管理制度，例如我组织小测验来测试团队成员对比赛规则的了解程度。虽然有些成员非常反对我的管理方式，但无可争议的是在这些制度实施后整个团队进展更为顺利，并且也少了很多分歧。我常常认为自己是一个友善而心软的人，但我很快意识到我有能力面对周围的批评声，并在帮助他人的同时专注我自己的工作。

领导力不只是具有发号施令的能力，优秀的领导者能用合理的规划和创意带领一支团队实现最后的目标，并充分挖掘发挥每一个团队成员的潜能。此外，当领导者充分展现出他的工作热情和团结团队成员的能力时，周围的人会被这种影响持续感化。通过机器人比赛的这段经验，我很自豪地看到一路上自己给整个团队带来的正能量以及我个人的成长。

2. 文书题目：Every person has a creative side, and it can be expressed in many ways: problem solving, original and innovative thinking, and artistically, to name a few. Describe how you express your creative side.

每个人都有创造力，创造力可以体现在许多方面：解决问题的能力、创新思维、艺术创造，等等。请描述你是如何展示你的创造力的。

范文作者：Frank，被加州大学洛杉矶分校录取

From designers to musicians to the Queen, everyone needs a splash of mathematics in their lives. From vector multiplication to Lissajous curves to Cauchy-Schwarz inequality, these seemingly "unpractical" mathematical concepts in fact have pivotal applications in our real lives. Mathematics is essential for society and our human development, yet we often take math for granted.

In year 11, I decided to direct a short video on the theme of "our world needs math" with my film-making team. We decorated an abandoned room with blackboards and archive boxes to look like a mathematician's office. We recruited drama students to act as people from different walks of life, who all come to me, "the mathematician", for help. We planned every scene and every cheeky transition. And the plot was especially interesting to write. At the beginning, I essentially used one number — four thirds — to help making a musical beat, designing a logo, and reducing plastic usage. As the video progressed, I used increasingly complex models to answer questions such as why your friends have more friends than you do and why some websites get ranked first on Google while others end up on page 46. At the end of the video, I hoped some might even learn how to dazzle his/her secret crush with a math equation.

It was a tremendously fun project. As much as I hoped the video would entertain and inspire others, I know for sure that I was entertained and inspired creating the film. It was a great medium to communicate my passion for mathematics.

Seeing many of my friends dropping out of math classes in senior school, my prime motivation was to promote the idea that math can be cool and beautiful as well as useful. Most students do not have a positive view of mathematics, and I aimed to break that perception. I wanted to demonstrate to my peers and broader society that we need mathematics.

We entered our film into the ChooseMath Video Awards competition, organized by Australian Mathematical Sciences Institute. Out of over 2000 entries, our video stood out and won the award.

范文作者: Bambi, 被加州大学伯克利分校录取

"Why are you staring at the ground again?" Mom never understands why ten-year-old me loves squatting to observe bugs. "Never mind," I tell myself, "adults have no idea of my magic."

Zoom in, then out. That's my trick, my creative skill. See that beetle crawling along the blade of grass? Zooming in, I imagine I'm its size and the beetle becomes king of his kind. Zooming out: my mind speeds free from gravity and into space. Amidst the grand universe, I feel I'm in the middle of nowhere. But there's beauty in this empty wholeness, or "Kong" as Chinese philosopher Laozi called it, which incorporates the immensely big and infinitely small.

As I've grown up, my "zooming" magic faded into memories. I relinquished my magic and chose to decipher the world's wonders with science.

Last year, I won a plant physiology research opportunity in Peking University. I investigated i the biomechanics of cucumber plant's spring-like tendrils to see why they twist and climb. Kneeling in a muddy plot, I harvested tendrils of different lengths. Then I witnessed the green tendrils turn pale after being submerged in a chemical bath of dimethylbenzene. After purifying the dehydrated samples in bubbling half-liquid-half-gas carbon dioxide, I finally put them under the scanning electron microscope.

The black-and-white images on the computer screen astonished me. A world invisible to human eyes revealed itself. Fluffy tendrils became thorny tentacles, as terrifying as the giant octopus that haunted the Nautilus. Stomata (air holes) looked like the wide-open blowhole of Moby Dick. Cells formed a dense surface, just like Robinson Crusoe's stone fort, protecting cells from being disturbed.

Science revealed a world more magical than fiction. It reactivated my childhood magic. Zooming-in, I visualize the recombining double-helix DNA behind cucumber tendrils. Zooming-out, I think of how, as Darwinians argued, gene mutation makes natural selection possible. These tendrils, though teeny-tiny, epitomize nature's flawed failures and heroic victories.

Chinese philosopher Zhuangzi described people's attempt to look into the universe as "the very small trying to comprehend the very large." I'm eager to explore the world whether it's with microscopes or creative imagination.

范文作者：LXJ，被加州大学伯克利分校录取

To me, creativity means approaching problems from a new perspective and breaking with conventional thinking when necessary. When I was in the Model United Nations club, I was responsible for the organization of club activities at the annual Arts Festival. Previously the club organized Q&A games, which were easy to prepare but elicited little enthusiasm. I designed a new role-playing game, which allowed players to act as historical figures and make decisions based on different historical scenarios. The feedback was great: the game was so popular that there was a long queue at the club stall during the Festival. Through breaking obsolete "traditions" and showing creativity at the Arts Festival, I was able to turn my ideas and interests into a fun, interactive game, and increased student awareness of the MUN club.

I try to be creative in my approach to everyday life. For example, I used to feel very stressed before exams. I tried to review all the material, but my anxiety would often prevent me from being able to focus. My solution was to alternate between building models and test preparation. This allowed me to take a step back from the grind of studying and relax my mind. Building models the day before a test may be an odd way to prepare, but it did calm me. Once my anxiety were relieved, I was able to study more efficiently and I approached the upcoming test with more confidence.

Being creative in the service of others is also gratifying. My grandfather takes care of a persimmon tree in the yard of my home. Due to health issues he cannot climb trees. To help my grandfather pick the persimmons I devised a contraption using a long pole and discarded soda cans. It lets my grandfather pick fruit more conveniently with less effort.

Combining information from a variety of sources, academic disciplines and personal experience is the heart of creativity. My ideas may not always appear to be breakthroughs, but the process of reflecting and refining of ideas helps to build the foundation from which all great ideas originate.

对我来说，创造力意味着在必要时打破常规、从全新的角度思考和解决问题。当我在模拟联合国社团时，我参与组织社团在年度艺术节时的摊位活动。之前社团经常组织快问快答系列活动，这种活动易于组织和准备，但缺乏新意。我设计了一种全新的角色模拟游戏：玩家扮演不同的历史人物并在不同的历史场景中作出选择和决策，最终解决历史危机顺利通关。玩家们的反响很热烈，我们的摊位在艺术节当天很快就排起了长队。在艺术节活动的组织策划中通过打破传统思维，我把我的创意和兴趣融入了一个有趣、互动性强的历史游戏中，并提高了社团在学校里的声望。

我在日常生活中也充分展现、活用创造力。例如，考试前我常常会非常紧张，翻来覆去地复习相关资料，但焦虑会使得我难以集中注意力。这时候，我会交替着复习考试、搭建模型，这使得我从紧张学习中暂时脱身并放松身心。在考试前一天搭建模型或许是一种奇怪的备考方式，但它能抚平我的心智，一旦焦虑得以缓解，我就能更高效地学习并以更自信的状态迎考。

用自己的创造力来帮助他人给我带来很多成就感。我爷爷在院子里养了一棵柿子树，但因为身体原因他爬不了树。为了帮他采集柿子，我用长竹竿和废弃汽水罐做了一个勾引装置，使他能轻松地摘果子。

融合不同的想法、学术领域或是个人经历是创意创新的核心。我的想法不一定是最有突破性的，但思考和精炼想法的过程是所有伟大发现的基石。

3. 文书题目：Describe the most significant challenge you have faced and the steps you have taken to overcome this challenge. How has this challenge affected your academic achievement?

描述你遇到过的最大挑战，以及为克服这一挑战所采取的措施。你是如何战胜挑战的？这一挑战对你的学业有何积极影响。

范文作者：Jerry，被加州大学洛杉矶分校录取

In Grade 10, I found a professor in Tong Ji University as my adviser on a bridge engineering project. This was my first time to conduct a research, and it turned out to be the most difficult academic task I have ever encountered.

First I spent a couple of days brainstorming some research topics. However, they were mostly rejected by the professor because they seemed too difficult for a high school student (such as the vacuum tube transportation). The professor suggested I focus on some easier ones. I browsed websites and newspapers and found that a bridge in Shanghai had almost been destroyed by flooding rain water. I decided to research a flood-resistant bridge. The professor gave green light to this topic.

But the more difficult part was yet to come. I had never taken bridge engineering courses before, therefore I did not know what type of model I should experiment on. I began to look for external help. I was lucky to find that a graduate student in the bridge engineering department had enough know-how to help me out. He helped me to choose one type from 3D design, wooden and paper models and taught me how to make them. I chose the wooden model and with wood, glue and knives, I built two models, on which I could test if they could resist the flooding.

Over the next 2 months, I conducted experiments, perfected the models in my high school lab and discussed data analysis with the professor. I made a lot of mistakes at first in data analysis, but I gradually collected enough reliable data and finished an essay describing the whole research process and results.

Through this project, I not only learned research skills, but also experienced the spirit of scientific research. I came to know that to learn something totally new is not as daunting as I thought. I also learned that I needed to exploit every resource I could find to achieve the result. I believe that I am now more prepared for my college research with my new learning through this challenging project.

在10年级时，我找到了同济大学的一位教授作为桥梁工程项目的顾问。这是我第一次进行学术研究，也是我遇到过的最困难的学术任务。

首先，我花了几天的时间进行头脑风暴，寻找一些可以研究的主题。但是，它们大多遭到了教授的拒绝，因为其中很多对高中生来说似乎太困难了(如真空管运输)。教授建议我专注于一些简单的事情。我浏览了网站和阅读了报纸，发现上海的一座桥曾经被暴雨形成的洪水淹没，险些被冲断。我决定研究一座防洪桥梁。教授听后认为这个题目很适合高中生。

但是，更困难的部分尚未到来。我以前从未学习过桥梁工程课程，因此我不知道应该尝试哪种类型的模型。我开始寻求外部帮助。我很幸运地发现桥梁工程系的一名研究生有足够的专业知识可以帮助我。他帮助我进行3D设计，木制和纸质模型中的选择，并教我如何制作它们。我选择了木制模型，并用木头、胶水和刀子制作了两个模型，可以在上面测试它们是否可以抵抗洪水。

在接下来的两个月中，我投入实验中，在高中实验室中完善了模型，并与教授讨论了数据。一开始我在数据分析中犯了很多错误，但是我逐渐收集了可靠的数据，并完成了一篇描述整个研究过程和结果的论文。

通过这个项目，我不仅学习了研究技能，而且还体验了科学研究的精神。我知道，学习全新的东西并不像我想的那么艰巨。我还认识到，我需要利用我能找到的所有资源来实现结果。我相信通过这个具有挑战性的项目，我将获得新的学习机会，从而为大学的研究做好准备。

4. 文书题目：Think about an academic subject that inspires you. Describe how you have furthered this interest inside and/or outside of the classroom.

描述你最喜欢的学科，描述你是如何在课内外发展这一兴趣的。

范文作者：Frank，被加州大学洛杉矶分校录取

Mathematics is beautiful.

Most people don’t agree. But it is.

I’ve been obsessed with mathematics and have pursued my passion ever since primary school. I learned to appreciate the subject by seeing the intricate connections between different mathematical concepts at work. After the muddy complications of very high-level mathematics, the result is often simple and elegant. When I worked out the general formula for the maximum number of pieces that can be obtained from x n-dimensional spaces cutting a n+1-dimensional space, I sat there in disbelief. I could not imagine that a month of work came down to one line of equation. Yet it was magically real, as if the equation itself was waving its hand at me, saying “glad you found me.”

These kinds of Eureka moments, big or small, happen all the time. One night at the Math Olympiad Selection Camp, we were all sitting in a classroom for a “relaxing” lecture. An hour later, we were on our feet, jumping up and down with excitement. It was about Wythoff’s Game that connects with a special “golden string” sequence, which also connects with Fibonacci numbers, the golden ratio, and Lindenmayer systems. What could be better than that!

To explore its elegant beauty, mathematics extends far beyond any classroom. With three years of Olympiad training, Melbourne University enrichment classes, national and international competitions, I have equipped myself with many creative problem-solving tools. I won "Best in State" and was one of four students who won a medal in the Australian Mathematics Competition. I won a Silver in the Australian Mathematical Olympiad and was selected as one of fourteen top mathematicians in Australia to participate in the Olympiad Selection Camp.

Beyond that, I also want to show everyone the beauty of mathematics. That's why I started a math club in school and made an award-winning short film called "the Mathematician".

These experiences have always satisfied my curiosity, my creativity, and my passion. But they are merely the beginning. I am sure that there are innumerable sequences of advanced mathematics that I can begin to tackle throughout my life.

范文作者：Bambi，被加州大学伯克利分校录取

Language is about culture. Culture is about identity. Languages convey messages beyond phonemes, alphabets or ideograms, even if the medium is the message — and this is what attracts me to Linguistics.

Communication. I love challenging myself to communicate, even when there's a difference in language. During my summer program, in a local market in Hyderabad, India, I drew with a twig in the sand, bargaining with a vendor who spoke Telugu. We locked eyes and he nodded. "Deal!" I yelled, and he shouted something in Telugu simultaneously. We looked at each other, the language barrier forgotten. We smiled — deal done. Communication works, with a bit of guessing, an understanding of linguistic patterns, and, most importantly, a curious and open mind.

Culture. I'm eager to help others recognize their cultural background through language. Rapping in Sichuan dialect, I give my audience a taste of the fun of folk culture. Using phonology theories in linguistics, I realized that it's the special syllabification in Sichuan dialect that makes rhyming easy, contrary to Mandarin's frequent ambisyllabicity. I encourage younger students to communicate with grandparents who speak in dialects that are gradually being replaced by Mandarin. Hopefully, these students would rediscover their culture as they chat with their "gaga" and "gagong" ("grandma" and "grandpa" in Sichuan dialect).

Identity. I'm part of Manchu, a Chinese minority group, yet I rarely defined myself as Manchu until I began to self-study its language. Awkwardly holding my pen to practice writing the Manchu alphabet, I connected to my ancestors from the tenuous and curving strokes of Manchu words. The excitement of perfecting the sweeping curve of "abka," the Manchu word for "sky" and the name of the sky deity, inspired me to preserve this endangered language. I also learned to find my place in contemporary Chinese-dominated society. When I compared Manchu oral history gathered in memoirs and records in Old Manchu Archive with the high school textbook version, I realized how a revisionist history has deprived the young Manchu generation of our identities.

Linguistics lets me see how people's backgrounds shape their words, and how words shape their minds.

范文作者：LXJ，被加州大学伯克利分校录取

I have long been fascinated by the study of mathematics. Through the study of elementary number theory, I learn to quickly find underlying patterns behind figures and equations; through the study of deductive reasoning in geometry, I enhanced my logical reasoning and insights into complicated questions. The subject greatly influences my way of thinking, and inspires me to apply mathematical reasoning to other academic disciplines and to commercial interests.

I am an avid learner and have challenged myself by taking the highest level math courses in my high school. I have also demonstrated dedication to math by going beyond the assigned class readings and proactively furthering my knowledge of the subject. On my own, I have read many math books, such as Proofs from the Book, by Martin Aigner, and have studied Number Theory, including Fermat's Last Theorem. More than just proving the theorem itself, mathematicians discovered many important Number Theory concepts like ideal number and built connections between some previously unrelated fields of study. I had always taken it for granted that the aim of studying mathematics was to find a "solution" to a problem, but through the study of Fermat's Last Theorem, I realize that the essence of mathematics lay in the process of thinking and making new discoveries. Mathematics inspires me to focus on the process of problem solving and ways of thinking rather than just on the final result.

In addition to learning theoretical knowledge, I took an active part in applying math knowledge through math modeling contests. Building math models enabled me to apply my mathematical knowledge and way of thinking to real-life situations. This brought me a sense of achievement, since I was able to see the tangible changes created in the process, and led me to want to work in applied fields as a future career goal. During the modeling process, I was excited to find a close connection between mathematics and other fields of study, like economics and computer science. It is mathematics that opened my eyes and inspires me to use interdisciplinary methods to solve real-life problems.

一直以来我对数学都很感兴趣。通过学习数论，我能快速了解数字和公式背后的规律和奥秘；通过学习平面和解析几何，我掌握了进行严密演绎推理和洞察困难问题的能力。数学这门学科极大地影响了我的思维方式，并启发我在别的学术领域和兴趣爱好中运用数学收获的逻辑推理能力。

我是个充满热情的学生，并不断通过挑战学校里最难的数学课来提高自己。此外，我在课外也积极深化我对这门学科的认识。我自行阅读了许多课外数学书籍，如马丁·艾格纳的《数学天书中的证明》，并从中学习了很多数论相关的内容（如费马大定理的证明历程）。在试图证明这个定理的过程中，数学家们发现了许多额外的数论领域的重要成果，如理想数的概念，并建立了数论与其他数学领域间的联系。我过去一直认为数学学习的目标是找到一个问题的解，但透过这个故事我意识到数学的本质在于思维和发现的过程。数学这门学科激发我关注解题的过程、思维方式，而非只关注最终结果。

除了学习理论知识，我还在数学建模竞赛中运用学到的数学知识。数学建模的过程使得我有机会在现实世界的问题中发挥数学思维和能力，建模过程中显著可见的突破和进展也给我带来一种成就感，并使我有了未来在应用领域工作的想法。在建模过程中，我非常兴奋地发现数学和不少其他学科之间的联系，如经济学、计算机科学。总体来说，数学开阔我的眼界，并激发我去用一种跨学科的思维解决现实世界中的问题。

范文作者：Jerry，被加州大学洛杉矶分校录取

I am most passionate about physics, especially astrophysics. Physics aims at explaining how the world works and is fundamental for other subjects, like chemistry and engineering. Astrophysics specifically focuses on celestial bodies' features and motion. I want to explore the world's ultimate secrets to satisfy my own curiosity and help improve scientific research.

When I was still in kindergarten, I asked the adults why my piano could produce sound. One year later, I found the answer from junior science lessons in primary school. The textbook introduced the definition of force, explained sound production and unveiled the relation of force and motion. I got to know when the hammers in my piano hit the strings, the strings vibrated and spread sound waves in the air, which is the medium. When I finished junior middle school, I could already understand simple general daily life scenes with knowledge of traditional physics theories.

After entering high school, I read a lot of scientific magazines and online articles written by various researchers. I got to know that in the previous century, Einstein proved Newton's mistakes and established new theories with other physicists. Decades later, today's researchers go on to perfect their theories and models and meditate what they should do next. Physics welcomes a revolution all the time. I am eager to join the crusade to discover the truth. Furthermore, the mysterious stars, planets and black holes captured my mind; I became even more determined to study astrophysics.

Physics shows me that there is a way to understand the world, presents me infinite possibilities for improvement, and inspires me to pursue scientific research in the future. It shapes me into a curious person with a flexible mind. I would like to follow my curiosity to discover the unknown. I believe in science and hope that I can climb on the shoulders of past researchers to approach the ultimate secrets inside the stars and my piano. In physics I have found a lifetime goal.

我对物理学,特别是对天体物理学非常感兴趣。物理学的目的是解释世界如何运转,并且是化学和工程学等其他学科的基础。天体物理学着重关注天体的特征和运动,我想探索世界的终极秘密,以满足自己的好奇心,帮助推进科学研究。

当我还在幼儿园时,我问大人们为什么我的钢琴可以发出那样的声音。几年后,我从小学的科学课中找到了答案。教科书介绍了力的定义,解释了声音的产生,并揭示了力与运动的关系。我知道了当钢琴中的锤子敲击琴弦时,琴弦振动并在空气中传播声波,空气则是声音传播的介质。当我读初中时,我已经可以利用传统物理学理论知识来理解简单的日常生活场景。

进入高中后,我阅读了许多研究人员撰写的文书,知道了在20世纪,爱因斯坦证明了牛顿的错误理论,并与其他物理学家建立了新的理论。几十年后,今天的研究人员继续完善他们的理论和模型,并思考下一步该做什么。物理学一直在恭候一场革命。我渴望参加科学的征途,以发现真相。此外,神秘的恒星、行星和黑洞吸引了我的注意力。我下定决心要学习天体物理学。

物理学向我展示了一种了解世界的方式,为我提供了无限的探索目标,并激发了我从事未来的科学研究。它使我变成一个头脑灵活且富有好奇心的人。我想跟随我的兴趣去发现未知的事物。我坚信科学，并希望我能站在前辈研究人员的肩膀上，探索大到恒星，小到钢琴内部的终极秘密。在物理学中，我找到了可以奋斗终生的目标。

5. 文书题目：What have you done to make your school or your community a better place?

请描述你做过的使你的学校或社区变得更好的事情。

范文作者：Frank，被加州大学洛杉矶分校录取

“We’re in that moment in history where we desperately need inclusion to be a verb，not a value；to act，not to hesitate；to reach out，and not to retreat.”

Hearing this at the 2019 Special Olympics World Games opening ceremony was not only an inspiration，but also a reflection of my own experiences.

Coming from a Chinese background and having to merge into the Australian culture wasn’t easy. That’s why I can appreciate the value and necessity of inclusion. With this firm belief in mind，I started a Global Citizen Committee in my school.

The committee organises different cultural events to celebrate diverse festivals around the world. Our projects ranged from Eid al-fitr to Day of the Dead to Chinese Moon Festival. We organised movie nights，theme dinners，and even a cultural trip to China，all in the hope that through understanding and appreciation we can also accept other cultures.

Ever since the committee’s founding，we’ve received positive responses and support. Just like the name suggests，our committee body consists of global citizens from a wide array of backgrounds. And working in such a diverse group was an enlightening experience，as there’re so many ideas floating around — traditions that I wasn’t familiar with but nonetheless grew fond of. Whilst our hope was to promote inclusivity in the school, I, too, learned invaluable lessons from other members.

But of course, inclusion isn't just about different races and cultures, it extends to the whole of humanity. That's why I volunteered in Special Olympics and made two promotional films for them.

At first, intellectual disability was a fuzzy concept to me. I had no concrete comprehension of what it encompassed. Meeting the athletes was therefore an incredibly empowering experience. They were resilient, determined, and unstoppable. In many ways, they are not different from us. And in some ways, their innocence and purity are far more human than most of us.

By cheering them on in the bleachers and by embracing their identity, we have demonstrated inclusion at work.

The arc of history bends towards justice, and so, too, it bends towards inclusion.

范文作者：Bambi，被加州大学伯克利分校录取

6:50 A.M., bathed in sunlight, I water cucumbers, pumpkins, and beans in the school vegetable garden. Whenever I feel stressed, the beautiful creatures here — busy bumblebees, alighted sparrows, and a sleeping white cat — help me meditate. My hands produce food, and my mind composes poetry. But this little garden isn't just my Utopia. It's also my portal to connect with people and build a community.

Once a biology teacher dropped by and asked for some of my bean pods to use in her experiments. Together, we squatted in my patch and discussed how seeds pop out of pods when they mature. Eager to learn more, I enrolled in her course during spring semester. Early in April, I practiced anatomizing strawberry flowers and lily buds she brought to class. Looking at their cellular structure under a microscope, I learned to observe nature through science.

I met a school janitor who lives in a shed near my garden. He grows green onions in little flowerpots around his shed. Seeing me cultivating our school's long-abandoned vegetable garden, he was surprised and happy. From him, I learned tricks to save water and make most out of the limited space. Though having a hard time understanding his dialect, I enjoyed listening when he talks about how he left his vegetable garden in his village for a better life in Beijing but now misses his happy old days.

Now, we three often work together. We pull weeds, water vegetables and worry about the upcoming rainstorm. When we're working, my biology teacher looks for every subtle change in the leaves' colors, while the janitor laughs and brags about the high-quality vegetables grown in his hometown. I engage in one of my favorite activities, composing poems: eulogies singing the lost beauty of nature and encomiums about three human beings bringing nature back to life among twenty million people dwelling in Beijing.

The garden nourishes our bodies and souls. We belong to a community that allows us to share what we produce with others, whether it's vegetables, poems, or science.

范文作者：Jerry，被加州大学洛杉矶分校录取

In my country, the National University Entrance Examinations (Gaokao) are the only way students' academic abilities are evaluated to decide which university he/she is qualified for. Most teachers and students, therefore, only focus on test scores. Even in my school, which emphasizes the spirit of scientific research and the importance of extracurricular activities, students are usually unwilling to spend a lot of time in clubs.

As a member of my school's robotics team, a teen researcher in the labs and the Chief Negotiation Officer of a charity organization, I participated in many events with my friends to promote the benefits of extracurricular involvement. For instance, we held public presentations on our campus and at other schools to advertise the robotics competitions held by FIRST (a robotics competition organization) so that more teenagers would learn to work like engineers; I talked with younger students about my personal bridge engineering projects to encourage them to participate in research like scientists; and I passed on my position in the charity group to new students and instructed them on how to raise funds. Many of the students we spoke to started to work on their interests, and I was able to help some of them in their efforts. I gave lessons on tool usage and management in the robotics team and shared my ideas with teen researchers on project topic selection. I use my knowledge and experience to assist upcoming students so that they can learn more quickly.

I believe that if those young people attend different activities, they can develop their leadership, research and presentation skills, as well as other abilities and the experience of working as a member of a team. This would enable them to identify and pursue their interests and to develop more holistically.

In all, I hope that more students in my country can realize that their lives are not only about exams, but can also be fun by getting involved in activities that will shape them into more well-rounded people and unfold more possibilities for their future. Thus, I will continue spreading the message to help my peer students.

在我国,标化考试是评估学生学术能力以决定他获得大学入学资格的主要指标。因此,大多数师生只关注考试成绩。即使在学校强调科研精神和课外活动重要性的情况下,学生通常也不愿在社团活动花费很多时间。

作为学校机器人团队的成员,实验室的青少年研究员以及一家慈善组织的首席谈判官,我与朋友们参加了许多活动,以推广参与课外活动的好处。例如,我们在自己的校园和其他学校举行了公开演讲,宣传国际青少年机器人挑战赛,以便更多的青少年像工程师一样学习工作;我与低年级的学生讨论我的个人桥梁工程项目,以鼓励他们像科学家一样参加研究。我将自己在慈善团体中的经验传授给了新生,并指导他们如何筹集资金。我们与之交谈的许多学生开始致力于他们的项目，我能够帮助其中的一些人。我在机器人团队中提供了有关工具使用和管理的课程，并与青少年研究人员就项目主题选择分享了我的想法。我利用自己的知识和经验来协助即将到来的学生，使他们可以更快地学习、进步。

我相信，如果这些年轻人参加各种各样的活动，他们可以锻炼自己的领导才能，提升演讲技巧，以及其他能力，获得团队协作经验。这将使他们能够确定和追求自己的发展方向，并全面发展自己的能力。

总而言之，我希望更多的学生能够意识到他们的生活不仅与考试有关，还可以通过参与各种活动使他们变得更全面，并为他们的未来展现更多的可能性和趣味性。因此，我将继续用自己的经历来帮助我身边的同学们。

范文作者：LXJ，被加州大学伯克利分校录取

My concern for the mentally handicapped originated from my participation in unified sports. Before interacting with them, I was just like everyone else in the society, filled with antipathy or fear towards disabled people. I was paired with handicapped students during practices of the “three-legged race”. I gradually came to recognize them as individuals and better understood their unique challenges. Their goals and ambitions in life were similar to mine and their competitiveness impressed me. After this experience, I was determined to help them be embraced by our society and live a normal life.

Shortly thereafter, I volunteered as a helper for the Special Olympics in Austria. Working at the information booth, I realized that I served not only as a reliable source of information, but also a patient listener and instructor that brought hope and encouragement to the athletes. I could feel a genuine sense of happiness and pride through their gratitude and innocent smiles even when I performed a small favor. I surprisingly found that my dedication to encourage and help others changed me, as well. I have always considered myself to be shy and introverted. This self-image discouraged me from displaying myself with full confidence. However, when I was with the athletes I discovered that I do have the power to affect people around me when I fully engage with others. Furthermore, I noticed that the athletes recognized their own limitations but nevertheless competed with fervor and self-confidence. This spirit impressed me deeply and inspired me to learn from the athletes while at the same time helping them.

Upon my return I devoted myself to publicizing the needs of the mentally handicapped community to my friends and family. After delivering a speech in my English class, I, together with several other impressed classmates, started an initiative to give elementary classes in science and technology to students from the Pudong Special Needs Education School. When contributing my own efforts and knowledge to their community, I am excited to see my own personal growth along the way.

我对低智商人群的关注源于我参与融合运动一事。在和这些人接触之前，我和社会中的其他人一样，对残障人士充满了同情或是恐惧的心理。在练习“两人三足”运动的过程中，我和低智商学生们被分到一组。在这个过程中，我逐渐认识到他们也是社会中的一分子，并逐渐认识到他们所遇到的困难和挑战。和我一样，他们也有着自己的理想和人生追求，这种积极的人生观念打动了我。在这次经历之后，我愈发希望这个人群融入社会，过上正常人的生活。

不久以后，我在奥地利举行的残疾人奥林匹克运动会上担任志愿者，并被分配到信息中心工作。那段时间里，我意识到我不只是一个可靠的信息咨询员，更是一个耐心的倾听者和指引者，为运动员们带来希望和鼓励。即使只帮了他们一点小忙，我也能从运动员们的感谢和笑容中感受到无比的快乐和骄傲。渐渐地，我惊讶地发现我帮助他人的这份努力和投入也改变了我自己。我一直认为我是个害羞而内向的人，这种自我认知使我没有足够的信心充分表现我自己。然而，当我和运动员们在一起的时候，我发现充分的自我表现使得我有力量来感染周围的人。此外，运动员们也会意识到自己的能力界限，但仍在赛场上全力以赴，这种精神深深地感染了我，激发我在帮助他们的同时也从他们身上学到东西。

我从赛事志愿者的工作归来一直致力于向周围人宣传低智商人群的处境和需求。在英语课中我的一次介绍相关经历的演讲后，我和其他几个感兴趣的同学发起了一个在浦东特殊教育学校教授科技课程的倡议。在我向这个群体贡献自己知识的同时，我很高兴能看到我自己一路上的成长。

第三节

英国大学和学院招生服务中心文书鉴赏

文书题目: Write a personal statement that shows you'd be a great student — to persuade university and colleges to accept you on their course. Course tutors use personal statements to compare applicants, so try to make yours stand out. Remember it's the same personal statement for all courses you apply to, so avoid mentioning universities or colleges by name, and ideally choose similar subjects. If they're varied then write about common themes — like problem solving or creativity.

写一篇表明你会成为一名优秀学生的个人文书——说服大学和学院接受你的申请。当然,招生官会用文书来比较申请者,所以尽量让你的文书脱颖而出。记住,你所写的这一篇文书会用来申请你选择的所有专业,所以避免提及大学或学院的名字,并且最好选择相似的科目。如果是不同的科目,那么写一些共同的主题——比如解决问题或创造力。

范文作者: Frank,被牛津大学录取

I trace my obsession with algorithms, when, ten years ago, I squeezed into a classroom with nine not-so-typical students, all of whom survived multiple rounds of testing to be selected to the top experimental class. I distinctively remember examining patterns for points-cutting-a-line, lines-cutting-a-plane, and planes-cutting-a-space. The intricate connections between these pattern-finding problems were tantalising to my young mind.

Today, mathematics for me encompasses far more than a classroom. With three years of Olympiad training, Melbourne University enrichment classes, national and international competitions, I have equipped myself with many more creative problem-solving tools. I won “Best in State” and was one of four students in my year level who won a medal in the Australian Mathematics Competition. I won a silver in the Australian Mathematical Olympiad, and, having been selected as one of the top fourteen mathematicians in Australia, I participated in the Olympiad camp. One of my mathematical papers is submitted for publication in The Mathematical Association of NSW.

My Eureka moment came when I stumbled across the same question about planes cutting a 3D space again. Except this time, I went much further. I sought the patterns in higher dimensions and worked out formulas for 3D-spaces-cutting-a-4D-space and beyond. At first, the patterns seemed to be irregular polynomials. But my intuition was telling me that maybe those polynomials were somehow connected to combinations. Just a few days later, while investigating the circle-division combinatorial pattern using Euler's Characteristics, I was suddenly transfixed to my seat.

The circle-division pattern looked EXACTLY like the 3D-spaces-cutting-a-4D-space pattern. I worked backward and found the general combinatorial formulas for all dimensional cases. The pattern appeared to be so elegant that I just sat there in disbelief.

After pushing my way through the muddy complications of mathematics, I successfully discovered the elegance and simplicity behind it.

After my Eureka moment, I have become more committed to applying and sharing the elegant beauty of mathematics. I am doing research on AI that predicts long-term unemployment, which, unlike other automation programs that will eventually cause millions of people to become unemployed, actually helps them. My research also addresses how machine learning should be used ethically not just because "we can do it". My short film about math, which explores how some concepts like Lissajous curves, Cauchy-Schwarz inequality, and page rank vectors can be applied to our daily lives, won first place in Australia. Passing on my passion and continuing to sharpen my skills is what I plan to do when pursuing mathematics in the UK.

Apart from my passion in mathematics, I have made many contributions to the school community. I started a math club in year 10, in which I organise four sessions a week with over ten tutors and over thirty tutees. The math club has brought much-needed help for students and has promoted a positive attitude towards mathematics. Sports-wise, I am the captain for table tennis and an active player in the school soccer team. Based on my continuing participation in these activities and many more, I received Duke of Edinburgh Gold Award in 2018.

Even though I am an international student, I have studied in a UK-oriented education system for four years. And having achieved 45 on my official predicted IB score, 10/10 on my GPA, 1570 on my SAT, 800 on all three SAT subject tests, and 114 on my TOEFL, I feel fully committed and prepared for studying in the UK.

第四节
美国部分综合性大学辅文书赏析

哥伦比亚大学
Columbia University in the City of New York

范文作者：Frank，被哥伦比亚大学录取

In 150 words or fewer, please list a few words or phrases that describe your ideal college community:

请用不超过 150 词来描述你理想中的大学群体：

In an ideal college community, people would be from diverse backgrounds with different interests, values, and perspectives. Everyone would be willing to have friendly yet challenging conversations. And I can bump into strangers standing in the cafeteria line and make new friends. It would be a place where inclusion and equality are treated not as a value but as a verb.

It would be a place where frantic scribbling at midnight in Butler Library also leads to an engaging presentation. Everyone would aspire to make a positive difference — by taking a multi-disciplinary approach to apply theoretical knowledge to help our communities and the world to move forward.

But colleges should always improve. My ideal college wouldn't promise perfection. In my ideal college, I'll learn as much about "luminous details" as about grand narratives. Learning within a dynamic community will permit me to apply what I've learned throughout my life.

Please list the following (150 words or fewer for each question):

The titles of the required readings from courses during the school year or summer that you enjoyed most in the past year.

请列出以下内容(每个问题不超过 150 词):

过去一年中你最喜欢的课内或暑期必读书目。

A Doll's House by Henrik Ibsen; Medea by Euripides; Death of a Naturalist poem collection by Seamus Heaney; Othello by Shakespeare; Ethan Frome by Edith Wharton; Macbeth by Shakespeare; To Kill a Mockingbird by Harper Lee; Jasper Jones by Craig Silvey; Beowulf; Bel Canto by Ann Patchett; Lord of the Flies by William Golding; One flew over the Cuckoo's Nest by Ken Kesey; The Canterbury Tales by Geoffrey Chaucer

The titles of books read for pleasure that you enjoyed most in the past year.

过去一年中你闲暇时最爱读的书。

Our Mathematical Universe by Max Tegmark; Eleanor Oliphant is Completely Fine by Gail Honeyman; Flipped by Wendelin Van Draanen; 1984 by George Orwell; Thinking Fast and Slow by Daniel Kahneman; The Catcher in the Rye by J. D. Salinger; Sapiens: A Brief History of Humankind and Homo Deus: A Brief History of Tomorrow both by Yuval Noah Harari; Fahrenheit 451 by Ray Bradbury; All the Light We Cannot See by Anthony Doerr; Pride and Prejudice by Jane Austin; The Great Gatsby by F. Scott Fitzgerald; Silas Marner by George Eliot; Thinking in Numbers by Daniel Tammet; Animal Farm by George Orwell; Man vs. Math by Timothy Revell.

The titles of print or electronic publications you read regularly.

你经常阅读的书或电子出版物。

The Guardian; National Geographic; The Age; The Economist; Behance;

Nature Magazine; The New York Times.

And the titles of the films, concerts, shows, exhibits, lectures and other entertainments you enjoyed most in the past year.

以及过去一年中你最喜欢的电影、音乐会、表演、展览、讲座和其他娱乐活动。

Parasite; The Favourite; The Peanut Butter Falcon; ANDHADHUN; Jeux d'enfants; Paris, Je t'aime; L'accordeur; Les Revenants; Hacksaw Ridge; Shape of Water; Greenbook; Secret Superstar; Fermat's Last Theorem documentary; Black Mirror; Joker; Forever Young (WuWenXiDong); A Beautiful Mind; Darkest Hour; On the Basis of Sex; Hidden Figures; The Greatest Showman; Bohemian Rhapsody; Rocket Man; One Cut of the Dead; Avengers — End Game; Isle of Dogs; Harry Potter 1 - 7; Once Upon a Time in Hollywood.

Spartacus — the Australian Ballet; The Dawns Here are Quiet (Musical) — Chinese National Centre for the Performing Arts. National Gallery of Victoria — Terracotta Warriors & Cai Guo-Qiang/SO — IL Viewing China; Wings of Time; School Musical — Chicago; Ted Talks like “the long reach of reason”. Math channel 3Blue1Brown and Engineering channel Mark Rober on YouTube. Short films like Watch Towers of Turkey and travel videos by Sam Kolder.

Please answer the following short answer questions (300 words or fewer).

Please tell us what you value most about Columbia and why.

请回答以下简短问题(300 词)。

请告诉我们你最看重哥伦比亚大学的什么,以及为什么。

I'm attracted by Columbia's rich major options and its rigorous Core curriculum. From my experiences taking Theory of Knowledge in IB, I understand the value of discussing the philosophical limitations and implications of our knowledge. Columbia's Core curriculum would allow me to critically think and debate about the fundamental questions of our very existence — from the meaning of our lives to the structure of our societies. It would be rewarding to write a senior thesis on the relation between modern scientific discoveries and their philosophical implications to our lives. Furthermore, Columbia offers numerous interdisciplinary majors: Mathematics can be combined with statistics, economics, and computer science. I believe such an interdisciplinary approach is vital for exploring my future aspirations. I hope to join world-leading experts like Professor Goldfield and Professor Jacquet to research in analytic number theory and automorphic forms.

I'm also attracted to Columbia's commitment to community support — from First-in-Family Programs to Bias Response to Multicultural Affairs for different sexualities, nationalities, religions, and cultures. I've learned to appreciate communities that promote inclusion from my own experiences in founding the Global Citizen Committee and volunteering for the Special Olympics. I know I'll find a spot in Columbia's 350+ student groups. I can continue my filmmaking by joining Film Production or Double Exposure. I can also continue my support for people with mental health issues by joining Active Minds, or I can volunteer to improve the participation of underprivileged and underrepresented minorities in STEM by joining Sci-Inspire. I can even start my own club such as Mathematics and Filmmaking.

I also look forward to accessing New York libraries with my student ID, career support within and outside the campus, film festivals and revival houses, museums, and incomparable cuisine, such as, of course, a delicious dish of fried chicken in JJ's Place.

If you are applying to Columbia College, tell us what from your current and past experiences (either academic or personal) attracts you specifically to the field

or fields of study that you noted in the Member Questions section. If you are currently undecided, please write about any field or fields in which you may have an interest at this time.

如果你申请的是哥伦比亚学院，请告诉我们你现在和过去的经历(学术或个人经历)中有哪些影响吸引你在学术领域中做出选择。如果你目前还没有决定，请写下你可能感兴趣的领域。

I've been fascinated by mathematics ever since primary school, where I was enrolled in gifted classes. This allowed me to practice more advanced mathematics at a very early stage. I've since developed an appetite for math and a deeper appreciation for its inner elegance. I've continued to take high-level mathematics all the way through high school. I've also participated in many Math Olympiad trainings and competitions at national and international levels and won numerous awards. These experiences equipped me with many creative and rigorous problem-solving tools.

One night at the Math Olympiad Selection Camp, we were sitting in a classroom for a "relaxing" lecture. We started with a mathematical game called Wythoff's Game and investigated a rather clever winning strategy. We then looked at a special Golden String sequence, where we discovered some connections with Fibonacci numbers and Golden Ratio. In the last 5 minutes, however, all these concepts turned out to be linked in a most elegant way — the winning positions can be used to generate the Golden String, and both can be expressed through Golden Ratio. What could be better than that!? Soon, we were on our feet, jumping up and down with excitement!

Sir Andrew Wiles compares solving a mathematical conundrum to walking down a path to explore a garden, designed by the great landscape architect Capability Brown. And "the real thrill is in this surprise element of suddenly seeing everything clarified and beautiful."

I believe the math courses at Columbia will allow me to continue my passion for mathematics through learning modern theories as well as exploring particular topics like number theory. The Department of Mathematics also offers joint degrees with many other disciplines that depend on math. Columbia's programs will prepare me with skills to make significant contributions in my field of study.

范文作者: Bambi,被哥伦比亚大学录取

Since Darwin's theory, various explanations have been offered for the morphology of Nepenthes, one of a number of carnivorous plants commonly known as "pitcher plants."

The Nepenthes insect trap is a highly specialized leaf. To look into details on a morphological level, we used scanning electron microscopy, stereomicroscopy, and paraffin section (should this be "sectioning" or possibly "sections"?) to describe the leaf development in Nepenthes x ventrata (a carnivorous plant). (Haven't you already said it is a carnivorous plant?) This process, since I am unsure about the grammar here do you mean from leaf initiation to the pitcher opening up, is divided into 7 stages (P0 - P6). In stage P1, two primordia rise on the ventral side of the leaf primordium, growing towards each other, which will develop into the lid and the pitcher. The lid primordium grows slower later, so the pitcher part seems significantly larger. It is speculated that it is the leaf primordium ectopic development that results in the three-dimensional pitcher structure.

To determine whether Nepenthes leaves are simple leaves or compound leaves, we cloned the KNOX1 homologous gene in Nepenthes and found new evidence on a molecular level. Expressing in complex primordia and remaining absent in simple primordia, KNOX1 is not just an important regulating factor for meristem activities, but also an important indicator piece of evidence to address this question. We obtained the 3' end cDNA from a 3'RACE experiment and obtained a full-length cDNA sequence by comparing data with preliminary gene sequencing data. We used NCBI BLASTX and protein structure analysis and established a molecular phylogenetic tree to prove that the obtained sequence belongs to the KNOX1 gene subfamily. We analyzed its expression pattern and found that Nv KNOX1 expresses in the shoot apex meristem and leaf primordium at stage P2. We compared the pitcher formation process and KNOX1 expression pattern in Nepenthes to that in Sarracenia, another kind of pitcher plant, and the results substantiated this conclusion.

We concluded that the Nepenthes leaves are analogous to compound leaves. The Nepenthes pitcher's unique three-dimensional structure is caused by its unusual leaf initiation, resulting from an anomalous Nv KNOX1 gene expression. We will analyze the temporal, spatial and quantitative characters of Nv KNOX1 gene expression in detail, as we finish our current work on genome sequencing of Nepenthes.（研究论文的摘要）

Details (250 words): describes the duration of your research involvement and details regarding your specific role in and contributions to the research project.

用 250 词描述你参与过的一个研究项目，以及你在研究项目中的具体角色和贡献。

In 2014, I entered my school's Science Experimental Class and reached out to my biology teacher, Dr. Feng Li. I worked in his greenhouse every day and regularly wrote down my observations.

Captivated by how the carnivorous plants develop specialized leaves, I searched for articles on the morphology, energetics, and evolution of carnivorous plants. I came across The Carnivorous Plants by Francis Ernest Lloyd and realized how 20th century scientists had neglected some pertinent observations and hypotheses early scientists had made regarding the structure and development of Nepenthes leaf.

I decided to look for determinative evidence that would solve this debate. Having participated in the Science Talent Program, I was already familiar with scanning electron microscopy and paraffin section experiments. I learned about stereoscopy as I worked with my partner, Xiao Liu. We observed the Nepenthes leaf primordium systematically in the Shunong Bai lab at Peking University with Dr. Li.

Having analyzed the photos we took, I realized that morphological observation was not enough. Dr. Li introduced me to a Science article titled Homologies in Leaf Form Inferred from KNOXI Gene Expression During Development, which inspired me to use KNOX1 gene expression to determine whether Nepenthes leaves are simple leaves or compound leaves. I reached out to Ph. D. student Yuhan Fang (who worked in the Shunong Bai lab) and learned to design primers, conduct 3'RACE experiments and analyze the obtained sequence with NCBI database.

I submitted my paper to Dongrun-Yau Science Award in September 2016, and was selected for the national final round.

斯坦福大学
Stanford University

范文作者：Frank，被斯坦福大学录取

Briefly elaborate on one of your extracurricular activities or work or family responsibilities. (50 - 150 words)

简要阐述一下你的课外活动或工作或家庭责任(50～150 词)

"We desperately need inclusion to be a verb, not a value": 2019 Special Olympics World Games opening ceremony.

Initially, "intellectual disability" sounded like a negative concept. I had no concrete comprehension of what it encompassed until hearing about Special Olympics' 50th anniversary video competition. After attending training sessions, I came to understand the mission and values of the Special Olympics. Working alongside athletes and seeing their determination was an empowering experience. After winning the video competition, I attended the World Games.

I guided athletes to the venues and helped with translations and coordination; I documented many inspirational moments. But it felt more than that, I embraced their identity as individuals and as members of an underserved community. I continue working closely with the local club and I'm trying to connect my school with the organisation as well.

I'm proud to say that I made inclusion to be a verb.

What is the most significant challenge that society faces today? (50 words limit)

当今社会面临的最重大挑战是什么?(限 50 词)

Many scholars have shared concerns about technological advancements. As Yuval Noah Harari puts it: "We may be fast approaching a new singularity, when all the concepts that give meaning ... will become irrelevant." Thus, our most significant challenge is to deploy technology to best serve humanity with prudence and ethics.

How did you spend your last two summers? (50 words limit)

你过去的两个夏天是怎么过的?(限 50 词)

I practiced solving questions for Math Olympiad competitions, finished a promotional film for the local Special Olympics, and attended WowYoung's short film award ceremony, where I won four awards. I also visited a Thai orphanage to teach and construct a water tower. I sharpened my French skills in Alliance Française.

What historical moment or event do you wish you could have witnessed? (50 words limit)

你希望自己能目睹什么历史时刻或事件?(限 50 词)

I would like to witness the bridge fire incident in Hong Kong on November 17th, 2019, which marks the turning point when violence outweighed civil protests. Also, I would rather witness first-hand than hearing sensationalised stories because of the strikingly different ways in which different medias portray events.

What five words best describe you?

5 个词来形容自己:

Curious, Creative, Passionate, Witty, Leader

Imaginative

Aspiring

Thoughtful

Humane

Sherlocked

When the choice is yours, what do you read, listen to, or watch? (50 words limit)

如果可以选择,你会读什么,听什么,看什么? (限 50 词)

Stanford grad Grant Sanderson's math channel 3Blue1Brown

Award-winning short films and movies from Marvel to Art-House (filmmakers watch the weirdest ones).

Omnivorous reader, from "Thinking Fast and Slow" to "Our Mathematical Universe" to "All the Light We Cannot See".

Global news like The Guardian and The Age.

Name one thing you are looking forward to experiencing at Stanford. (50 words limit)

列举一件你期待在斯坦福经历的事情。(限 50 词)

Applying my theoretical mathematics and computer science knowledge into actual practice and to use them for promoting social good and improving our human condition. I would like to participate in numerous programs such as

“Data Science for Social Good Fellowship Program”, “The Institute for Human-Centered Artificial Intelligence”, and “CS+Social Good”.

Imagine you had an extra hour in the day — how would you spend that time? (50 words limit).

想象一下你一天多了一个小时，你会怎么度过这段时间？（限 50 词）

Each morning, I would devote thirty minutes to mindfulness, to reflect and let go of all thoughts. I would spend the other thirty minutes to have an in-person one-on-one conversation with a faculty member, a friend, or a stranger and to reclaim the human interactions taken away by technology.

The Stanford community is deeply curious and driven to learn in and out of the classroom. Reflect on an idea or experience that makes you genuinely excited about learning. (100 to 250 words)

斯坦福大学的社区对课堂内外的学习充满了好奇心和动力。讲述一个让你对学习真正感到兴奋的想法或经历。（100～250 词）

Machine learning used to be an unsolvable mystery to me. “Experts” talked about it, but I had yet to understand the process or the principles. So, I began to hunt for this “holy grail” of modern technology. I began by learning the basics — linear regression and gradient descent. I was fascinated by the fact that mathematics is so engrained in the fundamentals of machine learning. Just as mathematics stems from simple axioms, all the complicated models are founded on similar principles. To connect my mathematical knowledge with this new learning process was a joy in itself. I then started to investigate through an actual research project — “Data-driven approach for predicting and explaining the risk of long-term unemployment (LTU)”. I was not only drawn to building machine learning models but was more excited that this research could have a positive social impact. I successfully created a sophisticated model that outputs 81.2% accuracy in predicting LTU, which can help Social

Workers to allocate employment resources efficiently to tackle the problem of LTU.

But I didn't stop there. To be able to deploy such a model in public, I also needed to explain its predicative decisions and identify biases. Learning two additional skills required me to incorporate principles from mathematics and computer science with economics and the humanities. It was this necessary interdisciplinary approach that allowed me to appreciate the way in which algorithms can be made ethically accountable, transparent, and as fair as I can possibly make it — for now.

Virtually all of Stanford's undergraduates live on campus. Write a note to your future roommate that reveals something about you or that will help your roommate — and us — get to know you better. (100 - 250 words)

几乎所有斯坦福大学的本科生都住在校园里。给你未来的室友写一张便条，告诉他你的一些情况，使你的室友和我们更好地了解你。(100～250 词)

Dear U.N. Owen,

G'day Mate!

First of all, don't be worried if you see me asleep until noon on a weekend, there's no need for an ambulance, I'm not dead. I also have the habit of solving a simple sudoku puzzle when I wake up every morning. You might see me walking around the room mumbling while randomly twisting Rubik's cubes into one of 43 quintillion combinations when I try to memorise or think about something. And you might see me scratching my head repeatedly when I get stuck on a math question ...

You may occasionally see me staying up very late staring at a crash report from Adobe Premiere Pro. That's just me trying to edit a video about my life at Stanford. I will make sure I dim my screen brightness and not distract you with a super-duper drop from the soundtrack.

I hope I can convince you to watch some of my weird films and I hope you'll share a few of yours with me. Although I'm not an Olympic athlete, I would love to go hiking to the mountains or ski with a bunch of friends. And I would love to introduce you to the Aussi tasty steak on a barbie, but I also look forward to my first Thanksgiving turkey with you.

I do hope to have a life-long friendship with you, and I'm looking forward to learning from your background and expertise!

Yours,

Frank

Tell us about something that is meaningful to you and why. (100 to 250 words)

告诉我们一些对你有意义的事情，以及它为什么有意义。(100~250 词)

One day in the studio ...

"Key light ready! Subject in place! Shotgun mic turned on! Camera Rolling!"

"Action!"

Stanford AO: "So, tell us about something meaningful."

Frank: "Well, filmmaking has been very important to me as it is my creative outlet to convey important ideas and messages. I intend my films to be lenses for raising awareness, voicing opinions, and empowering others. My first ever short film — 'Smiling Depression' — explores the complexities of hiding depressive symptoms under a smile and has reached 350,000+ viewers. The directing and acting role help me to resonate with people who suffer from this rapidly growing symptom. In addition, my music video — 'True Colors' — uses music to get people to open up to others; my collaborative project 'Obsession' warns of the dangers of drug abuse. Two of my promotional films for Special Olympics, one local and one for the World Games, aim to break stereotypes and empower athletes with intellectual challenges, while spreading words of inclusion. I've also made a film about mathematics, in a creative attempt to showcase its elegance and to advocate Australian students to choose mathematics. All these short films in part stem from my values and experiences and are very close to my heart. They also allow me to collaborate with other talented students — music producers and actors alike. Many of these films stirred debates and raised awareness; more importantly, they influenced viewers in an intimate yet profound way. I hope they will help individuals and communities to move forward."

"Cut!"

范文作者：Bambi，被斯坦福大学录取

Stanford students possess an intellectual vitality. Reflect on an idea or experience that has been important to your intellectual development. (100 to 250 words)

斯坦福的学生在智力上非常活跃。描述一个对你智力发展至关重要的想法或经历。(100～250 词)

Outside the window was the hustle and bustle of Beijing. Yet, in Mr. Xie's Traditional Chinese Poetry class, I was immersed in rhyme and meter, couplets and stanzas. Enchanted by these verses I began wondering: Is poetry still alive in today's world? Drafting my own lines, I felt unsure. Could I, a modern city girl, still echo with this ancient art?

That was when the music started, soft and soothing. It was *guqin*, an ancient Chinese instrument. Mr. Xie twanged the strings, creating a melody on his fingertips. He chanted with the music, reading a poem written by an imprisoned emperor 1038 years ago. Bitter but captivating, the poem and accompanying *guqin* resonated in our classroom. I pictured the lonely emperor, lamenting his lost empire on a moonlit evening.

I became lost in thought. I remembered, after my sixteenth birthday party, a profound melancholy seized me as I walked down an empty alley. My shadow played with the moonlight, like in a silent film depicting loneliness in city life. That emperor must have felt the same, I thought. We humans share the urge to record, question, create, and, therefore, we share a passion towards poetry. I began to feel an irresistible impulse to write my own lines.

Looking outside the window, dazzled by the moonlight that has endured for millennia, I tapped into the stream of language connecting me with Adunis, Pablo Neruda, Edgar Allan Poe, and Murasaki Shikibu. Even in the hubbub of twenty-first century city life, poetry endures.

Virtually all of Stanford's undergraduates live on campus. Write a note to your future roommate that reveals something about you or that will help your roommate — and us — know you better. (250 word limit)

几乎所有斯坦福本科生都住在校园里。给你未来的室友写一个展示你自己某一方面的留言,以帮助你的室友——以及我们——更好的了解你。(250 词)

Hey, future roommate!

I'm Bambi. Looking forward to meeting you! Here're a few things about me.

Growing up, I loved learning to cook with Mom. My favorite dish was the chili hot pot, prepared according to my grandma's secret ingredients. What's even more exciting was our dinner table talk: Italo Calvino's style of writing, history of Quebec autonomy debate, the doomsday scenario in *Interstellar* — anything and everything. I hope you'll join me at Stanford Cooking Society workshops. And if you'd try Chinese dishes, I'd love to share my recipes. When we share meals together, who knows where our conversations will go?

By the way, I'm a morning person. Having been a happy gardener for three years, I'll get up early and spend my mornings at my plot in the BeWell Community Gardens. When I bring a few crunchy cucumbers back to our dorm, you'll definitely love their taste. If you're also an early bird and you'd like to join, I guarantee that watching the busy bumblebees or darting sparrows would help release your stress.

As you can tell, I like healthy living. Since I spend much of my free time reading or writing, I figured out a way to avoid neck, shoulder, or back pain. If you see me doing yoga moves with a Kindle in hand, don't panic. Stretching while reading looks silly, but it really works!

I'm so excited to get to know you. I hope we'll have lots of fun together!

All the best,

Bambi

What matters to you, and why? (100 to 250 words)

什么对你至关重要,为什么?(100～250 词)

When my cousin came to celebrate Spring Festival in Beijing last year, he brought me a scroll written in Manchu language. Staring blankly at the jagged script, I couldn't understand a word. I belong to Manchu, an ethnic minority in China, yet, having grown up away from my hometown, I barely knew anything about my language.

This moment inspired me to begin studying this endangered language. Awkwardly holding my pen to practice handwriting in Manchu alphabet, I connected with my ancestors from these tenuous strokes. The excitement of perfecting the sweeping curve of my Manchu name, *Juhe*, reminded me of when I was a little girl attracted to romantic Manchu folk stories.

The language enabled me to delve into history.

What started with a Spring Festival scroll has become a journey to search for my ethnic roots. During this journey, I recognize that my identity is not a definite point, as I once imagined. What if I allowed myself to assimilate? What if I never took the time to investigate? In this sense, my ethnic identity as a Manchu is, curiously, fragile and transitory. Yet, with each new finding, I am reconstructing its meaning and making it grow.

芝加哥大学
The University of Chicago

范文作者：Emma，被芝加哥大学录取

UChicago professor W. J. T. Mitchell entitled his 2005 book What Do Pictures Want?

Describe a picture, and explore what it wants.

— Inspired by Anna Andel

芝加哥大学教授 W. J. T. Mitchell 在 2005 年出版了《图片想要什么?》

描述一幅画，并探索它想要什么。

“Pathetic creatures, you are.” the full-length portrait scorned.

I raised my lantern to take a closer look at him. His lips were carved so finely and his eyes were a rippling blue. The label on the frame read *By Basil Hallward*, 1891.

“The world is such a place of endless wonders — yet you mortals, after a few years of glorious bloom, wither and creep, for the rest of your lives, in the ominous shadows of death.”

The young Adonis stood at ease, his left hand resting on the gilded back of a divan, casual but firm. Moonlight swelled in the small attic and he brimmed with all the vitality and power of youth.

“That’s a bleak future indeed, Mr. Gray.”

“The flush in my cheeks, the fire in my pupils, the pulse of joy in my veins — they are forever mine and live forever in the present. But for your kind, most passions are quenched before thirty. By the time you reach fifty, one can see how life’s like all the way to your grave.”

“Mr. Gray,” I interrupted him, “If passion is to last forever, will it still be as tempting? You have been trapped in that frame for 150 years, and shall remain so, as springs were swept away by autumn leaves and human society lurched forward — you were left stranded in solitude. I pity you in your vain search for exhilaration."

Outside, clouds sneaked up on the pale crescent and smothered the night sky. Darkness softened the edges of the portrait and his torso shimmered dimly under the lantern. When he spoke once more, his voice was weighed down with fatigue.

"But what is one to do? I've known no other way to live than the one of pursuing sensual fulfillment. All art is useless and beauty exists only to be adored. Nothing meant anything to me. I had been a hollow shell — a liar and a hypocrite. I had been taught to worship discord and despise harmony. Grace, youth, wealth — I had them. Yet I kept searching for new emotions. Every exploration was transcendence from morality and I thrilled at the sight of my own corruption. Immortality — such cruel punishment it was — took the excitement out of everything: the maiden's love, the extravagant dances, and even the imprudent assassin. I long for change but fear too much the ending. Tell me, how do you enjoy life with a body that's doomed? How do you survive the pains and persist, knowing that any effort shall not outlive your bones? How do you find sweetness in tranquility when every day was similar to every other? To see myself age, to acknowledge the gaping void of death, yet to struggle and fight still — I dare not embrace such mortality."

Wind rattled the windows, grating on the rusted bolts. Despite the outpouring of sentiments, his brows were fixed in the same relaxed pose. The paint glinted dully and the lines blurred in uncertainty.

"You grab onto everything and endow it with meaning. Art conveys messages, books serve moral purposes, music offers better upbringings — those misguided souls in the ivory tower claim. What is, then, the significance of your existence? A mere speck of dust in the galaxy, how do you face the vast unknown?"

"Mr. Gray, you ask such intimidating questions." "This is a desperate hour.”

“You are no man of triviality, sir. The rituals of ordinary life trample your aesthetic concepts. And yet the meaning of life lies expressly in the path of exploration, paved by the numerous, the masses — the common. You see only Socrates after truth, Archimedes after science, Solon after democracy. Most of us see Paris citizens after freedom, soldiers after peace, Arabian women after equality. Others, as it seems, exist not in names but as significant numbers in the history of our kind. From where you stand, their lives might as well have been all the same, leaving no trace.”

“— Do they know not, perhaps, their utter helplessness?” “Just the opposite — most of us are well aware.”

“Then, why pain yourself with useless efforts in the search for meaning? You might as well take an easier and more pleasurable path and squander your days.”

“But meaning is never the destination, Mr. Gray.” I gazed up into his face, “It can be anywhere on the road but the destination. When mid-19th century Chinese workers gazed across San Francisco Bay, they turned their backs on their home an ocean away. They fled a society of turbulence after a better future, only to be shunned again by the Chinese Exclusion Act. Many of them died along the railroads on a foreign soil before earning enough to have a home, leaving their search to their children and grandchildren. When Syrian refugees dragged their thin and pallid bodies across the borders, they saw hope and safety. They sat together, silent and humble, waiting for a chance to chase their dreams. As you have said, Mr. Gray, we are pathetic creatures. We are a mass without a title and individuals without names. We have no choice but to realize our values in our struggles — albeit for happiness, for the laws of nature, or for love. We challenge ourselves, we aim at higher ground, we take in the bigger picture — call it consolation if you want, but the search is what makes life worth living. It makes mortality bearable, even, at times welcoming."

"Goodnight, sir." I said, leaving him lingering in a forlorn dream. He stared into the beyond, longing, suffering — but, perhaps, a little more human.

宾夕法尼亚大学
University of Pennsylvania

范文作者：LXJ，被宾夕法尼亚大学录取

How will you explore your intellectual and academic interests at the University of Pennsylvania? Please answer this question given the specific undergraduate school to which you are applying. (400 - 650 words)

你将如何在宾夕法尼亚大学探索你的知识和学术兴趣？请根据你申请的本科学院来回答这个问题。(400～650 词)

I label myself as a "scholar", since I really enjoy learning and academics. The University of Pennsylvania, with its particularly strong academic atmosphere and distinctive educational philosophy, is an ideal place to further my academic exploration.

I'm really interested in the use of technology in a social context. I first realized the two-sidedness of technologies when I conducted a school project on the impact of online shopping. The success of online shopping has greatly disrupted traditional brick-and-mortar stores, threatening workers' job security and depressing wages. For my project, I designed an intelligent shopping system for brick-and-mortar retail stores to help them innovate and remain competitive in the marketplace. This sparked my interest in the interaction between technology and the human condition.

Combining my interests in physics and history, I would like to explore the relationship between scientific progress and social changes. One important topic I would like to study in college is how science and technology should be developed and used for the betterment of human society. Penn's distinctive Science, Technology and Society Undergraduate Program (STSC) would enable me to study sciences from the perspective of its historical development and rightful role in our society. I would like to enroll in Scientific Revolution with Professor Voelkel James to examine the historical background and transitional elements for pivotal scientific progress during the 16th and 17th century. I would also like to enroll in A Global Perspective of Science & Religion with Professor Kucuk Bekir to find out how religious traditions impacted the development of science throughout history. Course offerings at the History and Sociology of Science Department inspire me to think in an interdisciplinary way, combining knowledge in natural sciences and social sciences.

To become an expert in this field of science and technology and their impact on our society, more than technical knowledge and expertise in natural sciences is necessary. A solid understanding of humanities and social sciences is also essential. The General Education system at the University of Pennsylvania offers a broad, liberal education that would enable me to take a variety courses from academic disciplines in the humanities, natural sciences and social sciences. Exposure to top-notch physics courses would provide fundamental knowledge of the technologies I seek to assess. Together with the interdisciplinary courses offered by the one-of-a-kind STSC program, this would allow me to pursue my interests in how history and physics influence each other — to use historical experiences as the guiding light for future development of new technologies.

Beyond the classroom, I would like to further my exploration through internships. Located in the city of Philadelphia, the university provides its students with abundant resources in internships in many industries. I would like to experience working in consulting to help companies such as Ametek, the electronics manufacturer develop and use technologies for the betterment of the society. I am also interested in the Service Fellowship at the Fox Leadership Program where I could research on topics that are dear to me, such as how to help the mentally challenged reach their full potential.

At the same time, interacting with talented and intellectually engaged peers from diverse backgrounds and with professors who are top scholars would add greater depth and perspective to my studies. I am eager to learn from and at the same time contribute my own individual talents and perspectives to the Penn community.

由于热爱学术的缘故,我常常把自己称作一个"学者"。因此,有着浓郁学术气氛和独特教育理念的宾夕法尼亚大学正是我进一步追寻学术和爱好的理想场所。

我对科技在社会中的角色特别感兴趣。在开展一项关于网上购物对社会影响的研究课题时,我第一次认识到了科技发展的两面性:网上购物固然是一项由科技发展带来的充满进步意义的社会变革,但它的成功极其强烈地冲击了传统实体店的发展,威胁到了行业内人员的就业和薪资稳定。我在项目中设计了一套为实体店量身定做的智能购物系统,帮助这些店家降低运营成本、维持行业内的竞争力。这次研究经历激发了我对科技与人文关怀间关系的思考和兴趣。

今后的大学生涯里,我希望结合我在物理学和历史学方面的兴趣,进一步探索科技进步和社会变化之间的密切联系,尤其是研究科学和技术的发展如何才能被合理开发和用于社会进步。宾夕法尼亚大学独特的科学技术和社会研究项目(STSC)能激发我从历史意义和社会地位的角度来研究科学。我尤其想上弗尔克尔·詹姆斯教授的"科学革命"课,从中学习16~17世纪时重要科技进步的历史和变革性意义;此外,我对库库克·贝基尔教授的"科学与宗教的全球化视角"这门课也很感兴趣,希望能在课上探索历史上宗教对科学发展的影响。科学史和社会研究系开设的课程激发我以一种多学科的视角来思考问题,灵活运用自然科学、社会科学等多领域的知识。

为了成为研究科技及其社会影响方面的专家,光有自然科学方面的知识是不够的，人文和社会科学方面的知识也极为关键。宾夕法尼亚大学的通识教育为学生们设计了一套覆盖面广、自由的课程体系，涵盖了人文、自然科学、社会科学等多领域、多方面的内容。参与顶级的物理课程能帮助我熟练掌握我所希望研究的科技领域的基本知识，并和科技与社会研究项目中其他跨领域的课程一起激发我去研究物理学和历史学如何相互影响、相互联系，并运用历史经验来引导未来科技的进一步发展。

在课堂外，我希望通过实习等方式进一步深化自己的学术探索。宾夕法尼亚大学坐落于费城，为学生们提供了充裕的、多行业的实习机会。我希望能尝试体验咨询行业内的实习机会，帮助如 Ametek 一类的公司更好地研发促进社会进步的科技产品。此外，我对 Fox 领导者项目下的社会服务机会也很感兴趣。在这个项目里，我可以学习研究一些我非常熟悉的话题，例如如何帮助低智商人群充分实现自己的社会潜能。

与此同时，与聪明、有才能、拥有不同背景的同龄人一起学习生活，与作为该领域内顶级学者的教授们一起工作研究，这些都能拓宽我学术研究的深度和广度。我非常期待在从宾大社区中学习受益的同时贡献我自己的价值和才能。

康奈尔大学
Cornell University

范文作者：Jerry，被康奈尔大学录取

Describe two or three of your current intellectual interests and why they are exciting to you. Why will Cornell's College of Arts and Sciences be the right environment in which to pursue your interests? (650 words limit)

描述两到三个你的学术兴趣，以及它们为什么让你产生了兴趣。为什么康奈尔大学的文理学院适合你的兴趣追求。(650 词以内)

My first intellectual interest is theoretical physics, especially astrophysics. I believe physics is the inspiration and driving force for social development. Physics aims at explaining how the world works and therefore helps people search for more powerful energy resources and more efficient ways to harness them. Astrophysics seeks to model the universe, revealing the ultimate secrets of our cosmos. Its mystic nature awes me and propels me to delve deeper into this subject.

My passion for astrophysics comes from my physics class and reading. My physics teacher not only talked about the cosmos from our textbook, but also showed us documentaries like *The Journey to the Edge of the Universe*, which became my favorite. I am an avid reader of magazines like *New Discovery* for more than two years, and I read *A Brief History of Time* four times. Though I still cannot understand everything from these readings, I did learn some basic theories and research methods. Recently, the breakthrough in gravitational wave detection pumped up my adrenaline to a new high level. Gradually, I also became interested in the practical applications of scientific knowledge. Working in the robotics club, for example, I could not help thinking about why motors were designed the way they were. Ultimately, however, knowledge cannot be applied until it is discovered, and my passion continues to be finding the secrets behind the starry night.

Cornell abounds with great astrophysics resources. Professors like Liam McAllister, Maxim Perelstein and Henry Tye, who study supersymmetry, extra dimensions of space and new strong interactions are attractive to me, not to mention Nobel laureate Hans Bethe, who explained how stars shine by converting hydrogen to helium. Cornell's Physics Department maintains outstanding facilities and communicates with many world famous labs and telescopes, such as the Arecibo Observatory, where the 1993 Nobel winner Russell Alan Hulse found proof for the existence of gravitational waves in 1974; and the SLAC National Accelerator Laboratory's equipment that Cornell helped to improve. I believe these resources and the University's active role in scientific research frontier will benefit me tremendously for future opportunities and keep me posted on the latest trend.

My other interests are science, as well as law and philosophy. These subjects deal with human beings' beliefs and society's regulations, which affect today's scientific research a lot. Recently, science has developed to such an advanced level that it has raised people's fears and doubts for the future. For example, scientists who designed the first atomic bombs still regret the destruction of Hiroshima and Nagasaki. Even today, people are still questioning the nuclear power grids for possible disasters and are wrapped by nuclear fear. Meanwhile, frightening discoveries go on even now in artificial intelligence, quantum computers, cloning, and other scientific fields. The development of physics will definitely trigger a lot more social debates on ethical dilemmas. I want to learn more about these controversies.

Furthermore, at a summer program at Cornell on Captive Raptor Management I learned that raptor researchers need to integrate social opinions, laws and ethics into their projects, which enlightened me that science is not a stand-alone but an interdisciplinary work. I hope that Cornell's CAS courses, like those offered by the law and society program and the philosophy and social science departments, can help me understand the relationship between scientific research and other social studies better.

For me, the breadth and depth of academic offerings and the long academic research record of the College of Arts and Sciences are the most important factors that drive me to apply to Cornell. I want to investigate astrophysics, as well as legal, societal, and ethical issues in depth, while at the same time pursuing a broad-based liberal arts education at Cornell's CAS.

我主要的学术兴趣是理论物理学,尤其是天体物理学。我相信物理学是社会发展的灵感源泉和原动力。物理学旨在解释世界如何运转,从而帮助人们寻找更强大的能源和更有效的能源利用方式。天体物理学试图为宇宙建模,揭示我们宇宙的终极秘密。它的神秘特质令我敬畏,并促使我更深入地研究这个主题。

我对天体物理学的热情来自我的物理课和阅读。我的物理老师不仅讲解了我们教科书中的宇宙，还向我们展示了《宇宙之旅》之类的纪录片，这成了我的最爱。我是《新发现》等杂志的狂热读者，两年里没有错过一期，并且我读了四遍《时间简史》。尽管我仍然无法理解这些阅读物中的所有内容，但我确实学习了一些基本理论和研究方法。最近，引力波探测技术的突破让我非常兴奋。在学习中，我也对科学知识的实际应用产生了兴趣。例如，在机器人社团工作时，我不禁思考为什么要按原样设计电动机。最终，知识只有在被发现之后才能应用，而我的激情仍然是在繁星之夜中寻找秘密。

康奈尔大学拥有大量的物理学师资和研究资源。像利亚姆·麦卡利斯特，马克西姆·佩雷斯坦和亨利·泰这样的教授对超对称性、高维空间以及新的强相互作用理论进行了研究，这对我很有吸引力，还有鼎鼎大名已故的诺贝尔奖获得者汉斯·贝特了。康奈尔大学物理系拥有出色的实验设备，并与许多世界著名的实验室和天文台有过合作，例如 1993 年诺贝尔奖获得者拉塞尔·艾伦·赫尔塞在阿雷西博天文台于 1974 年找到了存在引力波的证据。康奈尔大学也曾帮助改进 SLAC 国家加速器实验室的设备。我相信这些资源和康奈尔大学在科学研究领域的积极作用将使我受益匪浅，为我带来很多的机会，并让我了解最新的科研趋势。

我同时也对其他自然科学以及法律和哲学有学习兴趣。这些主题涉及人类的信仰和社会法规，极大地影响了当今的科学研究。近年来，科学发展到了如此先进的水平，引起了人们对未来的恐惧和怀疑。例如，设计第一枚原子弹的科学家仍然对广岛和长崎的毁坏感到遗憾。即使到了今天，人们仍在向核电网质疑可能会发生的灾难，并被核恐惧包裹着。同时，人工智能、量子计算机、克隆和其他科学领域中也有惊人的发现，但它们可能引起社会的恐慌。科学的发展无疑将引发更多关于伦理困境的社会争论。我想了解更多有关这些争议的信息。

此外，在康奈尔大学关于“猛禽管理”的一个夏季课程中，我了解到猛禽研究人员需要将社会观点、法律和道德观念纳入他们的考量之中，这使我认识到科学不是独立的，而是跨学科的。我希望康奈尔大学的文理学院课程（如法律、哲学以及社会科学系提供的课程）能够帮助我更好地理解科学研究与其他社会研究之间的关系。

对我来说，学术研究的广度和深度以及长期的学术研究记录是促使我申请康奈尔大学的最重要因素。我想深入研究天体物理学，并另外辅修法律、社会和伦理课程，在康奈尔大学的文理学院体验知识面广泛的文理教育。

范文作者：奥特曼，被康奈尔大学录取

Students in Arts and Sciences embrace the opportunity to delve into multifaceted academic interests，embodying in 21st century terms Ezra Cornell's "any person ... any study" founding vision. Tell us about the areas of study you are excited to explore，and specifically why you wish to pursue them in our College. (650 words)

文理学院的学生有机会钻研多方面的学术兴趣，这也是叶尔扎·康奈尔“任何人，任何研究”的创始理念在21世纪的体现。告诉我们你想探索的学习领域，以及你为什么想在我们学院学习这些。(650 词)

My first intellectual interest is math. Initially，I was fascinated with competitions and believed they prove ultimate strength. However，after competing for a long time，I began to doubt why I love math in the first place. In my junior year，I received，as a reward for the all-school Mathematics Prize，Cornell Professor Steven Strogatz's Infinite Powers. The book characterizes calculus as the language God used to program the universe. Calculus also interlinks different fields of science，philosophy，and economics，which encouraged me to rekindle my curiosity in the application of math.

Intrigued by the omnipresence of math in our world，I studied the algorithm and real-life applications of Page Rank in an independent research project. During my research，I came across an internet lecture on Page Rank published by Cornell's Department of Mathematics. Using mathematical concepts I encountered before，the lecture illuminated the concepts of stochastic processes and random dynamical systems，integral ideas in probability theory. Throughout the project，extensiveness of Page Rank's application fascinated me. Scholars have fused probabilistic methods and ideas from modifications of Page Rank into music information retrieval, sports analysis, social media studies, among other areas. Having scratched the surface of probability theory, I am eager to delve deeper into the subject and explore how it explains seemingly random phenomena in the world.

At Cornell, I will have access to a wide range of opportunities to further my interest in probability theory. For example, having encountered some very simple dynamical systems in my research project, I can't wait to explore more in the class Nonlinear Dynamics and Chaos. Moreover, I hope to join the research group in probability and statistics with Professor Lionel Levine, who focuses on how large-scale patterns emerge from local rules. From this particular branch of research, I wish to use probability to discover the most fundamental explanations for complex phenomena we encounter regularly in nature, finance, and other areas. Last, I am looking forward to participating in probability seminars, where I can discuss the newest findings in probability with scholars from around the world. With all these opportunities, I hope to gain insight into mathematical interpretations of reality and enjoy math even more.

My second intellectual interest is philosophy, mainly inspired by my ancient philosophy class. Great philosophers like Aristotle inspired the rise of mathematics because it is the most outstanding exemplar of rationality and logic. William Thomson Baron Kelvin once said "Mathematics is the only good metaphysics." As I discover the intimate connection between philosophy and mathematics, I am particularly interested in the philosophy of mathematics. At Cornell, I look forward to the class Foundation of Mathematics, where I can further explore how and why math arose from philosophy. Second, I will have the opportunity to work with Professor Harold Theodore Hodes, who specializes in logic and mathematics of logic. Researching the philosophy of math with him, I hope to understand how mathematics shapes human rationality and how mathematical rationality impacts our behaviors, decisions, and relationships. I believe mathematics allows us to obtain knowledge of the universe, so I am particularly interested in how math shapes human consciousness and morality.

I want to apply my knowledge from the classroom and contribute to Logos, Cornell's renowned philosophy journal. I also wish to further my passion for the beauty and truth in music an continue with cello, through Midday Music recitals and touring with the orchestra in Taipei on Cornell's broad, international music platform. Hopefully I can also continue music tutoring and encourage students around me to inspire more people in the greater community through music.

For me, philosophy and mathematics, like numbers, like human thoughts, collide with each other, and fuse into a unified order. As a passionate student, musician, and pursuer of dreams, I know in my heart that Cornell, where I can explore truths across interconnected disciplines of philosophy and math, is where I truly belong.

首先，数学是我的第一兴趣。之前，我一直对竞赛着迷，认为竞赛是对实力的绝对证明。然而，在参加了很长一段时间的数学竞赛后，我开始怀疑自己为什么要学习和热爱数学。在我十一年级快结束的时候，拿到了全校优秀数学奖，奖品是康奈尔大学教授史蒂文·斯特罗加茨的《无限的力量》，这本书将微积分描述为上帝的语言，上帝用它来编辑宇宙。当我们对计算机代码理解得越多，我们就越了解我们的宇宙。微积分还将科学、哲学和经济学在不同领域联系在一起，这鼓励了我重新发现数学的价值，并重新点燃了我对数学应用真正的好奇心。

对于数学在我们的世界中无处不在的证明，其实在我十一年级的线性代数课就做了一个相关的独立研究项目，项目研究了网页排序的算法和现实生活中的应用，在我的研究过程中，偶尔看到了康奈尔大学数学系一个关于网页排名的互联网讲座，讲座使用到了我之前学过的数学概念：随机过程和随机动力系统，这是概率论中特别令我感兴趣的部分，并帮助我加深了对研究项目的理解。在整个项目中，网页排序在无数不同领域的广泛应用深深吸引了我，使我着迷。在触及概率论的皮毛之后，我一直非常渴望更深入地研究这个主题，探索它是如何解释我们日常生活中看似随机的现象的。在康奈尔大学，我将能够得到更多更广泛的机会，使自己进一步提高对概率论的认识。康奈尔大学数学系有着全面的数学课程，例如在我研究的项目中遇到了非常简单的动力系统，那么在康奈尔大学的非线性动力学和混沌这门课上，我可以探索更多关于许多科学领域的动力系统知识。我也很渴望可以成为莱昂内尔·莱文教授的概率与统计学小组的一员，专注研究大规模趋势和模式是如何从现有规则中产生，这个特定的研究分支，是我们人类在自然界、金融和许多其他领域中经常遇到的复杂现象的最根本解释。最后，我希望在康奈尔参加更多的概率论研讨会，可以和来自各地的高级学者学习和讨论概率论方面的最新发现。有了这些机会，我希望能观察到数学对现实的解释，并且更加喜欢数学。

哲学是我的第二个兴趣所在，这主要是受到了今年古代哲学课的启发。自古希腊以来，亚里士多德等在现实中追求真理的伟大哲学家激发了数学的兴起，因为它是理性和逻辑最杰出的典范。威廉·汤姆森·卡尔曾经说过："数学是唯一好的形而上学。"在古代哲学中，数学和哲学之间就有着密切联系，这让我对数学哲学产生了浓厚的兴趣。我期待着在康奈尔大学参加数学基础这门课，在这门课中，可以进一步探索数学是如何以及为什么源于哲学。或许，我还将有机会和哈罗德·西奥多·霍德斯教授合作，在研究数学哲学的同时，了解数学如何影响我们的行为、决策和关系。我相信数学可以让我们获得宇宙的知识，数学可以塑造人类的意识和道德。

除此之外，我希望把课堂上的知识带到康奈尔大学著名的哲学杂志 *logos* 上，为杂志提供更多相关文书。我还会进一步展示对音乐的热情，带着我的大提琴在午间音乐会上独奏，和康奈尔大学乐团一起巡回演出，我也希望可以继续辅导音乐，鼓励身边和我一样有共同兴趣爱好的同学通过音乐来激励更多的人。

对我来说，哲学和数学就像数字，像人类的思想，相互碰撞，又融合为一体。作为一个充满激情的学生、音乐人和追梦者，我深知康奈尔是我真正的归属，在那里我可以在数学与哲学的交叉领域里追寻真理。

范德堡大学
Vanderbilt University

范文作者：Louisa，被范德堡大学录取

Please briefly elaborate on one of your extracurricular activities or work experiences.（150－400 words）

请简要说明你的课外活动或工作经历。（150～400 词）

When I stepped through the doors of my summer internship, my supervisor barely looked up from his computer. “As you can see, we are very busy here so I’m going to give you a project to work on for the next month.” It was clear he wasn’t interested in mentoring me.

My assignment was to find a pair of shoes with the worst sales rate and try to sell them. Since I’ve never done marketing, I was very confused. Standing in the factory between rows of storage shelves, I learned how orders are taken, how products are packed, and how packages sent from the warehouses arrive at the customer’s doorstep the next day. I’ve always been fascinated by supply chains, but I still did not know how to sell. Since my supervisor wouldn’t help me, I determined I would find out myself.

The process took weeks, and it was far from effortless. I did my own research and found several sales methods that had worked with other products. I combined them with the features of this product and found some solutions. I even bought a pair of the shoes myself and shot photographs, trying to make them look good.

From the experience, I learned that I thrive in that type of high-pressure environment. I also realized that just because I don’t have previous experience with something doesn’t mean I can’t be successful at it. Challenging myself to continuously move beyond my comfort zone enabled me to successfully sell the unpopular sneakers.

埃默里大学
Emory University

范文作者：邵文奕，被埃默里大学录取

What motivates you to study? (150 words)

什么促使你学习？(150 词)

When it comes to the subjects that interest me, I'm naturally motivated. The long, complicated biology vocabularies always appeal to me somehow. Every time I learn a new piece of knowledge from the microscopic view of the organisms, I feel the satisfaction of placing a piece of puzzle on the correct spot of the grand picture. Hitting the last punctuation of a story I wrote — or even just an essay — thrills me in a different way, yet is as fulfilling. Scrolling up to review my writing, I see not letters, but a work of art.

Still, some classes are less intriguing. However, I know they're the necessary steps to increase the probability I'd realize my dream. If I need to be in these classes anyway, why not utilize the time fully? I simply can't help pushing myself to see where my limit lies.

Favorite fiction/nonfiction? (150 words)

最喜欢的虚构/非虚构作品？(150 词)

I never imagined myself finishing the two-inch thick biography of Steve Jobs before. The surprising facts that the founder of Apple was better at designing than programming, that he uses tears to reach his purpose, and that his ability to focus on work both made him and killed him prompted me to read. I remember one detail especially well: John Sculley's wife once said to Jobs that, when she looked into his eyes, she saw a "bottomless pit" instead of a soul.

Did Jobs lose his soul while focusing on "make a dent in the universe?" I kept thinking. Did we, humans, lose what we call souls during the endless pursuit of knowledge? Are we meant to pay a price for our dreams, and can we gain back the lost? One way or another, I believe Jobs had a soul, for he never forgot being called soulless.

范文作者：Nijedan，被埃默里大学录取

"Reflections" Category (150 words)

"反思"(150 字)

Share about a time when you questioned something that you believed to be true.

你是否曾质疑过某个你一度信以为真的事情？请分享给我们。

As a teenager, I loved watching Kingdom of Heaven and was drawn by the character of Guy de Lusignan. The rags-to-riches story, accompanied with elements like love, honor, and spoils of war, romanticized the Crusaders, depicting them as fearless and faithful warriors.

Through reading Christopher Tyerman's God's War, however, I began to learn about religious fanaticism behind the Crusades. Amin Maalouf's The Crusades Through Arab Eyes told the tale from a different angle, as Frankish invaders took advantage of a fragile and decentralized Muslim world and brought destruction to the local populace. These books changed my perception on the political and religious conflicts in the Middle East.

Reading on, I was awed by the raw depictions of the Arab World, haunted by the legacy of the Holy Wars while displaying remarkable cultural resilience. The multifaceted nature of history reminded me not to rush to judgement on civilizations before thorough investigations.

"Tell us about you" Category (150 words)

和我们聊聊你自己(150 词)

If you could witness a historic event first-hand, what would it be, and why?

如果你能够亲历一个历史事件，你觉得会是哪个事件？为什么？

I want to witness Hernando de Alarcón's 1540 expedition, where he travelled along the Colorado River and scouted a vast landmass now known as California.

During his first encounter with the local Quechans, he "started making signs of peace, casting down his sword," as his boat approached the shore, declaring that he had no ill intent. The tribesmen received him amicably, as they warmly embraced and then exchanged souvenirs.

It was rare in the history of the Americas that the interaction between Europeans and indigenous people did not result in hostility. Columbus, Cortés, and Pizzaro arrived with the intent to conquer, loot, kill, and enslave.

I want to observe how Alarcón and the Quechans managed to communicate with each other, and form bonds so tight that some even volunteered to travel with him. Perhaps, Alarcón's story may help us create bridges in today's increasingly polarized society.

乔治城大学
Georgetown University

范文作者：Nijedan，被乔治城大学录取

As Georgetown is a diverse community, the Admissions Committee would like to know more about you in your own words. Please submit a brief essay, either personal or creative, which you feel best describes you.

乔治城大学是一个多元的集体，招生委员会想要通过你自己的话加深对你的了解。请提交一篇短文，要求根据自己的情况选择体现个人特色或创意性。

In the past four years, home gradually became a vague concept to me: a midnight phone call abruptly interrupted by a playful freshman's prank, or a deck of dust-laden polaroid photos that sat on top of my bookshelf, perhaps a brief text message hastily read before the tournament started and left unreplied ever since.

The retro catonese tones in my playlist disappeared, replaced by indie rock bands. The red-patterned sweater knitted by my grandma slipped away from my closet, while the baggy, school-logoed hoodie came on instead. The "where are you really from?"s and "what's your actual name?"s came up less and less often. And I became one with the crowd.

Or so I thought.

A singular identity sounds constraining and suffocating to me. I refuse to be linear, or one-dimensional, since intersectionality runs deep in my mind. Sometimes, I can't help but wonder: the red-bricked dorm houses, emerald-green hills, and refreshing pine-tree aroma, are they really my home? The smoke-filled "Longtang"s, the daunting highrises, and the briskly appearing and reappearing streams of passers-by, are they really far away? Both, I'd imagine. A piece of this, a part of that, a glimpse of this, a snapshot of that — organically and miraculously assembled into the flesh-and-blood "me".

I am passionate and visionary, but also realistic and practical. Earlier this year, a few friends and I co-founded Hope Humanities, an online journal platform that helps high school students pursue their passions in academic writing and publication. Like my peers, I tend to think big, determined to utilize our initiative to promote cross-cultural understanding and build a close-knit community of young scholars around the world. Meanwhile, I also focused on the logistics: whether it is to design a fair and structured system to review submissions, seek cooperation opportunities with nonprofits and social media influencers to gain more publicity, or to organize writing competitions and workshops to reach more targeted audiences.

I find my passions for the past, but also set my eyes for the future. On one side, I am intrigued by the prolonged cultural and religious history of different geopolitical regions; at the same time, I aspire to utilize my historical knowledge to analyze, assess, and address contemporary socio-political challenges. Reading Machiavelli, Montesquieu, and John Locke inspired me to learn more about Renaissance and Enlightenment political theories and their lasting impacts on our modern society. Studying the writings of Thomas Jefferson, Aaron Burr, and Barry Goldwater provided insights into the roles these ideologies played in different stages of American history. Using financial modeling and statistical sciences to perform an independent study on New York City's transportation system demonstrates the intersection between economics and public policy in a modern, cosmopolitan urban space. Through reading, learning, and exchanging ideas with peers, my perception of civilizations and societies around the globe became more complete and multi-faceted.

Sometimes, I write as a journalist and a scholar, armed with astute observations. Interning at Shanghai Daily, I covered a news story on the economic impacts of Super Bowl LII and wrote an opinion article on the 2018-2019 federal government shutdown. For my government and US history course, I conducted independent research and wrote essays on the Nicaraguan civil war, comparing and analyzing Carter and Reagan administration's different diplomatic approaches. On other occasions, I am a poet and creative writer, abstractionist, romantic, and imaginative. I wrote about a love saga set in the brutish scenes of a 1970s Central American civil war (108 days in San Cádiz, a historical novella I wrote and published on amazon), or "the sound of seagulls, bluefish, and a stranded lighthouse," (North Carolina, a poem I wrote on an east-coast road trip) or perhaps "The bronze sculpture of an aged/General on the horseback" who "is wearing/A mask, too." (In Time of Plague, another poem I composed in the midst of the pandemic)

Instead of feeling the inevitable clash of distinct cultures or values, however, I now felt complete, as if my different identities, cultures, passions, and traits were interlocked — in a cohesive, harmonious manner, like "yin" and "yang". My home remains the same; The temperate little boy in my grandma's eyes never departed. My "transformation" wasn't just about the way I dress, the music I listen to, or the language I compose in — Rather, what changed the most was how I saw the world, its many societies, and the numerous people within. Learning history helped me understand the "habits of mind" of different civilizations, the customs and traditions ingrained in their cultures. Working in the news industry helped me gain perspectives on misinformation, government censorship, and partisan bias in today's mass media — what we came across online were, on many occasions, fabricated and filtered versions of reality. Finally, creative writing was not only my way of self-expression but also my means to explore and envision the alternative — a different path that a government, a society, or a character could have taken, as well as its possible outcome.

Perhaps, our world, shattered, fueled, polarized, needs exactly that kind of intersectionality.

卡耐基梅隆大学
Carnegie Mellon University

范文作者：LXJ，被卡耐基梅隆大学录取

Please submit a one-page, single-spaced essay that explains why you have chosen Carnegie Mellon and your particular major(s), department(s) or program(s). This essay should include the reasons why you've chosen the major(s), any goals or relevant work plans and any other information you would like us to know. For freshmen applying to more than one college or program, please mention each college or program to which you are applying. Because our admission committees review applicants by college and program, your essay can impact our final decision. Candidates applying for early decision or transfer may apply to only one college and department.

请提交一篇文书，解释你为什么选择卡耐基梅隆大学和你选择的专业、系或

项目。这篇文书包括你选择专业的原因，任何目标或相关的工作计划，以及你想让我们知道的任何其他信息。对于申请多个学院或项目的新生，请注明你申请的每个学院或项目。因为我们的招生委员会会根据学院和课程对申请人进行审查，所以你的文书会影响我们的最终决定。早申请或转学的申请者只能申请一个学院和系。

Mellon College of Science，Physics.

I love immersing myself in the study of physics and exploring the nature of the universe. My interest originated from learning quantum physics. By reading Does God Play Dice? A History of Quantum Physics by Tianyuan Cao，I became fascinated by atomic models and quantum theories. Later，I furthered my exploration in the discipline by taking the highest level physics courses in my high school and entering the USAD competition.

The physics department at Carnegie Mellon University is an ideal place for me to further my education. My passion for robotics and math modeling has fueled my interest in the computational physics track. I look forward to applying programming and modeling skills to the study of physics. In addition，I find many of the physics course offerings very interesting，including Physics for Future Presidents，which goes beyond doing calculations and instead discusses the social and political impact of physics，and Science and Science Fiction.

Beyond the classroom，I plan to apply and further my understanding of physics through research and internships. I am particularly interested in Professor Robert H. Swendsen's research，focusing on computer simulations in solid state physics and statistical mechanics. I also intend to use the services of the Career and Professional Development Center（CPDC），which provides students resources to find their career goal through internship opportunities.

Dietrich College of Humanities and Social Sciences，Statistics.

In addition to the study of physics，I also intend to major in Statistics at the Dietrich College of Humanities and Social Sciences. Statistical thinking and data analysis are increasingly crucial in the era of big data. I am particularly drawn to the StatML joint major. The curriculum not only helps students lay a solid foundation in mathematics and data analysis, but also equips students with computing knowledge, which is critical for machine learning. I would love to participate in courses such as Statistical Computing and Algorithms and Advanced Data Structures. This interdisciplinary way of learning would prepare me for future applications of statistics in other fields, like computer science.

At the Statistics & Data Science Department, I could learn from and interact with eminent scholars. I would love to participate in the Privacy and Cyber-Security research group led by Professor Jay Kadane, and further my study of the use of statistical thinking in machine learning under the guidance of Professor Mark Schervish, an expert in statistical machine learning and its applications. Through research and internships, I would seek opportunities to apply knowledge to solve real-life problems.

Carnegie Mellon University is a community where I would find outstanding academic resources and a shared passion for obtaining knowledge and utilizing it for the betterment of our society. Surrounded by world-class professors and like-minded peers, I would feel a sense of belonging and a strong desire to contribute to the community.

List the books (if any) you've read this year for pleasure. Choose one and in a sentence describe its impact on you. (500s words limit)

列出你今年读过的书(如果有的话)。选出一本,用一句话描述它对你的影响。(500 词以内)

1453: The Holy War for Constantinople and the Clash of Islam and the West, by Roger Crowley.

Does God Play Dice? The History of Quantum Physics, by Tianyuan Cao.

The Decline and Fall of the Japanese Empire, by John Toland.

Utopia, by St. Thomas More.

The Prophet, by Kahlil Gibran.

The Plague, by Albert Camus.

Slaughterhouse-Five, by Kurt Vonnegut.

Animal Farm, by George Orwell.

The Three Body Problem, by Cixin Liu.

The Hitchhiker's Guide to the Galaxy, by Douglas Adams.

Reading 1453: The Holy War for Constantinople and the Clash of Islam and the West strengthened my view that people and societies that fail to adapt to new technologies and new circumstances will eventually be weeded out.

弗吉尼亚大学
University of Virginia

范文作者: Nijedan,被弗吉尼亚大学录取

What's your favorite word and why? (250 words)

什么是你最喜欢的词,为什么?(250 词)

The word "terminal" encompasses our past, present, future, and a metaphor for life.

"Terminal" is where you depart from your hometown, wave to your beloved, turn around, and take off to a distant land. I remember my first time stranded in an airport terminal, having to cut ties with the warmth and coziness of home, ready to leap off to a different continent to continue my education. "Terminal" marks our farewells to the past.

In addition, "terminal" is a connecting device in computers. Through terminals, we engaged in conversations and kept ourselves updated with news and stories around the globe; in some ways, a "terminal" is the key for us to maintain our membership in the ever-changing contemporary societies and not to be left behind, trapped in the dark and distant age of the past.

The word “Terminal” can also mean the end of a railway or transportation route, or an incurable disease. While some take off and depart, many more have just reached the end of their journeys, some exacerbated by sights of their native lands and others getting ready for a new start. With aspiration and ambition they had once set sail, and with peace and gratitude they now returned.

Thus, a “terminal” is a continuous and eternal loop of past, present, and future, of departing, pondering, and reaching the destination, in literal sense and in life as well. Perhaps, like a Möbius strip, the interconnected, repetitive nature gives “terminal” its unique and thought-provoking magic.

What work of art, music, science, mathematics, literature, or other media has surprised, unsettled, or inspired you, and in what way? (250 words)

什么样的艺术、音乐、科学、数学或文学作品让你感到惊讶、不安或挑战？(250 词)

In The Crusade in Arab Eyes, French-Lebanese scholar Amin Maalouf characterized the constant hostilities between Western civilizations and the Arab world as vengeance that originated in the age of the Crusades, saying “The Arab East still sees the West as a natural enemy,” fighting an old war under new causes. Maalouf’s perspective has remained particularly impactful for me since it extended my perception beyond a binary understanding of relationships between political entities.

Maalouf’s argument reminded me of the importance of comparative studies, prompting me to read the more theoretical writings of past political scientists such as Locke’s Second Treatise of Government and Rousseau’s The Social Contract. These Enlightenment era concepts, however, were inevitably limited by their historical contexts and Eurocentric mindsets. Rereading

Maalouf's work, however, inspired me to incorporate distinct perspectives across cultural and national lines into my study.

My research project focused on American politics under the Carter and Reagan administrations. Maalouf's refreshing interpretation of the Crusades through an Arab perspective encouraged me to read extensively on Latin American history, politics, and social structures. Ultimately, I decided to analyze the two presidents' divergent emphasis on foreign affairs and the international power dynamics of the Cold War not through the typical American perspective, but through lenses of Nicaraguans, Salvadorans, and Iranians.

Through the inspirations of Maalouf's work and my further reading, I wish to continue to explore global politics, especially in the Americas. I am eager to learn from local conditions and perspectives, re-evaluating orthodoxies from the ground up.

北卡罗来纳大学教堂山分校
University of North Carolina-Chapel Hill

范文作者：Nijedan，被北卡罗来纳大学教堂山分校录取

Expand on an aspect of your identity — for example, your religion, culture, race, sexual or gender identity, affinity group, etc. How has this aspect of your identity shaped your life experiences thus far? (250 words)

展开你身份的一方面（如宗教信仰、文化、种族、性别、社会活动等）。这一方面迄今为止是如何塑造你的人生体验的？（250 词）

Growing up in a traditional household in China, I was deeply immersed in a culture that valued strong family ties and emphasized "listening" rather than "talking." In school, we are organized into classes, close-knit communities that spend all time together. The teachers often adopt a lecture-based approach in education, simply transferring facts and formulas from one perspective directly to another.

Coming to the States all alone and starting high school there, I am immediately awestruck by the classroom layout, where a small group of students sit around round tables and self-organized discussions. The professor serves as a moderator instead of arbitrator during these conversations. In life, I am shocked to see how individuals can develop a personal path that stands different from their peers or against their parents' expectations.

The culture shock does not make me detest or abandon either of the cultures; Instead, I decide to look at them through an outside perspective and evaluate objectively. Rather, I have retained some elements — such as the willingness to listen, the effort to understand, and the need to uplift peers — in my home culture and embrace the parts of the new culture that best matched my vision: the importance to voice one's opinions, to make one's own decisions rather than bending to the pressures of others.

The intersection of two cultures and two ways of thinking is not bipolar or divisive, but cohesive: it provides insights to the choices I make and how I interact with others. Most importantly, it affects my style of leadership: leading the fencing team, I always embrace each player's suggestions while working to integrate the team by hosting events; being a senior prefect, I intend to encourage collaborations among my advisees while taking into account their individual talents. The mixed approach has worked out more effectively than the laissez-faire approach I've seen by other leaders here and more inspiring than the authoritarian management adopted by authoritative figures back home.

If you could change one thing about where you live, what would it be and why? (250 words)

如果你可以改变你住所的某一方面，会是什么？为什么？(250 词)

I grew up in Shanghai, a place with a rich and sophisticated cultural history. I remember galloping through the narrow alleyways, feeling the touches of the aged stone walls mixed with ancient Chinese embellishment and colonial outlooks, immersing myself in the deep condensation of local history, witnessing its growth from a fishing village, to a bustling trade port, and eventually to a cosmopolis filled with magical realism.

Attending high school in the States enabled me to see my home town from the outside. I was constantly awed by the metropolis' expansion both vertically and horizontally as well as its incorporation of high-techs such as 5G or Artificial Intelligence.

Interning at Shanghai Daily, I was given the task to report on the city's efforts to revitalize its historical sites, amidst criticism that it lacked a cultural identity. One of its projects was to refurbish and repurpose an old opera house, turning it into an interactive exhibition center stacked with VR games, giant TV screens, and modern dance performances.

To me, this was disappointing at best. Despite its goal of preserving history, the authorities wanted something impressive to tourists. However, this approach dismayed local residents, especially older ones. They preferred joyful rhythms and the soothing aroma of green tea inside a traditional opera house. The lack of connection between these grandiose projects and the local interest was painful and disheartening..

Back in the states, I saw many fabulous cases where local traditions and historical structures were preserved, immersed, and well-incorporated into modern societies. I witness Trinity Church standing alongside daunting skyscrapers, or Mardi Gras transitioning from a French, Christian ritual to a popular, cosmopolitan carnival.

In the future, I wish to utilize my study in history and politics, my experiences working at museums and publications, and the great examples I've seen in the States to promote a more natural and resonating representation of the local culture and history back home.

纽约大学
New York University

范文作者：M，被纽约大学录取

We would like to know more about your interest in NYU. What motivated you to apply to NYU? Why have you applied or expressed interest in a particular campus, school, college, program, and or area of study? If you have applied to more than one, please also tell us why you are interested in these additional areas of study or campuses. We want to understand — Why NYU? (400 words maximum)

我们想知道更多关于你对纽约大学的看法。是什么促使你申请纽约大学的？你为什么对某个校区、学院、专业或学习领域提出申请或表示出兴趣？如果你申请了不止一所学校，也请告诉我们你为什么对其他这些学习领域或校区感兴趣。我们想了解——为什么选择纽约大学？（最多400词）

NYU's visual arts and humanities programs prepare international students to become part of the global community by providing them with the classes, resources, and highest number of international students of any school in the US to learn from and be friends with. The student body as a whole is far more diverse than almost any university, as is the faculty and administration. I will be able to go to Berlin and Florence — my favorite cities — to attend the program sponsored by the classics department. I also hope to attend the Yeronisos Island Field School, gaining real-life archeological: surveying the field, cleaning artifacts, taking excavation photos — things I've I dreamed of since childhood.

Coming from Shanghai and visiting NYU, I felt both at home and like I had entered a world far (less) different than my own — skyscrapers dominate both skylines, the streets and metros packed during rush hour, the designer stores on Fifth Avenue and the Bund, restaurants with menus from all prices and countries.

But there also exist dramatic differences. While New York is a global in its demographics, Shanghai is still overwhelmingly Chinese. While the museums in New York contain many of the best art from around the world, Shanghai does not have museums that come close. Shanghai has the people's park which is known for arranging marriages and is nothing like Central Park, which is like entering a nature preserve in the midst of the city.

Lately, I've devoted myself to learning languages so I can become a global citizen. Already I've managed to text a Norwegian stranger using Norwegian for an hour, and at the very end she said; "If you go to Norway, you should come to my hometown, Bergen, it is so beautiful." I saw a door open: a door to her world, which not only transcended the difference in time zones and cultures, but also brought me into a new way of understanding.

Photography is my method to express my internal self to the external world. Every shot I take becomes my of world without "filters". I want to be the next Bill Cunningham. And to raise public awareness as did the Citizens of New York stories.

Walking through the NYU campus, I feel the energy of the city and the Village, but also know I have a lot I can bring to the community too.

纽约大学的视觉艺术和人文专业为国际生提供了各类课程、资源和来自美国各个学校的学生，让大家互相学习和互相认识对方，这使得国际学生能够融入全球性群体。总体来说，纽约大学的学生构成几乎比任何一所大学都要丰富，教职工和行政部门也是如此。我可以去我最喜欢的城市——柏林和佛罗伦萨，去参加古典学部门组织的各个项目，从而去做田野调查、整理史前器物、拍摄挖掘照片等我儿时就梦想做的事情。

当我探访纽约大学时，作为一名上海人，我对纽约感到如家一般的熟悉：和我所在的城市一样，这里有矗立云霄的摩天大楼，高峰时期拥挤的街道和地铁，第五大道上和外滩一样充斥着精品店，还有各式各样的餐厅，菜单上写着不同国家的语言和价格。

但纽约和上海也存在着极大的差别：纽约在人口构成上更加全球化，而上海还是来自各地的中国人居多；纽约的博物馆拥有来自全世界的佳品，而上海几乎没有能与之争锋的博物馆。上海的人民公园以它的相亲角著称，而到了中央公园却如同进入一个城市中的自然保护区。

近些年，我也致力于学习各种外语以成为一名国际公民。我曾经试着和一位挪威陌生人用挪威语发了一个小时的信息，最后她说：“如果你去挪威，一定要去我的家乡卑尔根看看，那里很美。”我感觉自己推开了一扇门：一扇通往她世界的门，这并不只是超越了时区和文化的差异，同时也带给我一种理解事物的新的角度。

摄影是我把内在的自我传达给外在世界的媒介。我拍的每一张照片组成了不带滤镜的自我世界。我希望成为下一个比尔·库宁汉，并像他这位讲述纽约故事的市民一样用我的照片来引起公众的注意。

漫步在纽约大学，我感受到来自城市和大学本身的活力，我也知道自己可以给这个集体带来很多东西。

第五节

美国部分文理学院辅文书鉴赏

阿默斯特学院
Amherst College

范文作者：Frank，被阿默斯特学院录取

第一题 **At Amherst we know that identity is more than checkboxes. If you would like to share more about your identity, background, family, culture or community, please tell us more here. (Maximum: 175 words)**

在阿默斯特，我们知道身份不仅仅是复选框。如果你想分享更多关于你的身份、背景、家庭、文化或社区的信息，请告诉我们。（最多175词）

I come from a multi-cultural background.

Having studied in a Chinese educational system for 8 years, my transition to Australia was difficult. From the occasional Aussi slang to disparate political ideologies to different life choices, I was initially overwhelmed. Yet, I made every effort to communicate with my Australian friends and quickly adapted to its culture.

I've now integrated myself into Aussi academic and social life. Then, I began to explore the idea of intellectual challenges while making videos for Special Olympics. I soon belonged to a more inclusive community. The athletes were at home on the sporting field: skilful, resilient, and determined, which moved all the spectators. Yet, there's still prejudice towards them by many.

Belonging to one's own micro-background is easy but belonging to a wider world is challenging. That's why I made two films for Special Olympics — to break stereotypes while foregrounding inclusion. That's also why I founded the Global Citizen Committee — to promote acceptance of different cultures and perspectives.

I aspire to bring people together in inclusive and supportive ways.

第二题　If you have engaged in significant research in the natural sciences, mathematics, computer science, social sciences or humanities that was undertaken independently of your high school curriculum, please provide a brief description of the research project: (50 - 75 words)

如果你在自然科学、数学、计算机科学、社会科学或人文科学领域从事过高中课程之外的研究,请简要说明所研究的项目:(50～75 词)

I constructed advanced ensemble machine-learning models (81.2% accuracy) to predict citizens' risks of becoming long-term unemployed using national-level data. I also examined how to dissect black-box models both locally and globally, revealing contributing factors of long-term unemployment. I also addressed an under-explored question in AI, that is, the inherent bias in machine learning model predictions. My research helps public employment services to profile and prioritise employment resources in an accountable, transparent, and ethical way.

第三题　Please briefly elaborate on an extracurricular activity or work experience of particular significance to you. (Maximum: 175 words)

请简要说明对你有特殊意义的课外活动或工作经历。(最多 175 词)

Filmmaking is one way I've contributed to my school and wider audiences. I intended my films to be lenses for raising awareness, voicing opinions, and empowering marginalized groups.

I've made promotional films for the school charity, for promoting educational programs, and our rowing team. I also helped the refugee club and my own Global Citizen Committee to spread words of inclusion.

My short film "Smiling Depression", viewed by over 350,000, explores the complexities of hiding depressive symptoms under a smile. In addition, my music video — "True Colors" — uses music to get people to open up to others. My collaborative project "Obsession" warns about drug abuse. Two of my films for Special Olympics, one local and one for the World Games, aim to break stereotypes and empower athletes with intellectual challenges. I've also made a film about mathematics, in a creative attempt to showcase its elegance and to advocate Australian students to choose mathematics courses.

Many of these films stirred debate and raised awareness. And I believe they have helped individuals and communities to move forward.

第四题 "Difficulty need not foreshadow despair or defeat. Rather achievement can be all the more satisfying because of obstacles surmounted." (300 words)

Attributed to William Hastie, Amherst Class of 1925, the first African-American to serve as a judge for the United States Court of Appeals

困难不必预示绝望或失败。相反,由于克服了障碍,成就会更加令人满意。(300 词)

来自阿默斯特学院 1925 届的威廉·黑斯蒂,第一位担任美国上诉法院法官的非裔美国人。

Timbertop: 230 students lived for a year in a rural Australian mountain range. We had no access to any technology. Our lives were filled with hiking, cross-country running, chopping wood, and community service, nestled alongside a demanding academic program.

The initial excitement about setting up tents or cooking on portable stoves was short-lived. We shared the pain of hiking 30 kilometers for 4 consecutive days with a 25-kilogram pack on our backs.

Starting our 4-Day Hike, the sun was shining brightly. As we gained altitude, it started to rain and soon it changed to snow. We had to camp, cook, and sleep in the thickening snow. That night, I had to fill up my water bottle from a narrow mountain stream, and the only way to do so was dipping my hands in piercingly cold water.

No doubt, it was difficult. But when I saw the sun setting on one side of the mountain and the moon rising on the other simultaneously, I was in awe by the spectacularly rare golden-hour view. Our achievements were certainly "all the more satisfying".

Literally, we shed blood and tears, but ended up saying it was the best year of our lives.

Indeed, there were many surprises along the way — a rare bowl of chicken curry for dinner, running every single step up a mountain ridge, telling stories around bonfires, or simply watching a possum scurrying away from our noise. The surmounted obstacles allowed us to grow into young adults while supporting each other and appreciating the journey we went through.

I still remember the sweat and pain and ache after our 33-kilometer marathon. But I also remember the deep bonds, the unyielding determination, and the year we call Timbertop. It inspires me to be resilient and persistent, taking on challenges with confident equanimity.

克莱蒙特·麦肯纳学院
Claremont Mckenna College

范文作者：小李，被克莱蒙特·麦肯纳学院录取

Why do you want to attend CMC? (Min: 150 words/Max: 250 words)

你为什么要加入克莱蒙特·麦肯纳学院？(最少 150 词，最多 250 词)

What excites me most about CMC is the strong spirit of leadership on campus. I know exactly what I want in college: (1) to meet inspiring leaders, (2) to be immersed in a liberal arts environment where debates and bold plans are embraced, and (3) to be serious about my broad-based and flexible academic studies, while spending considerable time solving real-world problems. I will find them all at CMC!

The majority of influential figures I have spoken with, including the mayor of Honolulu and the special advisers of UNDP, are people I met at meetings and dinners. So the Athenaeum of CMC caught my attention. I want to talk to Ramona Vosburg about how I feel atheism is hurting my country's mental health, and ask Peter Hayes: is a holocaust still likely to happen in today's world? Or new types of disasters, in cyberspace or in a virtual world, will emerge? I cannot wait to discuss issues like these with motivated friends and faculty at CMC and other Claremont Colleges. Under the balmy sunshine of California, we are going to utilize the plentiful resources in the Claremont Consortium, and address the problems in new and creative ways.

克莱蒙特·麦肯纳学院最吸引我之处在于其所倡导的领导力精神。我的大学生活目标非常清楚：(1) 结识各领域的领袖；(2) 在一个自由的环境中大胆地表达与辩论；(3) 在认真学习理论知识的同时，花时间踏入社会学习处理真实的社会问题。克莱蒙特·麦肯纳学院可以让我达到这些目标。

我曾接触过一些很有影响力的人物，如夏威夷火奴鲁鲁市市长和联合国发展规划署特别顾问。通常我都在参加会议或晚宴时见到这些人。正因此我很喜欢克莱蒙特的 Athenaeum。我想要与罗姆纳·沃斯伯格探讨宗教在中国的角色，我还想要问彼得·海斯当今世界仍然会出现大规模的战争吗。还是说冲突会更多地发生在网络或虚拟空间？我期待能够与克莱蒙特·麦肯纳学院以及学校的其他同学和教授一起讨论这些问题。在加州温暖的阳光下，希望我能够充分利用克莱蒙特联盟的资源，学习用创新思维解决问题的能力。

注释：

Athenaeum：一个类似于 TED 的演讲活动，学期间学校在每个工作日邀请各领域的专家学者和学生共进晚餐并分享自己对一个话题的见解。

罗姆纳·沃斯伯格和彼得·海斯是将要参加 Athenaeum 的两位学者。

华盛顿与李大学
University of Washington and Lee

范文作者：Nijedan，被华盛顿与李大学录取

Please describe how you have familiarized yourself with Washington and Lee University and what aspects of W&L's community are most exciting to you. (250 words)

请描述你是如何了解华盛顿与李大学的，以及我校社区的哪些方面最令你激动。(250 词)

From early on, I have been intrigued by the political dynamics in the U.S., reading about personal politics in the early republic era, or analyzing the polarized contemporary society. Hosting one of the nation's most prestigious electoral mock conventions, Washington and Lee University caught my attention, which led me to do more research and take a virtual tour.

Hoping to pursue intersectional studies of politics, history, and economics, I found the Williams School particularly appealing due to its interdisciplinary coursework. The American Political Thought seminar, for example, would allow me to review different "systems of thought" in American history and their lasting influences, seeking answers for the ultimate question of "morality versus expediency" in politics. The possibility to spend a term at the national capital also excites me, as I hope to gain hands-on experiences and apply my classroom learnings through intern opportunities.

At W&L, I will get the unique chance to experience a world-class liberal arts education while taking courses from the graduate law program. I envision pursuing the Law, Justice, and Society minor, which would connect my understanding of political theories to my concerns on social issues, opening up more career opportunities.

Outside the classroom, I hope to engage in intellectual conversations with peers through the Alexander Hamilton Society and utilize my past experiences with journalism and publications to contribute to The Columns. In addition, I want to meet like-minded people and continue my passions in leadership and service through W&L's Greek system.

Please describe an aspect of your life outside of school that is important to you, such as an extracurricular activity, a job or a family responsibility. How does your involvement impact you and those around you? (250 words)

请描述在你课余生活中对你至关重要的某一方面，如课外活动、打工或家庭责任。你的参与是如何影响你自己和你身边的人的？(250 词)

Earlier this year, a few friends and I founded Hope Humanities, an online journal platform, to help high school students pursue their passion in writing and publication amidst the pandemic.

I picked the name "Hope" for our platform: after all, it is the gleam of light in times of difficulties and also stands for "Humanities Online Platform for Everyone." In a few months, our organization grew to a team of over 100 students, representing over 70 institutions across five countries. Aside from publishing monthly selections of research papers, prose, and poetry, we also started hosting workshops and organizing competitions to promote humanities and cross-cultural understanding. I particularly enjoyed the opportunity to collaborate with many students from diverse cultural and educational backgrounds, brought together by the common passion in humanities.

Despite my previous experiences in media and publications, I encountered many new challenges heading the political commentaries department: How do I adopt a more objective stance when reviewing submissions? Should I publish an article that might be misconstrued as offensive to the readers? Suddenly, the principles and guidelines I learned from my journalism class seemed misplaced and too vague for me to take actions. The conventional approach would be to balance out the different perspectives; however, would that necessarily constitute fairness and equality? The best I could do was to stay open-minded, discuss with team members, host peer review sessions, and most importantly, create a space of pluralism, where all meritorious and respectful voices across platforms and ideologies could be heard.

戴维森学院
Davidson college

范文作者：Nijedan，被戴维森学院录取

Why Davidson? (250 - 300 Suggested Words Limit)

为什么选择戴维森学院？（限 250～300 词）

Having spent my past four years at a boarding school, I was hesitant before my visit to Davidson, fearing I might be trapped in a small bubble with homogenous voices.

My perception immediately changed when I began my tour. A young man with a genuine smile, my tour guide had similar backgrounds as myself: both Asian international students, both attended a boarding school, and shared a passion in history and political science with a global insight.

Our first stop was a beautiful lawn with scattered students sitting around; he explained, in times of presidential elections and other political events, clubs representing different platforms and interests would organize debates and encourage conversations, where I could have my beliefs challenged by the diverse voices of my peers.

Stepping down the staircase of E. Craig Wall Jr. Academic Center, he explained to me the significance of honor code, a principle most important to Davidson students and a part of their citizenship and commitment to the campus community.

Walking through the long hallways in the Chambers Building, I envisioned the courses I might take as a Davidson student. Maybe, I would be exploring factors such as proxy wars, post-colonial economic exploitations, and widening income gap and their impacts on the rise of terrorism in the Global War on Terror seminar. Or perhaps, I would find myself in the U.S.-Latin American Relations class, analyzing Latin America's strategic significance during the cold war and the negative influences that U. S. intervention had brought to the democratization of Latin American nations. When the bell tolled and discussion came to end, I would pick up my pen, combining my academic interests with my passions in publications, through writing Op ED articles for Davidsonian, or reviewing the submission for Libertas, the art and literary student publication.

List the books you have read in the past year for school or leisure. Place an asterisk by those books required for classes you have taken.

列出你在去年读过的课堂或课外读物。在课程要求的书目旁用星号(＊)标注。

History of Political Thoughts: Why and how should we govern?

(1) **Affairs of Honor*, written by Joanne B. Freeman, on the concept of "personal honor" and the various political maneuvers in the early Republic, which culminated at the election of 1776 and 1800 and began to decline.

(2) **The Great Debate: Edmund Burke, Thomas Paine, and the Birth*

of Right and Left, written by Yuval Levin, which discusses the background and beliefs of Burke and Paine, how these factors affect their attitudes towards revolution and social change, and how their debate is relevant to the partisan split in America.

(3) * On Politics: A History of Political Thought from Herodotus to the Present, written by Alan Ryan, which explored a plethora of classical, renaissance, and enlightenment political theories, such as Plato, Machiavelli, Thomas More, Hobbes, and Locke.

(4) *The Conscience of a Conservative*, written by Barry Goldwater, enabled me to explore the roots and principles of political and economic conservatism in America and shed lights on the 1964 presidential election between Goldwater and Johnson.

Colonial History of the Americas and Its Lasting Impacts:

(1) * *Brazil: The Troubled Rise of a Global Power*, written by Michael Reid, which recounted the nation's unique and fascinating history (long and persistent practice of slavery, inheritance of a monarchial system post-indepedence, acceptance of miscegenation), its diverse and vibrant society, as well as its seemingly promising yet often-times stagnant economic development.

(2) *A Voyage Long and Strange: Rediscovering the New World*, written by Tony Horwitz, which detailed the Viking, Spanish, and French colonial history in North America before the departure of Mayflower in 1620 as well as its impacts on the "habit of mind" of contemporary Americans.

(3) *Guns, Germs, and Steel: The Fates of Human Societies*, written by Jared Diamond, a work that had sparked controversies and considerable debate among historians as it emphasized the roles of technologies and immunity in the successful conquests of Eurasian civilizations, as their geographical locations provided more possibilities of contact, trade, and

exchange.

History of Wars and Conflicts: How did they rise? What are their legacies?

(1) *The Crusades through Arab Eyes*, by Amin Maalouf, which presented an interesting and rare voice in the discussion of the crusades, connecting the historical grievances to the present-day conflict in the Middle East.

(2) *A Mad Catastrophe: The Outbreak of World War I and the Collapse of the Habsburg Empire*, by Geoffrey Wawro, attributed the fall of the Habsburg Empire, whose power loomed over Europe for centuries until the Prussia-Austria War, to its corrupt and obsolete government, its outdated and poorly equipped military, as well as its inherent shortcoming — being home to dozens of different ethnic groups during the rise of nationalism in Europe.

(3) *King John: And the Road to Magna Carta*, Stephen Church, discussed King John's life and his unsuccessful wars in Normandy and Aquitaine, filled in the gap in my historical understanding, and sketched a more complete picture surrounding the origin and development of the Magna Carta, a document that shed lights on modern constitutional democracy.

(4) *City of Fortune: How Venice Ruled the Seas*, Roger Crowley, helped me understand how political construct, social hierarchy, and military expansions work within medieval merchant republics while exposing its dependency on the broader Mediterrean market and its inability to integrate overseas colonies, a few reasons which contributed to its eventual decline and collapse.

Literature and Non-fictions: Power of Societal Reflections.

(1) * *Kindred*, Octavia E. Butler, a mix-and-match of science fiction and discussions of slavery, which juxtopsed the stories of an interracial couple in 1970s California and lives on a plantation in a slave state during antebellum era.

(2) *A Good Man is Hard to Find: And Other Stories*, Flannery O'Connor, a collection of short stories reflecting various themes — family, religion, and race — in the southern society from the early-to-mid twentieth century, depicted through O'Connor's unique lenses as a moralistic, Roman Catholic woman.

(3) *Hillbilly Elegy: A Memoir of A Family and Culture in Crisis*, J.D. Vance, another controversial non-fiction that emphasized the roots of the Applachian culture, the decline of manufacture-based industries on the rust belt, the causes of working class poverty, as well as the generational shift in political leaning (from establishment to populistic), core family values, and work ethics. Again, the author's personal experience might not be as valid as he claims but nevertheless provides a good opening to some largely ignored societal problems among blue collar Americans.

(4) *The Gangs of New York*, Herbert Asbury, an entertaining yet sometimes revolting (whenever it comes to poor condition and hygiene of the slum) read about the corrupt and nasty underworld of New York City, which helped me understand the success of Tammany Hall and Boss Tweed and starkly juxtaposed NYC in contemporary eyes.

Please briefly elaborate on one of your extracurricular activities or work experiences. (200 Words Limit)

请简述你的一个课外活动或工作经历(限 200 词)

In the midst of the pandemic, a few friends and I founded a journal platform for high school students, hoping to help our peers continue their passions as extracurricular activities become less accessible.

I picked the name "Hope" for our platform. It not only represents a gleam of light in times of great despair but also stands for "Humanities Online Platform for Everyone." In a few months, our team grew to over a hundred members from over 70 institutions, spanning three continents.

Despite my previous experiences in publications, I encountered many new problems heading HOPE's political commentaries department: How do I adopt a less biased perspective when reviewing submissions with strong political leanings? How should I judge a work that might be deemed offensive? The purpose of journalism is to deliver the truth with accuracy, I learned, but such a principle is difficult to follow in real life. What I did was to create a space of liberty and pluralism, where all meritorious and respectful voices across platforms and ideologies could be heard.

More importantly, I was able to find my own "community" and collaborate with many students from diverse backgrounds, brought together by the common passion in humanities.'

附录

附录1 申请美国大学前的三个关键

在申请美国大学前，如何做到步步为营？以下三个关键步骤家长们一定要重视。

第一个关键——高中课程的选择与表现

高中课程的选择对学生来说至关重要，这关乎学生在高中阶段的知识吸收速度、个性的成长和学习成绩，以及未来出国后对国外体系的适应速度。

每个学生都有适合他的课程体系。绝大部分学生都是接受九年制义务教育通过中考进入高中。对于这一部分学生要进行分类，对于那些学习能力和时间管理能力非常强，在保证学校课业成绩优秀的情况下，依然能有时间去参加课外活动和比赛的学生继续体制内路线是一种不错的选择。在体制内高中课程中，他所能学到的理科知识相对是有优势的。但是体制内课程的压力也会带来可能的劣势，主要是学生需要额外时间来提升英语水平和做课外活动。

另外，体制内课程是高考导向型，而美国申请是侧重课内一贯的表现。这个不同就会让体制内的同学面临尴尬的境地。体制内课程老师为了让学生意识到高考时的差距，平时考查要求严苛，难度很大，从而成绩看起来平平。平均分 50 分或 60 分也是很常见的。

在平均分只有 50 分或 60 分时，70 分或 80 分确实很不错了。可是 70 分或 80 分这个成绩在提交美国大学的成绩单上只有 2.0 或 3.0（满分 4.0），这个分数就可能让学生的申请材料尚未被招生官读到就被拒绝了。

对于学习能力非常强，英语能力突出的学生就建议学习 IBDP 课程，高一的时候学习 IGCSE 和 PreIB 都可以。IBDP 的优势是能很好地过渡到美国大学的课程体系和英语能力的提升，劣势是需要学生花费大量时间进行适应并且完成很大的课程量。

A-Level 十一年级后科目数量要求不高，且国内开设的课程主要是理科。对于比较偏科理科的学生是不错的选择。

AP 不是课程体系而是考试类型。所以，对于 AP 考生，无论是科目还是考试数量，选择空间比较大，有能力就能冲刺更多门的 AP 考试。对于那些学习能力很强的学生，大学前就能探求多方向学科，收获证实自己实力的许多门 AP，加速未来方向的选择。AP 和 IB 达到一定分数，都能在大一时换学分。

美国大学对 IB、AP 和 A-level 都接受，但最终取决于对于本校课程难度的挑战和课程成绩。有成绩没有难度和有难度没有成绩，都会成为进入梦想学校的阻碍。

第二个关键——标化考试成绩

标化考试成绩是帮助大学招生官评判不同学校学生的水平的。对于不为大学招生官熟悉的学校而言，标化考试的作用更加重要。

标化考试分为语言考试和学习能力测试。语言考试为托福、雅思、多邻国等学校承认的英语考试。学习能力测试为 SAT，ACT。语言是基础，是必须首先突破的。如果托福没有达到一定程度就开始其他考试，就好比蛇吞象的效果，会造成消化不良，产生效果低下的结果。

标化考试最重要的是时间安排。特别是 SAT 考试是需要出境考试的，考试次数需要控制，时间规划更加重要。

第三个关键——课外活动的选择

美国大学对学生的评价，不仅仅局限于学术成绩，同时也会对个性以及未来的发展潜力做出评估。同时，美国大学强调学生不仅仅向老师学习，也需要向身边的同学学习。所以，美国大学希望录取的学生是各种各样的，有不同的背景和态度，从而在潜移默化中推动学生的成长。

如何评判学生的个性特质和潜力，主要是通过课外活动、奖项、文书、推荐信和面试获得。

活动的作用，首先是提供学生成长的平台。学生在活动中不断发现自我，并获得提升。其次，活动需要呈现孩子的热情、能力以及与其他学生的差异性。

活动的选择上，主要分为两块，一块是参与活动的时间，一块是参与什么活动。活动的选择应该从兴趣、优势、资源 3 个方面综合考量。

如果是九年级学生，时间比较宽裕，可以大范围地接触多种类、多方向的活动，进行初步筛选。十年级开始应该集中 1～3 个方向，各种活动围绕这几个方向推广。十一年级应该在 1～2 个方向上深度推进，并取得成绩。十二年级持续最重要的活动。

活动应该是校内校外资源结合运用，学术和慈善、艺术或体育项目等兼顾。

活动是培养软实力的沃土。时间管理、领导力管理、沟通能力、团队合作等等都是我们给予孩子最好的礼物。

附录 2　从初三暑假到录取——美国大学申请规划理想时间表

九年级　基础期

体验生活,自我探索,开阔视野,寻找兴趣,培养个人爱好

具体行动:

1. 积极拓展,参与学校各种社团活动,包括慈善、志愿者活动

2. 发展个人兴趣爱好(艺术、科技、体育、阅读)

3. 利用寒暑期参加夏令营/冬令营,体验国际课程

4. 读英文原版小说,培养阅读习惯

5. 开始提高英语水平,强化托福练习

十年级　发展期

打好学术基础,发展个人活动,增强领导力,确定未来的大方向

具体行动:

1. 尽快适应高中生活,挑战有一定难度的课程并保证 GPA

2. 在保证校内学术成绩良好的情况下,拓展校内外其他学科或学术类活动

3. 坚持大批量英文原版阅读,强化英语练习

4. 争取托福过关,开始 SAT 培训

5. 逐步明确专业方向,参与或创立相关社团,并培养团队合作精神和领导力

6. 坚持志愿者活动和个人兴趣活动

7. 寒暑期参与学校(修学分)/专业相关的实习/志愿者

十一年级　冲刺期

提升亮点活动，发展个人兴趣，展示领导力，建构学术方向

具体行动：

1. 争取高分完成有挑战性的课程
2. 取得具有竞争力的标化考试成绩(SAT/ACT，AP)
3. 继续参加学术型活动，争取学术性奖项，全面展示学术能力及领导力
4. 暑假参与竞争力强的暑期项目或进行研究性实习或科研活动
5. 培养领导力，在1～2个社团获得领导职位
6. 坚持志愿者活动和个人兴趣活动
7. 寒暑假参观大学，进行初步选校定位
8. 十一升十二年级的暑期开始文书写作

十二年级　总结期

确定目标学校和申请方向，全面展示学术能力及活动能力，完成升学申请工作

具体行动：

1. 保持有竞争力的学科成绩
2. 完成高中学业及相关考试。拓展其他学科，为大学学分换算做好准备
3. 管理自己的团队，持续参加原有的活动，推动社区变革
4. 完成文书、面试和申请系统的填写和申请工作
5. 跟踪申请结果，补交学校要求的材料
6. 确认入学的大学，并根据学校要求完成各项大学入学准备工作
7. 为高中生活写上圆满的句号

附录 3　申请后小贴士两则

申请后小贴士 1：成功进入理想学校后，第一份实习如何找？又该如何准备申请研究生？

从拿到录取通知书到正式入住学校宿舍，很多学生都松了一口气，感觉放飞自我的四年开始了，然而真的是这样吗？其实很多大学给你创造的机会就这样被浪费了。

以就业来说，学校为了能给学生更好的就业率，绝大部分学校都会一年举办两场实习招聘会(career fair)。每一场招聘会都会提前几个月通知并告知每一家公司所需要的实习职位和岗位，招聘会也不单单是为毕业生准备的，很多公司会需要暑期实习生。通过参与学校的招聘会能够直面公司的人力资源部(HR)。很多来到学校的公司 HR 都是本校毕业生或者公司的老板是学校毕业生，这样的公司往往也更愿意给出实习的机会，但是需要学生对各个公司有着足够的了解。缺乏资料的学生除了通过网站搜索外，也可以去学校里一个叫作职业指导中心(career center)的地方询问更多的信息。几乎每一个学校都会专门开设职业指导中心给到学生更多的资料以及可能比招聘会更多的实习岗位。很多学校为了鼓励学生实习，甚至暑期的实习还会给学生学分(毕竟很多实习公司都不给钱)让学生更快地毕业。还有一些学校(如达特茅斯学院)，允许学生自由选择时间段，申请春秋季去实习，来增强竞争机会。这些都是学生刚入学就应该去了解的。

对于一些比较善于交际的学生也可以确定一个自己的求职意向，通过学校的邮箱给学校校友发送求职实习邮件，或者是通过当地的校友会找到实习单位。中国学生脸皮薄可能一开始不倾向于这么做，但是校友资源往往是美国大学能给到一个学生最好的资源之一，善于利用这一资源往往得到的会比你想到的更多！

在申请实习之前，不仅仅需要了解目标公司和职位，还需要做好自我的准备：简历和求职信。这是公司接触到你的第一部分信息。学校的职业指导中心都会提供帮助，指导你如何把简历做到最好。当然简历除了排版漂亮，内容更加重要。简历涵盖专业、成绩、校内活动/职位以及完成的实习机会。美国大四毕业后拿到的工作录取通知大部分来自大三升大四暑期的实习单位。所以，大三暑期的实习非常重要。大三暑期的实习大部分是大三上学期申请到的，少部分是大三下学期拿到的。当然也有少数优秀同学在大二升大三的暑期就拿下了实习机会。大三前如果在美国没能拿下实习机会，就应该尽量在国内拿到实习机会，让未来的公司看到你在不断地提升自我。进入大学后，实习的时间管理也是强烈推荐学生关注的。

当然也会有很多学生不满足于本科这个学历，希望追求更高的学历，那么应该怎么做呢？

在美国，如果目标是学术研究，未来进入大学或研究机构，一般直接申请读博士。如果目标是研究生后进入企业，就应该申请硕士研究生项目。大部分硕士研究生项目是职业导向，少量研究生项目是偏学术型，为博士申请做准备的。如果目标是律师 JD，大四上学期需要考 LSAT 并申请法学院。如果目标是做医生，大四前需要考 MCAT，然后申请医学院。上述所有研究项目申请，GPA 都是第 1 位的。其他的申请基础是标化考试，包括 GRE、GMAT、LSAT 和 MCAT。考哪一个，需要看具体项目的要求。除了法学院，相关实习经历尤为重要，研究生/博士申请中，研究经历和教授推荐信变得非常重要。

每一个学校，不管是文理学院还是综合型大学，都会给本科生以科研机会。文理学院虽然小，但是没有研究生在竞争，拿到研究机会比较大。大型研究型大学，虽然研究项目不少，但是争取的学生也多，更加需要学生积极主动地去争取。大二或大三是申请研究项目的最佳时间点。大型研究型大学还提供暑期研究项目，有一些大学甚至对外校学生提供研究项目的机会。这些都是可以去抓住的机会。

大学科研项目往往是教授带着学生一起进行的。有些学校是有系统公示研究项目和申请要求的，同学们应该提早关注。当然也建议和一些喜爱的教授多喝茶沟通或发邮件，向教授询问是否平时或者暑期有这些研究科研机会可以参与和学习。教授在这方面是有权力决定要谁进组做研究的。

总结一下，大学不是一个松懈的理由，相反的应该是更愉快的忙碌。

志向直接工作的，需要抓住学校能提供的招聘会，职业指导中心，校友等资源从实习开始，美国企业往往喜欢实习生多年转正的套路，在美实习也能让美国企业更放心地录用你工作。

而志向研究生或者博士生的，就应该早早的开始科研，和教授打好关系，并进行细化专业的研究和匹配。考试成绩到最后大家都差不多，丰富的科研经济和教授一篇充满赞扬的推荐信也就更能帮助学生本身。

申请后小贴士 2：未能进入“梦校”，这样做“曲线救国”，转学还能搏一回！

曲线救国，也就是大学转学，是一种高效而又方便还省钱的进入梦想学校的方式。

美国大学一般课程设置均为大一大二进行“general education”学习，也就是通识课的学习，每一个学生都要学习人文社科，自然科学，艺术，体育等多方面课程，当然也有一些课程的专业前置课会放在大一大二学习，然后大二下半学期填写表格正式申请专业，大三正式进入专业，大三大四主要以专业课为主。根据这样的设计，是能支持同学转学的。

一般转学有两种方式，一种是大学直接邀请你大二再去。比如佐治亚理工学院会给学生直接发大二转学录取通知，学生直接去另一个学校读一年，只要保证一定的 GPA，大二可以直接转校进来。第二种也是最常见的，学生直接自己申请转学。很多学校会接受大一转大二，也有一些学校只接受大二转大三。一般不接受大三转大四。

大一转大二，一开始就需要了解目标学校的转学课程和学分要求，避免因为不了解而错过要求。同时确保高 GPA，积极探索学校的活动资源，让目标学校的老师看到你能快速适应和融于新的学习环境。很多学生其实大一大二的课程难度并不大，专业课程的学习也不会很多，在校的成绩也相对较高。美国大学也非常乐意招收这一部分已经完成了基础课程学习，成绩上佳并且有了非常明确的专业意向的学生。

大部分学生是大二转大三，特别对于高中成绩不够理想的同学，是比较适合大二转大三的。这个时候的转校，对于国际学生，托福是必须的。但是很多学校不再要求SAT成绩。SAT成绩不理想但是大学GPA很漂亮的学生，比较适合大二转大三。这个时候的转学，目标学校一般会要求学生明确希望选择的专业。所以在大一大二的选课中，需要根据目标学校专业的要求，上足“pre-request”课程。在绝大部分的美国大学，或许3.0/4.0不是一个难以取得的分数，但是3.5+/4.0就是一个相对来说更难拿到的分数，这个分数能让大学看到是一个上进的，学习能力强的学生。

转学时需要提交申请文书、成绩单，还需要老师推荐信。所以，在大一大二上学期，需要至少和一位授课教授搞好关系，能让教授同意为你提交推荐信。

附录 4　不要盲目崇拜大学排行榜

做好了申请美国大学前的准备后，为自己选择目标学校成了最重要的事情，在此要多提醒一句：大学排行榜只能作为参考，而不能盲目崇拜。

现在市面上各个排行榜的参考依据相差甚大，导致同一所大学在不同排行榜上的排名可能相差甚远。例如，华盛顿西雅图大学在 2020 年 *U.S. News* 美国排名中位列第 62 位，而在 *U.S. News* 世界排名第 10 位。那么为什么这两个排名的差距会相差那么大呢？这是因为两个排行榜所考量的全面性不同，关注的侧重点不同。我们可以看一下这两个排行榜的考量依据(见附表 4.1)。

附表 4.1　*U.S. News* 大学排名参考指标对比

U.S. News 美国大学排名		*U.S. News* 世界大学排名	
参考指标	权重	参考指标	权重
毕业率和留校率	22%	全球学术声誉	12.5%
专家意见	20%	地区学术声誉	12.5%
师资力量	20%	论文发表	10%
学生表现	10%	图书刊物	2.5%
财政资源	10%	会议	2.5%
毕业率表现	8%	标准化论文引用影响指数	10%
校友捐赠	5%	论文引用数	7.5%
社会流动	5%	被引用最多的 10%的出版物数量	12.5%
		出版物占被引用最多 10%的比率	10%
		国际协作	10%
		代表领域中出版物被引用最多 1%的数量	5%
		出版物占被引用最多 1%的比率	5%

(资料来源：*U.S. News* 官网 https://www.usnews.com/education)

由此可见，*U.S. News* 世界排名更偏重学术成就，其中包括出版物和学术论文，更加注重学术研究对国际的影响。而 *U.S. News* 美国大学排名则更加注重对学生全面综合的教育，学校的声誉，毕业生的反馈，以及师资力量，等等。不同的排名考量会带来截然不同的学校排名，因此在选择学校时，排行榜只能作为参考，适合自己的学校才是最正确的选择。

当下的中国社会，用人单位很看重应聘者毕业院校的排名或者知名度，在很大程度上据此来判断应聘者的能力。并且，有很多中国家长认为排名是评价学校的唯一标准。而在美国人眼里，学校排名虽然重要，但只可作参考标准之一，他们更崇尚学生在申请院校时找到更适合、更匹配自己的学校。例如，加州大学戴维斯分校招生办主任沃特·罗宾森在《环球时报》中说道："学生找到适合自己的，满足自身需求的大学才最重要。"留学生应该在了解大学排名的基础上，对学校进行更深度地了解，如这所学校是否有自己感兴趣的专业，这所学校是否能为学生提供丰富的科研以及社会实践的机会，其教学质量、生活环境是否多元化等。

著名的专栏作家托马斯·弗里德曼在《纽约时报》上发表过两篇文书，分享了世界上最受尊敬的企业之一——谷歌公司的人力资源总监关于招聘的一些见解。出乎意料的是，谷歌并不会特别关注那些名牌大学的毕业生。这位总监说道："现如今，一个人的才能可以有多种多样的形式，并且可以通过很多其他渠道培养出来。人事部需要通过大学的品牌，洞察学生的实质。"文书还表明："一个人的工作能力并不取决于他的学历。这个社会只关注他能如何运用所学知识，并为这种能力买单，而不会在意他是如何学到的。"一位谷歌的招聘官也说道："当我阅读应聘者的简历时，他们是否有大学学位确实很重要，但我从来不会特别关注他们的毕业院校。"

同样地，《华尔街日报》刊登过一篇研究薪酬与学校、专业之间关系的文书。该文书称，职业生涯平均收入最高的是理工科毕业生，学校排名对其影响非常小。除此之外，就业以及收入情况与学校的地理位置关系更加密切，其影响要大于学校的排名。例如，根据美国专业招聘平台 Jobvite 显示，最受硅谷高科技公司青睐的 20 所大学中一大半位于加州，而排名第一的是地理位置得天独厚的圣何塞州立大学，其排名无法进入 *U.S. News* 综合排行榜，只在区域大学中位列第24位。

因此,在选择学校时,排名固然重要,但仅可作为参考。学生应该花更多的时间来研究学校的教学质量、开设的专业、科研和工作机会等,找到真正和自己匹配的学校。

附表4.2 2022 *U.S. News* 美国综合大学排名

排名	学校名称	中文名称
1	Princeton University	普林斯顿大学
2	Harvard University	哈佛大学
2	Columbia University	哥伦比亚大学
2	Massachusetts Institute of Technology	麻省理工学院
5	Yale University	耶鲁大学
6	Stanford University	斯坦福大学
6	University of Chicago	芝加哥大学
8	University of Pennsylvania	宾夕法尼亚大学
9	Northwestern University	西北大学
9	Johns Hopkins University	约翰霍普金斯大学
9	California Institute of Technology	加州理工学院
9	Duke University	杜克大学
13	Dartmouth College	达特茅斯学院
14	Brown University	布朗大学
14	Vanderbilt University	范德堡大学
14	Washington University in St. Louis	圣路易斯华盛顿大学
17	Rice University	莱斯大学
17	Cornell University	康奈尔大学
19	University of Notre Dame	圣母大学
20	University of California-Los Angeles	加州大学洛杉矶分校
21	Emory University	埃默里大学
22	University of California-Berkeley	加州大学伯克利分校
23	Georgetown University	乔治城大学

续 表

排名	学 校 名 称	中 文 名 称
23	University of Michigan-Ann Arbor	密歇根大学安娜堡分校
25	Carnegie Mellon University	卡耐基梅隆大学
25	University of Virginia	弗吉尼亚大学
27	University of Southern California	南加州大学
28	Wake Forest University	维克森林大学
28	University of North Carolina-Chapel Hill	北卡罗来纳大学教堂山分校
28	New York University	纽约大学
28	Tufts University	塔夫茨大学
28	University of California-Santa Barbara	加州大学圣芭芭拉分校
28	University of Florida	佛罗里达大学
34	University of Rochester	罗切斯特大学
34	University of California-San Diego	加州大学圣迭戈分校
36	University of California-Irvine	加州大学欧文分校
36	Boston College	波士顿学院
38	Georgia Institute of Technology	佐治亚理工学院
38	University of California-Davis	加州大学戴维斯分校
38	College of William & Mary	威廉玛丽学院
38	University of Texas-Austin	得克萨斯大学奥斯汀分校
42	Tulane University	杜兰大学
42	Boston University	波士顿大学
42	Brandeis University	布兰迪斯大学
42	Case Western Reserve University	凯斯西储大学
42	University of Wisconsin-Madison	威斯康星大学麦迪逊分校
47	University of Illinois-Urbana-Champaign	伊利诺伊大学厄巴纳香槟分校
48	University of Georgia	佐治亚大学
49	Northeastern University	东北大学

续 表

排名	学 校 名 称	中 文 名 称
49	Lehigh University	里海大学
49	Pepperdine University	佩伯代因大学
49	Villanova University	维拉诺瓦大学
49	Ohio State University-Columbus	俄亥俄州立大学哥伦布分校
49	Purdue University-West Lafayette	普渡大学西拉法叶校
55	University of Miami	迈阿密大学
55	Rensselaer Polytechnic Institute	伦斯勒理工学院
55	Santa Clara University	圣塔克拉拉大学
55	Florida State University	佛罗里达州立大学
59	Syracuse University	雪城大学
59	University of Pittsburgh	匹兹堡大学
59	University of Maryland-College Park	马里兰大学帕克分校
59	University of Washington	华盛顿大学
63	Rutgers University-New Brunswick	罗格斯大学新伯朗士威校区
63	University of Connecticut	康涅狄格大学
63	Pennsylvania State University-University Park	宾州州立大学帕克分校
63	Worcester Polytechnic Institute	伍斯特理工学院
63	George Washington University	乔治华盛顿大学
68	Fordham University	福德汉姆大学
68	Indiana University-Bloomington	印第安纳大学伯明顿分校
68	Southern Methodist University	南卫理公会大学
68	University of Massachusetts-Amherst	麻省大学阿默斯特分校
68	University of Minnesota-Twin Cities	明尼苏达大学双城分校
68	Yeshiva University	耶什华大学
75	Baylor University	贝勒大学
75	Clemson University	克莱姆森大学

续 表

排名	学校名称	中文名称
75	Loyola Marymount University	洛约拉马利蒙特大学
75	Virginia Tech	弗吉尼亚理工学院
79	American University	美利坚大学
79	Brigham Young University-Provo	杨博翰大学普罗沃分校
79	Gonzaga University	贡萨加大学
79	North Carolina State University-Raleigh	北卡罗来纳州立大学
83	Binghamton University-SUNY	纽约州立大学宾汉姆顿大学
83	Colorado School of Mines	科罗拉多矿业大学
83	Elon University	依隆大学
83	Howard University	霍华德大学
83	Marquette University	马凯特大学
83	Michigan State University	密歇根州立大学
83	Stevens Institute of Technology	斯蒂文斯理工学院
83	Texas Christian University	得克萨斯基督教大学
83	University of California-Riverside	加州大学河滨分校
83	University of Iowa	爱荷华大学
93	Stony Brook University-SUNY	纽约州立大学石溪分校
93	University at Buffalo-SUNY	纽约州立大学布法罗分校
93	University of California，Merced	加州大学美熹德分校
93	University of Delaware	特拉华大学
93	University of Denver	丹佛大学
93	University of San Diego	圣迭戈大学
99	Auburn University	奥本大学
99	University of Colorado Boulder	科罗拉多大学波尔得分校
99	University of Oregon	俄勒冈大学
99	The University of Utah	犹他大学

（资料来源：*U.S. News* 官网 https://www.usnews.com/best-colleges/rankings/national-universities）

附表 4.3 2022 *U.S. News* 美国文理学院排名

排名	学 校 名 称	中 文 名 称
1	Williams College	威廉姆斯学院
2	Amherst College	阿默斯特学院
3	Swarthmore College	斯沃斯莫尔学院
4	Pomona College	波莫纳学院
5	Wellesley College	韦尔斯利学院
6	Bowdoin College	鲍登学院
6	United States Naval Academy	美国海军学院
8	Claremont Mckenna College	克莱蒙特·麦肯纳学院
9	Carleton College	卡尔顿学院
9	Middlebury College	明德学院
11	United States Military Academy	美国军事学院
11	Washington and Lee University	华盛顿与李大学
13	Davidson College	戴维森学院
13	Grinnell College	格林内尔学院
13	Hamilton College	汉密尔顿学院
16	Haverford College	哈弗福德学院
17	Barnard College	巴纳德学院
17	Colby College	科比学院
17	Colgate University	卡尔盖特大学
17	Smith College	史密斯学院
17	Wesleyan University	卫斯理安大学
22	United States Air Force Academy	美国空军学院
22	University of Richmond	里士满大学
22	Vassar College	瓦萨学院
25	Bates College	贝茨学院
26	Colorado College	科罗拉多学院

续 表

排名	学 校 名 称	中 文 名 称
27	Macalester College	麦卡斯利特学院
28	Harvey Mudd College	哈维穆德学院
29	Soka University of America	美国创价大学
30	Berea College	伯理亚学院
30	Bryn Mawr College	布林茅尔学院
30	Kenyon College	凯尼恩学院
30	Mount Holyoke College	曼荷莲学院
30	Scripps College	斯克里斯普学院
35	College of the Holy Cross	圣十字学院
35	Pitzer College	匹泽学院
37	Oberlin College and Conservatory	澳博林大学音乐学院
38	Bucknell University	巴科内尔大学
38	Lafayette College	拉法叶学院
38	Skidmore College	斯基德莫尔学院
38	Whitman College	惠特曼学院
42	Denison University	丹尼森大学
42	Franklin and Marshall College	富兰克林与马歇尔学院
42	Occidental College	西方学院
42	Thomas Aquinas College	托马斯阿奎那斯学院
46	DePauw University	迪堡大学
46	Furman University	福尔曼大学
46	Hillsdale College	希尔斯代尔学院
46	Trinity College	圣三一学院
50	Connecticut College	康涅狄格学院

(资料来源：*U.S. News* 官网 https://www.usnews.com/best-colleges/rankings/national-liberal-arts-colleges)

附表 4.4　2022 *U.S. News* 世界大学排名

排名	学校名称	中文名称	所属国家和地区
1	Harvard University	哈佛大学	美国
2	Massachusetts Institute of Technology	麻省理工学院	美国
3	Stanford University	斯坦福大学	美国
4	University of California-Berkeley	加州大学伯克利分校	美国
5	University of Oxford	牛津大学	英国
6	Columbia University	哥伦比亚大学	美国
7	University of Washington	华盛顿大学	美国
8	University of Cambridge	剑桥大学	英国
9	California Institute of Technology	加州理工学院	美国
9	Johns Hopkins University	约翰霍普金斯大学	美国
11	University of California-San Francisco	加州大学旧金山分校	美国
12	Yale University	耶鲁大学	美国
13	University of Pennsylvania	宾夕法尼亚大学	美国
14	University of California-Los Angeles	加州大学洛杉矶分校	美国
15	University of Chicago	芝加哥大学	美国
16	Princeton University	普林斯顿大学	美国
16	University College London	伦敦大学学院	英国
16	University of Toronto	多伦多大学	加拿大
19	University of Michigan-Ann Arbor	密西根大学安娜堡分校	美国
20	Imperial College London	伦敦帝国理工学院	英国
21	University of California-San Diego	加州大学圣迭戈分校	美国
22	Cornell University	康奈尔大学	美国
23	Duke University	杜克大学	美国
24	Northwestern University	西北大学	美国
25	University of Melbourne	墨尔本大学	澳大利亚
26	Swiss Federal Institute of Technology Zurich	瑞士苏黎世联邦理工学院	瑞士

续 表

排名	学校名称	中文名称	所属国家和地区
26	Tsinghua University	清华大学	中国
28	University of Sydney	悉尼大学	澳大利亚
29	National University of Singapore	新加坡国立大学	新加坡
30	New York University	纽约大学	美国
31	Washington University in St. Louis	圣路易斯华盛顿大学	美国
32	University of Edinburgh	爱丁堡大学	英国
33	King's College London	伦敦国王学院	英国
33	Nanyang Technological University	南洋理工大学	新加坡
35	University of British Columbia	不列颠哥伦比亚大学	加拿大
36	University of Queensland Australia	澳大利亚昆士兰大学	澳大利亚
37	University of Copenhagen	哥本哈根大学	丹麦
38	University of Amsterdam	阿姆斯特丹大学	荷兰
39	University of North Carolina-Chapel Hill	北卡罗来纳大学教堂山分校	美国
40	Monash University	莫纳什大学	澳大利亚
41	University of New South Wales	新南威尔士大学	澳大利亚
42	University of Pittsburgh	匹兹堡大学	美国
43	University of Texas-Austin	得克萨斯大学奥斯汀分校	美国
44	King Abdulaziz University	阿卜杜勒阿齐兹国王大学	沙特阿拉伯
45	Peking University	北京大学	中国
46	Sorbonne Universite	索邦大学	法国
46	University of Munich	慕尼黑大学	德国
48	Catholic University of Leuven	鲁汶天主教大学	比利时
48	Karolinska Institute	卡罗林斯卡学院	瑞典
48	Utrecht University	乌得勒支大学	荷兰
51	McGill University	麦吉尔大学	加拿大
52	Ohio State University-Columbus	俄亥俄州立大学哥伦布分校	美国

续 表

排名	学 校 名 称	中 文 名 称	所属国家和地区
52	University of Wisconsin-Madison	威斯康星大学麦迪逊分校	美国
54	Heidelberg University	海德堡大学	德国
55	University of Minnesota-Twin Cities	明尼苏达大学双城分校	美国
56	Australian National University	澳大利亚国立大学	澳大利亚
57	Icahn School of Medicine at Mount Sinai	西奈山伊坎医学院	美国
58	Georgia Institute of Technology	佐治亚理工学院	美国
58	University of Manchester	曼彻斯特大学	英国
60	Universite Paris Saclay	巴黎萨克雷大学	法国
60	University of Maryland-College Park	马里兰大学帕克校区	美国
62	Erasmus University Rotterdam	鹿特丹伊拉斯姆斯大学	荷兰
62	University of Colorado-Boulder	科罗拉多大学博尔德分校	美国
64	University of Zurich	苏黎世大学	瑞士
65	Boston University	波士顿大学	美国
66	University of Adelaide	阿德莱德大学	澳大利亚
67	Université de Paris	巴黎大学	法国
67	University of California-Davis	加州大学戴维斯分校	美国
67	University of California-Santa Barbara	加州大学圣巴巴拉分校	美国
70	École Polytechnique Federale of Lausanne	洛桑联邦理工学院	瑞士
70	University of Southern California	南加州大学	美国
72	University of Illinois-Urbana-Champaign	伊利诺伊大学香槟分校	美国
73	Vanderbilt University	范德堡大学	美国
74	Emory University	埃默里大学	美国
74	Technical University of Munich	慕尼黑工业大学	德国
76	University of Hong Kong	香港大学	中国香港地区
77	University of Tokyo	东京大学	日本

续 表

排名	学 校 名 称	中 文 名 称	所属国家和地区
78	Humboldt-Universität zu Berlin	柏林洪堡大学	德国
78	University of Western Australia	西澳大学	澳大利亚
80	Pennsylvania State University-University Park	宾夕法尼亚州立大学	美国
80	Wageningen University and Research Center	瓦赫宁根大学和研究中心	荷兰
82	Chinese University Hong Kong	香港中文大学	中国香港地区
82	Leiden University	莱顿大学	荷兰
84	University of Glasgow	格拉斯哥大学	英国
84	Vrije Universiteit Amsterdam	阿姆斯特丹自由大学	荷兰
86	University of California-Irvine	加州大学欧文分校	美国
87	University of Barcelona	巴塞罗那大学	西班牙
88	University of Groningen	格罗宁根大学	荷兰
89	Rockefeller University	洛克菲勒大学	美国
90	University of Oslo	奥斯陆大学	挪威
91	University of Birmingham	伯明翰大学	英国
92	Ghent University	根特大学	比利时
92	University of Bristol	布里斯托大学	英国
94	University of Helsinki	赫尔辛基大学	芬兰
95	Freie Universität Berlin	柏林自由大学	德国
95	Lund University	隆德大学	瑞典
97	King Abdullah University of Science and Technology	阿卜杜拉国王科技大学	沙特阿拉伯
97	University of Southampton	南安普敦大学	英国
99	University of Arizona	亚利桑那大学	美国
99	University of Florida	弗罗里达大学	美国

(资料来源：*U.S. News* 官网 https://www.usnews.com/education/best-global-universities/rankings)

后 记

本书于 2021 年 5 月完成初稿，刚好是 2021 申请季结束的时候。今年受疫情的影响，美国大学申请变得更加艰难。在这个申请季刚刚开始不久，大家都预测今年的申请季可能会是史上最简单的一次，然而结果显示，今年很多美国顶尖大学的录取率仅有个位数。

同样在申请季前，有人预测说，由于今年大部分学校采取了标化考试可选(test-optional)政策，课外活动也因为疫情的影响无法正常完成，那么文书一定会在整个申请中比以往更为重要。许多中国家长听到了这个消息，一门心思希望通过各种方式让孩子写出好的文书，企图复制各种牛娃的文书创意、构思方式，期待自己的孩子也能搞点惊天动地的东西出来，一脚踏进名校大门。

但申请美国大学这个事情，四海之内真的没有一套标准。就像大家常说的，美国本科申请没有公式可言，不是人家怎么做，你就一定要怎么做，人家说这样做好，你就一定要这样做。文书更是如此，是没有捷径可走的。从更好理解的话来说，文书是一篇没有体裁的自我展示，就是讲述关于孩子自己的故事，而这个故事的听众就是招生官。招生官就是想通过各类不同主题的文书，了解你个性中的他们想要看到的许多方面，建立一个关于你的较为立体多面的形象，以便为自己的学校挑选合适的学生。

美国大学的招生官也知道，在这个世界上天才是屈指可数的，能有几个爱因斯坦，又能有几个霍金呢？他们能理解，也能接受每一个孩子的平凡，但平凡不等同于平庸，平凡的孩子也终能发掘自己与众不同的特质，终能展示自己独一无二的那一面，而招生官希望看到的正是这位学生是不是这样一块“终会发光的金子”。

这个世界上不会有两块一模一样的玉，同样，不会有两个孩子拥有全然相同的个性与生活。每一个孩子独有的经历和性格正是大家苦苦寻找的文书题材的“原石”，而在峰越教育，无论是中方老师还是外籍老师，都会不断基于这个“原石”去加工、打磨孩子们的文书。最终，文书所呈现的也会是拥有孩子本身“纹路”、带有自己“原色”的内容。所以这也是为什么，我们在每一位学生写作文书前，都会和学生进行大量的头脑风暴，因为我们要引导孩子去回忆自己过往那些特殊的经历，发现自己真实的性格。

本书的末尾收录了许多峰越教育过往优秀学生的真实文书。在此，我也想正式表达对他们的感谢，谢谢他们愿意分享自己的生活，自己的反思，愿意分享相对私人的叙事，以帮助以后的学生进行文书写作。在这些学生中，有的写了教社区小朋友大提琴的经历，有的写了自己在解一道数学题的经历，有的写了对摄影的热爱，等等。这些经历看上去并不是惊天动地的，但这正是一个 18 岁中国学生的画像，是他们的日常生活，他们的喜怒哀乐，他们的兴趣爱好。这就是名校招生官们最想看到的内容。书中外籍老师们的每一次建议，每一次指导，都是基于孩子兴趣的本身。所以，各位看到此书的家长，请尊重每一个孩子原有的个性，不要引导孩子用什么猎奇的心态去刻意制造某种不属于自己的文书创意。让孩子写出他最熟悉、最真实的自己，或许那是一个看起来平平常常的故事，但却描绘了他不普通的人生、不普通的自我。这一点也正符合峰越教育所坚持的“发现你、打造你、成就你”，而非“改变你”。我们致力于成为值得信赖、充满激情、专业卓越的升学指导机构，通过中外顾问结合的模式，有针对性地了解、发掘每一位孩子，帮助他们更了解自我，更善于展现自我，最终为自己争取一个更好的未来。

峰越教育创始人
李　锦
微信号：Jin_li_Abest